Basic

THE M & E HANDBOOK SERIES

Basic Accounting

J O Magee, FCA

*Formerly Principal Lecturer in Accountancy at the
Polytechnic of North London*

SECOND EDITION

Pitman Publishing
128 Long Acre, London WC2E 9AN

A Longman Group Company

First published 1973
Reprinted 1974, 1975, 1976
Second edition 1979
Reprinted 1983, 1986, 1988

© Macdonald & Evans Ltd 1973, 1979

A CIP catalogue record for this book is available from the
British Library.

ISBN 0 7121 0284 1

Founding Editor: P W D Redmond

Typeset, printed and bound in Great Britain by
Richard Clay Ltd, Bungay, Suffolk

Preface

In the Preface to my most recent HANDBOOK, *Basic Book-keeping*, I said that the intention was that that book in conjunction with this present work should provide full cover for students who were preparing for examinations in book-keeping and accounting principles at elementary or intermediate level. I went on to say that the two books, taken together, were aimed at giving a sound basis of study for the examinations of the leading professional bodies. I have tried to link the two books by means of an introductory chapter showing the close affinity that book-keeping has with accounting, and emphasising the immense importance of book-keeping as a tool in the hands of the accountant.

As before, I have used the technique of small steps wherever possible and have tried not to take anything for granted. This approach may cause the bright student to become impatient at times and for this I apologise. However, my object is to instil into the mind of the average student the rationality of the subject and to encourage him to appreciate that the difficulties inherent in the study of accounting can be mastered if the will to work is present. With the need for practical application in mind, questions taken largely from various examining bodies have been inserted at the end of each chapter and, in most cases, fully worked answers have been given in Appendix II. Experience leads me to believe that the full workings of problems is something which students find helpful. It is often of really material assistance and helps to overcome fear of certain aspects of the subject. So far as possible the questions have been placed in ascending order of difficulty.

Because this book is a "basic" study of accounting both partnership and company accounts have been omitted. Essentially, they are not *basic* matters either of accounting practice or principle; both fall under the heading of "specific types" of business problems and both are fully covered in separate HANDBOOKS entitled *Partnership Accounts* and *Company Accounts* respectively. For the student who wishes to study the subject of accounting more deeply these books should be of some help.

Many of the examples given in the text or to be used for practical work by the student have been taken from recent examination papers set by the professional and academic bodies listed below. To each of these I wish to express my gratitude for permission to make use of their material. Those questions bearing no acknowledgment are of my own devising. I accept full responsibility for the worked solutions given in Appendix II.

July 1973   J. O. MAGEE

PREFACE TO THE SECOND EDITION

In this second edition the original structure of the book has remained unchanged but two new chapters have been added. The first of these is entitled "Fundamental Accounting Concepts" and is largely based on the *Statement of Standard Accounting Practice* (S.S.A.P.2) issued by the Institute of Chartered Accountants in England and Wales. I am greatly indebted to the Institute. The second new chapter aims to show the student that much important information can be gained by the use of ratios as long as they are selected intelligently. I have been less concerned with those ratios used in the field of investment analysis and have concentrated more on those which are of use to management. This does not mean that the former have been entirely omitted but greater stress has been laid on the internal aids that certain ratios can give the managers of businesses. Finally I have pointed out to the student that the study of ratios can open up a new and fascinating dimension of accountancy, and I hope that a study of this chapter will be of help.

August 1979   J. O. MAGEE

Acknowledgements

The Chartered Association of Certified Accountants (A.C.C.A.)
Institute of Chartered Secretaries and Administrators (I.C.S.A.)
Institute of Chartered Accountants in England and Wales (I.C.A.)
The Chartered Institute of Management Accountants (C.I.M.A.)
Chartered Institute of Bankers (C.I.B.)
Royal Society of Arts (R.S.A.)
Southern Universities Joint Board (S.U.J.B.)
Welsh Joint Education Committee (W.J.E.C.)
Union of Lancashire and Cheshire Institutes (U.L.C.I.)
East Midland Educational Union (E.M.E.U.)

NOTE: All dates in examination questions have been standardised with the permission of the relevant authorities to agree with the texts.

Bibliography

Stott, J. Randall: *An Introduction to Accounts*, Edward Arnold (Publishers) Ltd, 1970.
Edey, Harold C.: *Introduction to Accounting*, Hutchinson University Library, 1973.
Favell, A. J.: *Practical Book Keeping and Accounts*, University Tutorial Press Ltd, 1976.
Castle, E. F. and Owens, N. P.: *Principles of Accounts*, Macdonald and Evans Ltd, fifth edition, 1978.
Baston, Andrew: *Elements of Accounts*, Cassell and Co. Ltd, ninth edition, 1968.
Castle, E. F.: *Principles of Accounts,* University Tutorial Press Ltd, seventh edition, 1983.
Magee, B.: *Accounting*, Gee and Co. (Publishers) Ltd, ninth edition, 1979.

Contents

CHAPTER I

Book-keeping and Accounting

THE FUNDAMENTAL INTERRELATIONSHIP

1. The difference between book-keeping and accounting. How does book-keeping differ from accounting? This question is often asked by students and as this chapter is intended to link the earlier book, *Basic Book-keeping*, with this present one it is appropriate that an attempt to be made to explain this difference.

Book-keeping may, with reasonable accuracy, be defined as the skill of recording business transactions in terms of money according to a commonly accepted pattern.

Accounting may be defined as the application of the combination of book-keeping and analysis techniques to specific *types* of business problems, e.g., the production of financial statements required by management.

2. The link between book-keeping and accounting. In the earlier book in this series, *Basic Book-keeping*, we proceeded to develop a logical pattern of events showing the interaction of entries and how, from a base of given information, we could finally produce the result of a period of trading in the shape of the net profit. At the same time, as an automatic result of our double-entry book-keeping, we were able to set out the overall position of the business in the form of a Balance Sheet.

Because a very large part of what is known as accounting is based upon the principles of double-entry book-keeping it is of supreme importance that an accountancy student acquires a thoroughly sound knowledge of those principles. In addition, it is imperative that his knowledge extends to the practical application of these principles since accounting is essentially a practical subject. Furthermore, it is vital that constant practice in working problems is obtained, for it is only by much practice that competence in this subject is attained.

3. What is meant by the term "accountancy"? The two words "accounting" and "accountancy" are frequently regarded as being interchangeable. There is, however, a difference. "Accounting" has been defined above. "Accountancy" is the profession, in its widest sense, carried on by an accountant. In general a professional accountant's role in the business sphere can be said to fall into two categories:

(a) that of the professional accountant in the capacity of auditor, financial expert, tax adviser, business consultant, etc.;

(b) that of the commercial or industrial accountant.

The Australian Commercial Dictionary defines the word "accountancy" in the following terms:

"*Accountancy*. The profession of accounting. The concepts governing the process of book-keeping and accounting; the concepts underlying the recording, classifying, analysing and summarising in a sytematic manner of transactions having a monetary basis and the interpretation and presentation of the results of these operations. One who engaged in such practice is known as an accountant."

A SUBJECT BASED ON LOGIC

4. The logical and rational aspects of accounting. "The study of accounting as a means of mental training and discipline has not been as widely appreciated as it deserves to be." "Accounting is, in effect, a study in *applied logic* and unless a student understands and appreciates this aspect of the subject he must lose much of the valuable *training in logical thinking* which its study affords."

These two extracts are taken from *An Outline of Accounting* (Professor Louis Goldberg, The Law Book Company, Melbourne, 1966) and suggest, with very good reason, that accounting can be regarded by anyone with a logical mind as being a subject of absorbing interest and of great intellectual and practical value. In its logical consistency it promotes intellectual satisfaction and develops a faculty for attention to detail which is an important quality in research.

As will be seen later in this book, the application of double-entry book-keeping plus the use of one's power of reasoning need to be employed when dealing with the many and varied problems the accountant may be faced with. Basically, most problems posed are capable of solution by the use of book-keeping alone and it is, therefore, absolutely essential that a sound knowledge of this aspect has been obtained. At this early stage there will be ample opportunities for the use of the student's powers of reasoning, but there will be few opportunities to employ analysis techniques. These tend to arise more in the practical field, under business conditions, than during study. As practical experience is gained ability in analysis will grow. It is something which is gained rather than learned, a sort of "know-how" which is acquired without the individual consciously realising it.

A glance through the chapter headings will convey some idea of the variety of types of accounting problems which may be encountered. The realisation that this book only deals with *basic* matters in the field of accounting should also give pause for thought.

5. The importance of constant practice. It is appropriate at this point to emphasise how immensely important it is for students to have as much practice at working problems as possible. Although reading is important and the student should, if possible, attend classes where verbal explanations of difficult points can be obtained, there is no substitute for practice. It is only by the practical expedient of working on problems on a strictly personal basis that real mastery of the subject will be achieved. That the student of accountancy "teaches himself" is undoubtedly true. As in mathematics, so in accountancy, the constant working of problems is the key to real understanding and a thorough grasp of the subject.

In the pages which follow as many problems as space has permitted have been set out at the end of each chapter. These are of varying difficulty but in Appendix II fully worked answers have been given in most cases. It is assumed, of course, that students who turn to this book will already have reached a fair degree of competence in book-keeping. If this has not yet been attained the earlier book in this series, *Basic Book-keeping*, is recommended as a primer in the subject.

PROGRESS TEST 1

Theory

1. How would you define the term "book-keeping"? **(1)**
2. What do you understand by the term "accounting"? **(1)**
3. In what way does "accountancy" differ from "accounting"? **(3)**

4. It is claimed that accounting is more than a technique. Quote an authority on this point. **(4)**

Practice

5. I trade in typewriters and adding machines, and my assets and liabilities on 30th September were:

	£
Cash held in the office	169
Bank overdraft	980
Stock of typewriters, worth	3,650
Stock of adding machines, worth	775
Equipment required by the business	688
Creditors: L. Wright	79
J. Gurney	143
R. Pickard	320
Debtors: J. Calne	435
B. Swift	17
K. Rogers	148
R. Makston	76

(a) Enter these balances in the relevant books of account.

(b) Record the transactions for the month of October (*see below*) in suitable books.

(c) Draw up a Trial Balance for 31st October (all cheques are paid into the bank on the day of receipt).

Transactions for October:

Oct. 1   Sold Elysium adding machine to J. Sanger for £145—paid for by cheque.

Oct. 5   Paid off L. Wright's account by cheque for £79.

Oct. 5   Paid off £50 from J. Gurney's account as part payment—cheque sent.

Oct. 9   K. Rogers sent a cheque for £148 to pay off his account.

Oct. 9   Paid Elysium Machine Co. £100 by cheque for two new machines.

Oct. 10   Paid £10 in cash for machine repair.

Oct. 11   Paid monthly rental of premises, by cheque, £29.

Oct. 14 Sold Eclipse typewriter to M. King for £85.
Deposit of £40 received by cheque, with balance to be paid within 30 days.
Oct. 16 Paid £5 cash for stationery.
Oct. 20 Bought National Insurance stamps for cash, £8.
Oct. 23 B. Swift sent his cheque for £17.
Oct. 26 Paid cleaner's wages—cheque for £15.
Oct. 28 J. Calne sent his cheque for £335.
Oct. 30 Paid electricity bill £8 by cash.

(S.U.J.B.)

6.*(a)* The following Trial Balance was taken from the books of R. Jones at 31st December 19–4 *after* the Trading and Profit and Loss Account had been prepared. From this Trial Balance, and from the additional notes, prepare the Balance Sheet of the business of Jones as at 31st December 19–4.

	Dr £	Cr £
Capital, 1st January 19–4		5,500
Premises	5,000	
Trade creditors		600
Goodwill	500	
Bank overdraft		900
Motor van, 1st January 19–4	350	
Rates paid for January–March 19–5	50	
Wages owing		12
Trade debtors	1,200	
Cash in hand	75	
Fixtures and fittings	300	
Drawings	1,000	
Stock, 31st December 19–4	400	
Net profit for 19–4		1,863
	£8,875	£8,875

NOTES:

(*i*) In calculating the net profit, agreed depreciation of 20 per cent on the motor van and 10 per cent on the fixtures and fittings had *not* been taken into account.

(*ii*) A provision for bad debts of 5 per cent of the trade debtors is to be made.

(*b*) Define briefly the following terms:

    (*i*) asset;

    (*ii*) liability;

    (*iii*) capital of a sole trader;

    (*iv*) Balance Sheet;

    (*v*) net profit.

(Union of Lancashire and Cheshire Institutes)

7. You have inherited £6,000 under the terms of your grandfather's will and decide to purchase a newsagent and tobacconist business which is for sale at £4,000. The stock, valued at £600, was purchased as a separate transaction.

You pay £5,000 of your inheritance into a Business Account which you open with the Counties Bank. The purchase price of £4,000 included shop fittings and equipment valued at £675; debtors for papers and magazines, £284; the lease of the shop which had seven years to run valued at £2,100, while the remainder was the cost of goodwill. You agree to accept the liability of £350 owed to creditors for goods supplied to the seller.

You draw a cheque for cash to give you a float for change, £30.

During the first four weeks of trading your cash sales amounted to £780, while sales on credit were £370. Your debtors paid you £350 during this period and you paid £620 by cheque to your suppliers. In this first four weeks you purchased goods on credit costing £1,040. In addition you made the following cheque payments: purchase of an office safe for £120; bought a second-hand car for £450 and paid a deposit of £150, the remainder to be paid by monthly instalments; paid rent, £20.

Cash payments were made as follows: wages for four weeks, £80; national insurance, £24; postage, £8; sundry expenses, £7; personal drawings, £100. The remainder of the cash takings were paid into the bank after retaining a float of £30 for change.

At the end of the period debtors owed £420; creditors were owed £770; closing stock at cost was valued at £674.

Record the above transactions in the ledger and take out a Trial Balance. When you have agreed this prepare the final accounts and a Balance Sheet.

8. Briefly explain the following methods of valuing assets for balance sheet purposes:

    (*i*) depreciation by the "straight line" method;

(*ii*) depreciation by the "diminishing balance" method;
(*iii*) revaluation.

In respect of each method mention one type of asset for which the method would be particularly appropriate.

9. P. Taylor is dissatisfied with the firm of accountants he employs and considers that it does not give him the service he feels he needs. He discusses the possibility of appointing you in place of this firm but before doing so he decides to test your ability.

He gives you a copy of the accounts prepared by his former accountants for the year ended 31st December 19–4, and the year ended 31st December 19–5, asking you to compare them and to advise him as to the conclusions you draw from the information provided. He feels that this is a service which professional accountants should give their clients. He asks you to pay particular attention to the figures set out below and to let him have your comments.

	19–4	19–5
Sales	£92,000	£108,000
Gross profit	30,360	32,400
Net profit	11,040	13,500

Show, in the form of a report to P. Taylor, the conclusions you reach.

10. The annual accounts of a trading firm were made up to Monday 31st March. Stocktaking was postponed until Saturday 5th April, when the stock-in-trade on the firm's premises amounted, at cost, to £25,370. There were no trading transactions on 5th April.

Goods held by customers on 5th April, on sale or return, amounted to £400 at selling price.

Goods sold for £184 on 31st March were not despatched to the customers until 7th April.

Sales for the period 1st to 4th April amounted to £2,840. All the goods were despatched in the same period with the exception of goods sold for £720 which were not sent off until 7th April.

In the period 1st to 4th April credit notes for returns inwards, amounting to £168 at selling price, were issued and the relevant goods were received in the same period.

Purchases for the period 1st to 4th April amounted to £1,835, and all the goods were received in the same period.

Goods purchased on 31st March for £123, and entered in the books on that date, were not received until 7th April.

The rate of gross profit is 25 per cent of the selling price of all goods.

You are required to prepare a statement showing the amount of the stock which should be included in the annual accounts made up to 31st March.

(I.C.S.A.)

CHAPTER II

Fundamental Accounting Concepts

ACCOUNTING CONVENTIONS: TERMS

1. Statement of Standard Accounting Practice 2. To understand financial accounts it is essential that those who use them be aware of the main assumptions on which such accounts are based. The Institute of Chartered Accountants in England and Wales has issued a *Statement of Standard Accounting Practice* (*S.S.A.P.2*) in an attempt to promote such understanding.

2. Accounting assumptions and conventions. The Trading and Profit and Loss Account of a business together with the Balance Sheet are prepared according to certain generally accepted conventions. They are produced in a manner which is acceptable for the people who *use* them for one purpose or another. In other words they meet with the approval of businessmen and as they conform to established lines of thought they may fairly be said to be understood universally in the business world.

These generally accepted matters really attain the status of rules, and, as such, fall under two main headings:

    (*a*) assumptions;
    (*b*) conventions.

It is thought better not to make any rigid dividing line between these two headings but to treat them as being part and parcel of "accounting concepts."

ACCOUNTING BASES

3. Assumptions and conventions. Over the course of many years a variety of accounting bases have been developed which provide an orderly and consistent framework for reporting periodically on the results of trading and setting out the financial position of a business.

There are four basic assumptions which form the bedrock of our present system of accounting. These are:

    (*a*) the *going concern* basis;

(b) the *accruals* basis;

(c) the *consistency* basis;

(d) the *prudence* basis.

S.S.A.P.2 defines these four assumptions as "fundamental accounting concepts" and continues, "these concepts have such general acceptance that they call for no explanation in published accounts and their observance is presumed unless stated otherwise. They are practical rules rather than theoretical ideals and are capable of variation and evolution as accounting thought and practice develops."

4. The "going concern" concept. We can liken the annual cycle of a business to a wheel which is continuously revolving. Starting at the beginning of the life of the business and assuming that the wheel will take one year precisely to complete a revolution, the pattern would be as follows:

(a) capital in the form of cash is paid in;

(b) this is used to buy fixed assets and stock;

(c) these are used to produce goods or to provide a service;

(d) goods or service are turned into cash;

(e) the cash is used to pay for the various expenses incurred;

(f) any profit resulting from these operations belongs to the owner and he will take out of this profit such money as he needs for his own use;

(g) the remainder he will leave in the business to encourage its growth.

In the following years the pattern would be repeated except for the first item, the investing of capital. We can thus envisage fairly clearly what is meant by a "going concern"; one that revolves continually on its axis and follows a clear pattern year after year.

Remember the idea of the "wheel".

5. The "accruals" concept. In order to determine the proper amount of profit a business has earned during a period of trading it is necessary to go beyond the receipts of cash from sales and the payments of cash for goods and expenses.

If the only data recorded was in respect of cash received and paid during an accounting period we would, almost certainly, be lacking some of the information needed to calculate *accurately* the profit earned. Adjustments will need to be made in the records to "provide" for accrued expenses, i.e. those expenses which have been incurred *during* the particular period of trading but which will not be paid for until the *following* period. For example, the telephone account for the last three months will not have been received by the last day of the trading year, and therefore an estimate of the amount "to be provided" in respect of this expense will need to be made. We refer to this as being an "accrued expense."

Precisely the same reasoning is applied to "payments in advance" (sometimes called "prepayments"). In these cases the operation is in the reverse direction to that of accrued expenses. Thus, if we take the Rent Account as an example, in order to show the correct *charge* for the year we would have to remove any amount which had been paid in advance by crediting this sum in the Rent Account and bringing it down as a debit balance, i.e. an asset in the balance sheet.

S.S.A.P.2 states that expenses are to be "accrued" as they are "incurred" and must not be related only to the date when they are paid. So long as the *expense has been incurred* it must appear in the Profit and Loss Account of that period. In the same way, any income which has fallen due but has not yet been *received* must be treated similarly.

Certain matters are less easy to decide as to whether or not they constitute "accruals". These fall under two headings as follows.

(*a*) *Where income is received* before *expenditure is incurred*. In certain trades cash is received from a sale to which conditions are attached for a limited period of time. For example, a guarantee may be given for a period of, say, three months, during which time any failure of the goods sold will be repaired free of charge.

(*b*) *Where heavy expenditure takes place before any cash benefit is received*. This is a problem which does sometimes arise affecting (more usually) some of the larger companies. High expenditure may be incurred on:

(*i*) research and development;
(*ii*) exploration costs;
(*iii*) advertising both in the press and on television.

All of the above expense headings have something in common, i.e. the outlay of comparatively large sums of money for which no reward will be forthcoming for some time in the future, e.g. oil exploration. Advertising expenditure is more likely to obtain results more rapidly than either of the other forms of expense.

6. The "consistency" concept. This is a straightforward concept which implies that "there is a consistency of accounting treatment of like items within each accounting period and from one period to the next" (S.S.A.P.2).

The aim of this convention is to ensure:

(a) that there is no distortion of figures by unjustifiable differences in *accounting treatment* between one period and another;

(b) that accounting information between one period and another should be comparable with a view to the proper interpretation of accounts.

Integrity among those concerned in the production of accounting records can thus be seen to be a matter of considerable importance.

7. The "prudence" concept. This is sometimes referred to as the "realisation" concept. Again, we have a straightforward and commonsense assumption to put into practice. In essence it means making the decision as to the point in time at which it is valid for the profit on any particular transaction to be counted as having been earned.

No problem arises in the case of a cash sale. The goods are sold and the money (which contains, of course, the element of profit in the transaction) is received. Where a sale on credit is involved the arrival of the cash may be delayed for some weeks. None the less, the convention is observed that the taking of the profit is justified even though there is some delay involved before the money is received. One can argue with conviction that the seller would not have parted with the goods at the time of sale unless he was reasonably certain that his money would be forthcoming in the fairly near future. Occasionally, bad debts *are* incurred under this system but these form only a minute fraction of the enormous volume of business which is transacted on credit.

Profits must *not* be anticipated and should only be recognised by inclusion in the Trading and Profit and Loss Account in the form of either cash or debtors (S.S.A.P.2).

In so far as liabilities are concerned, under the "prudence" concept S.S.A.P.2 states that, "provision should be made for all known liabilities, that is to say, expenses and losses, whether the amount of these is known with certainty or is a best estimate in the light of the information available."

THE ENTITY CONCEPT

8. The independent existence of a business. The law has conferred upon every limited company *a legal existence* completely distinct from that of the individual shareholders. The legal entity is thus a person in its own right and can enter into business transactions. Thus, what is known as "the entity concept" has been given legal blessing.

An important convention which is fundamental to accounting practice is that where transactions are entered into between a business and the general public, that business is regarded as being a person with a completely independent existence from that of the owner of the business. There is no question of *legal* recognition being given in these cases, but, none the less, the convention applies.

9. The owner and the business. It is most important that the student understands that the business, on the one hand, and the owner of the business, on the other hand, are to be regarded as though they were two completely separate and independent beings. The business is regarded as having a life of its own, thus fulfilling the "entity concept."

Human agency is required to bring a business into existence since, quite obviously, it cannot come into being by itself. Once created, however, it is regarded as having an *identity* of its own and is, therefore, capable of entering into transactions with other people *on its own account*. At the outset a business possesses absolutely nothing and must look to its founder to provide the necessary finance out of which it can purchase those assets which it needs. In the light of the "entity concept" it is not difficult to envisage the business and its founder entering into the *basic* transaction whereby the founder provides the business with its first asset, i.e. a certain amount of money. At the same time the business acquires its first liability in the form of the owner who becomes its first creditor.

10. The ledger holds the records of the business. In the ledger of the business is recorded any transactions into which the business has entered. *Personal* transactions of the owner which have nothing to do with the business are *not* recorded in the ledger. These are the owner's private concern. Thus, it follows that every entry in the ledger is recorded from the viewpoint of the business and not from that of the owner.

PROGRESS TEST 2

Theory

1. Name the four basic assumptions of accounting. **(3)**
2. Explain what you understand by the expression "going concern." **(4)**
3. What is meant by the term "accruals concept"? **(5)**
4. Give two examples of provisions for accrued expenses which could have an effect on the accounts of a firm for a year ahead. Give two examples which might affect the accounts over the next five years. **(5)**
5. "Consistency in accounting operations is necessary." Is this statement true and if so, why? **(6)**
6. What is meant by prudence in accounting? Give some examples which might affect a firm's accounts. **(7)**
7. What is meant by the "entity concept" and how does it operate? **(8, 9)**

Practice

8. How do you explain that two accountants may report different "profits" for a particular company in a given year although both follow accepted accounting conventions.

(I.C.A.)

9. What do you understand by the term "conservatism" in relation to accounting measurement? Discuss the extent to which the use of the convention of conservatism increases the accuracy of the calculation of profit.

(R.S.A.)

10. "Profit is normally calculated by matching costs against revenue." Discuss this statement and indicate how you would obtain the appropriate figures to complete the matching process.

(R.S.A.)

CHAPTER III

Bank Reconciliations

BUSINESS RECORDS AND THOSE OF THE BANKER

1. Introduction to Bank Reconciliations. The term "Bank Reconciliation" or "Bank Agreement" is used when referring to a check which is made periodically (it may be weekly, monthly or at longer intervals) between the Cash Book of the business, i.e. the Bank Account, and the Bank Statements provided by the bank.

First of all we must be perfectly clear as to the nature of the records with which we are dealing. There are two aspects which need to be considered in order to understand precisely what is involved.

(*a*) The Cash Book of our business contains a detailed record of all the money which we give to our banker to take care of during a period of trading and of all payments which the banker makes for us out of the funds so given to him. Every time we pay money into the bank we enter the details on the *debit* side of the Cash Book (showing that the banker is our debtor) and crediting, of course, the account of the person who gives us the money. So far as our books are concerned the double entry is thus completed. It is most important that the newcomer to book-keeping fully realises this fact.

(*b*) The banker keeps his own set of books and his records are completely independent of any books which our business maintains.

He, too, uses the double-entry system of book-keeping and so, when we give him some money of ours to look after, he has to make a double entry to record it in *his* books.

We therefore have *the same item of money* being recorded as a double entry in our business books and, at the same time, being recorded as a double entry in our banker's books. Each double entry, of course, is a self-contained double entry so far as each set of books is concerned, i.e. there is no question whatever of one part of the double entry being made in our business's books and the other part being made in the books of the bank.

2. The "reflection". We know what entries we would make in our books if we were recording the receipt of £100 by cheque from J. Snodgrass. We would simply make a debit entry in the Bank Account (Cash Book) and a corresponding credit entry in the personal account of J. Snodgrass.

What entries would our banker make in his books? He, too, operates the double-entry system of book-keeping although his manner of operation may be rather unfamiliar to commercial users. Nevertheless, the fact remains that our banker does use double entry and fundamentally it is exactly the same as our own. That being so, when we give him the £100 to look after he will record it as *a receipt* of money and therefore a debit entry will be made in his cash book. The corresponding credit entry will be made in the personal account in the name of our business which he keeps in his ledger.

What obvious conclusion can be drawn from this? Simply that the two sets of books, the banker's on the one hand and our own business's on the other, will contain the *same* double entries. Now, we are not concerned in general with the entries in the banker's cash book. We are, however, greatly concerned with the entries *in his ledger*, because they will be exactly the same as the entries we have made in our Cash Book.

In this way the Bank Account in our Cash Book is truly a "reflection" of our personal account in the banker's ledger; that is to say, the entries are equal and opposite; they are *reversed* just as a reflection in a mirror is reversed but remains at the same time the identical copy of the original. We, for our part show the banker as our debtor while he, from the entries he has had to make in his records, shows our business as his creditor.

To establish the above matter in the mind of the student only one item has been used, i.e., a payment into bank. But what was true for that item is true for all. It does not matter how many items we have to record; it does not matter whether they be receipts or payments; so long as they are items which have to be entered in *our* Bank Account (in the Cash Book) then they *must* be recorded in our personal account in the bank's ledger. We may, therefore, expect to find at any time that the balance according to the Bank Account (in our Cash Book) is *exactly equal to the* balance showing on our personal account in the Bank's ledger.

VERIFICATION OF CASH BOOK ENTRIES

3. Bank Statements. With the introduction of accounting machines into general use in banks the Bank Pass Book faded from the business scene. The Bank Pass Book was a small book which would fit conveniently into the pocket of a man's jacket. The book was ruled in ledger form with debit entries on the left-hand page and credit entries on the right. The Pass Book was, in fact, a handwritten copy of the customer's personal account as it appeared in the bank's ledger. Whenever the customer needed it for the purpose of checking entries in his own Cash Book he would collect it from the bank, returning it after use so that the bank could keep it written up in the future. For the purposes of the present study the important point for the student to appreciate is that the Pass Book was a copy of the customer's account in the bank's books.

Today, the Bank Pass Book has completely disappeared and has been replaced by loose sheets known as Bank Statements. These Bank Statements, like the old Bank Pass Books, are simply *copies* of the customers' accounts in the bank's ledger. The entries in these statements are now made by means of a computer and as many carbon copies as necessary can be taken. By this method both the bank's ledger and the customer's copy can be entered up at the same time by one operation and the danger of an error being made when a copy is taken is therefore eliminated. Another advantage of this sytem is that every time an entry is made the machine calculates the new balance which was something that could not conveniently be done in the old Pass Books.

4. Checking in detail. Before we can proceed with the reconciliation of the two balances we have to obtain the bank statements from the bank and check the items entered therein with the details which have been entered in the Cash Book. It is of vital importance that this detailed check be carried out most carefully and that each item in both the Cash Book and the Bank Statement is marked with a tick (preferably in coloured ink or pencil). As we satisfy ourselves that, for example, a cheque for £25 has appeared in both the Cash Book and the Bank Statement, we mark each entry—one in the Cash Book and the other in the Bank Statement—with a tick. When this has been carefully done we will find in all probability that there are a few items with no tick against them. Some will be in the Cash Book while others may appear in the Bank Statement.

Our next task is to deal with these unticked items according to their nature. The next section will show the nature of these items. When we have discussed these we will proceed with the next step towards the "Bank Reconciliation."

THE TIME FACTOR

5. The time lag. If it could be so arranged that the bank was able to make the relevant entries in our personal account (in the bank's ledger) *immediately* after we had made the entries in the Bank Account (in our Cash Book) we could then expect to find the balances in the respective accounts to be in agreement at all times. Unfortunately, this is not possible. The reason for this is that when we draw a cheque (write out and sign a cheque) in payment of a debt we owe to somebody, a certain period of time will elapse before our banker becomes aware of our action.

The following is the probable sequence of events.

(*a*) The cheque is drawn and sent through the post to the creditor.

(*b*) The creditor receives it within a day or so and pays it into his bank account.

(*c*) *His* bank sends the cheque to the Banker's Clearing House to be sorted.

(*d*) The cheque is sent from the Banker's Clearing House to our banker.

(*e*) *Our* banker debits the personal account of our business in his ledger and thus catches up with the entry we made on the credit side of our Cash Book when we first drew the cheque.

It thus becomes clear that a time lag of several days will occur between the entries being made in our business books and the entries made in the bank's books. During this period the balance on our Bank Account will not be in agreement with the balance which the banker shows on our business account in his ledger.

Those cheques which are still in transit are called *unpresented cheques.*

6. Cheques not yet credited by the bank. In much the same way it sometimes happens that if we pay money into the bank it is not credited immediately to our account in the bank's ledger. The usual reason is that the bank is busy and the detailed ledger entries are left until the next day before being posted. Consequently, if we wished to check and agree the balance which appeared in the Cash Book with the balance according to the bank's ledger account we would have to make an allowance for the amount which the bank had failed to credit to our account.

We refer to items of this nature as *cheques not yet credited*.

7. Other causes of differences. In addition there are several other items which may cause a temporary failure to agree the two balances. The following are the most usual causes.

(*a*) Bank charges entered in the Bank Statement but not entered in the Cash Book. In this case the bank would charge (i.e., debit) our account with the charge (usually made half-yearly) for keeping our account. No cheque would have been drawn by us for this item and consequently no entry would have been made in the Cash Book (on the credit side). The first information we would have of these charges would be when we checked the entries in detail between Cash Book and Bank Statement. The charge would appear in the Bank Statement but it would not have been entered in our Cash Book.

(*b*) Standing orders. Many people find that a most convenient way of making payments of the same amount at regular intervals is to authorise their banker to perform this service for them, debiting their account with the required amount on the date upon which it becomes due. This is known as "payment by Standing Order". The method is particularly suitable where goods are being bought on hire-purchase and a regular monthly payment of the same amount has to be made. It is also widely used to pay monthly instalments to building societies when a house is being purchased, and also in respect of monthly, quarterly and half-yearly life assurance premiums. The payment of annual subscriptions to professional associations, etc., is yet another example of settlement by Standing Order. In these cases it is usual to wait until the Bank Statement has been received before making the entries in the Cash Book.

(*c*) Dishonoured cheques. If a cheque has been received from a debtor and paid into a bank but is subsequently returned by the debtor's banker because of some defect (e.g., it may not have been signed, it may be dated wrongly, or there may be insufficient funds in the debtor's account to meet the cheque) it is possible that no credit entry would have been made in the Cash Book at the time When the cheque was paid into the bank in the first instance it was debited in the Cash Book If the cheque is returned then a credit entry must be made *cancelling* the original debit. People often fail to do this (since it is a comparatively unusual occurrence) and as a result they are unable to reconcile the Cash Book with the Bank Statement.

(*d*) Traders' Credits. This is a method of settling accounts between business houses. The debtor notifies his bank of the name and address of his creditor's banker and, in effect, instructs him to transfer the amount owed to the credit of his supplier's account. We sometimes come upon such an item in examination questions. Be careful to note in whose favour the Trader's Credit is: is it money coming in from a debtor or is it a payment which is being made to a creditor?

(*e*) Dividends and interest received. Sometimes we find that instructions have been given by shareholders to the effect that any dividends or interest are to be sent direct to their bank. In such cases the probability is that no entry will have been made in the Cash Book. The Bank Statement will, of course, show the item as a credit to the customer's account and, as a result, the necessary entry must be made in the Cash Book in order to effect reconciliation.

8. Examination problems. In almost every examination question which is set by the professional bodies we find that we are not given all the information which would be available if we were faced with the problem of preparing a bank reconciliation for a business in real life. If we were in business we would have the Cash Book in which the Bank Account was written up and, in addition, we would have the relevant Bank Statements. We would thus have at our disposal all the information necessary to prepare a bank reconciliation. Present-day examination problems are made a little more complicated. Most of the necessary information is stated in the question but one vital fact is generally omitted. As a rule the question fails to tell us the closing balance either in the Cash Book or in the Bank Statement. One or other of these balances is missing. As will shortly be shown the "pro forma" which we should use for a bank reconciliation contains:

(*a*) the balance appearing on the Bank Statement;

(*b*) details of any unpresented cheques;

(*c*) details of any cheques which have been paid into the bank but which have not yet been credited to the customer's account, and

(*d*) the balance which appears in the Cash Book (Bank Account).

Since the examination problem usually leaves out either (*a*) or (*d*), we are left with the task of ascertaining the amount of the missing balance before we can complete our answer.

PREPARING A BANK RECONCILIATION

9. Checking the Cash Book against the Bank Statement. If we were attempting to reconcile the Cash Book balance with that on the Bank Statement at the end of a period of, say, one month, we would, first of all, check each entry made during the period in the Cash Book with the corresponding entry in the Bank Statement, for we must remember at all times that the details which are entered in the Cash Book are simply a reflection of those self-same details in the Bank Statement. Bearing this in mind we will correctly conclude that if *all* the items entered in the Cash Book during the period correspond with *all* the items entered in the Bank Statement during the same period the balance in the Cash Book must be exactly the same as the balance in the Bank Statement.

EXAMPLE: The following items were entered in the Cash Book of Hunter & Sons. The bankers were Barclays Bank Ltd.

Bank Account

Capital A/c	£1,000	A. Black		£240
		T. Patterson		85
		The Post Office		10
		Balance c/d		665
	£1,000			£1,000
Balance b/d	£665			

In the Bank Statement (which is a copy of Hunter & Sons' personal account in the ledger of Barclays Bank) the following entries would appear:

Date	Details	Dr	Cr	Balance
	Cheque		£1,000	£1,000
	Black	£240		760
	Patterson	85		675
	The Post Office	10		665

NOTE: The columnar form of accounting is shown here for that is the one in general use by the banks. In the "Details" column above it must be pointed out that, in the majority of cases, only the cheque number appears, no name of the payee being shown, although most of the major banks give details of standing orders. The number of the cheque can be identified with its counterpart on the cheque stub, which should record details of the transaction.

As can be seen, the last item in the Balance column of the Bank Statement corresponds exactly with the balance on the Bank Account in the Cash Book.

If then we checked each entry in the Cash Book with each entry in the Bank Statement we would expect to find the balance in each case to be exactly the same although on opposite sides. And that is just what we should find provided that all additions or other calculations had been made correctly.

10. Unpresented cheques and bank charges. Let us now take another example but this time showing some unpresented cheques and bank charges.

EXAMPLE: The following entries appeared in the Cash Book of J. Snodgrass.

Cash Book (Bank Account)

Dec. 20 Balance b/f	£426		Dec. 23 H. Johnson		£100
Dec. 22 F. Richards	82		Dec. 29 Cash		20
Dec. 31			Dec. 30 Westpark		
T. Burtenshaw	105		Borough Council		51
			Dec. 31 N. Collins & Co		48
			Dec. 31 Balance c/d		394
	£613				£613
Balance b/d	£394				

When the Bank Statement was obtained on 2nd January the information on it was as follows:

Date	Details	Dr	Cr	Balance
Dec. 20	Balance			£426
Dec. 28	Cheque		£82	508
Dec. 29	Cash	£20		488
Dec. 30	Johnson	100		388
Dec. 31	Charges	14		374

In order to reconcile the balance shown on the Bank Statement with that shown in the Cash Book the first thing to do is to check in detail the items which appear in the Cash Book with those in the Bank Statement, placing a tick against each entry with a coloured pencil. A fairly bright colour is recommended, e.g., orange, green or light blue, since these stand out and can be clearly seen. Do not use an ordinary pencil as pencil marks can be erased easily.

Taking the debit side of the Cash Book we find that the item of £82 has been credited in the Bank Statement while the £105 item has not. On checking the credit entries in the Cash Book we find that the £20 and £100 cheques have been duly presented for payment and charged against Snodgrass's account in the bank's ledger. The cheques for £51 and £48 have not yet reached the bank. In other words, the bank, at the close of business on 31st December, is *not aware* that Snodgrass has drawn these two cheques. As a result, naturally enough, they do not appear in the Bank Statements as debits in Snodgrass's account.

We note, however, that in addition to the above matters the bank has debited him with £14 for Bank Charges. When we balanced the Cash Book we were not aware of this; we must now adjust the balance on the Cash Book. That is to say, we must enter in the Cash Book any items which *should* be in it but which, for one reason or another, are not. The only item which falls into this last category is the amount of £14 for Bank Charges. The revised balance on the Cash Book will, therefore, be ascertained in the following manner:

Bank Account

Dec. 31 Balance b/d	£394	Dec. 31 Bank Charges	£14
		Dec. 31 Balance c/d	380
	£394		£394
Balance b/d	£380		

Note how we have adjusted the balance on the Cash Book by entering the item Bank Charges on the credit side of the account.

NOTE:

 (a) We have *not* made any adjustment for the unpresented cheques.

 (b) We have *not* made any adjustment in respect of cheques we have paid *into* the bank but which the bank has not credited to Snodgrass's account.

These are points of very great importance which students frequently fail to appreciate. Only too often do we find them making adjustments for these items. This is utterly wrong. Once the items have been entered in the Cash Book no other action is necessary. The entries have already been made in the Cash Book and once this has been done we must *not* undo them.

11. Making the Reconciliation. The lay-out of the Bank Reconciliation Statement is very simple and should always be adhered to. It is regarded as good practice to start with the balance which appears on the Bank Statement and work down until the final balance is reached. This should be the balance which appears in the Cash Book.

Taking the details of the example in **10** our Reconciliation will appear as follows:

Balance per Bank Statement at 31 Dec.			£374
Less Unpresented cheques:			
	Westpark Borough Council	£51	
	N. Collins & Co	48	99
			275
Add	Cheques paid in but not yet credited by the bank		105
	Balance per Cash Book as adjusted		£380

DEALING WITH EXAMINATION PROBLEMS

12. Recommended method at the examination. At the examination the following procedure is recommended for dealing with questions. These vary, of course, in their requirements but one can be reasonably certain that their main feature will be to test a candidate's ability to make a reconciliation of the Cash Book and the Bank Statement.

13. The Cash Book. Certain items such as Bank Charges, Standing Orders, dividends paid into the bank, etc., will at first appear only in the Bank Statement. These must all be entered in the Cash Book so that every item which is in the Bank Statement now appears in the Cash Book. Having done this, calculate the revised balance on the Cash Book, enter it and carry it down as the corrected and final Cash Book balance. (This, of course, is what would be done, in actual practice, by the cashier of a firm.)

NOTE: On no account should you enter in the Cash Book the unpresented cheques or any amount which has been paid into the bank but which has not been credited to your account by the bank. These items are *already* in the Cash Book.

14. Ascertaining the Bank Statement balance. If the question does not state the amount of the balance on the Bank Statement the next task is to find out what this sum is. It is very helpful if a *memorandum account* for the Bank Statement is opened. Enter on the debit side the total of any unpresented cheques. On the credit side enter the amount of cheques paid in but not yet credited to your account by the bank. By making these two entries you are anticipating those entries which the bank must make in due course. Having already made all the adjusting entries in the Cash Book we can be sure that we have accounted for *every item* which appears in the Bank Statement. Now, having entered the unpresented cheques and the amounts not credited in the Bank Statement Account, we have made certain that every item in the Cash Book appears in the Bank Statement. As a result the two balances *must* be the same. (We already know from **13** above what the correct balance on the Cash Book amounts to.)

Now in the Bank Statement Account enter the final balance which we have ascertained for the Cash Book, on the *opposite* side to that shown in the Cash Book and carry it down. All that now remains is to total up both sides of the Bank Statement Account. The difference between the two sides *must be* the missing balance which the question failed to give.

15. The Bank Reconciliation. With the Bank Statement balance in our possession it is a simple task to set out the Bank Reconciliation. The following pro forma is recommended:

Bank Reconciliation

(*a*) Balance per Bank Statement   £

(*b*)   *Add:* Cheques paid in but not yet credited by the bank

(*c*)   *Less:* Cheques drawn but not yet presented for payment

(*d*) Balance per Cash Book

NOTE:

(*a*) The respective positions of the unpresented cheques and the cheques not yet credited may be reversed if so desired (see example in **11** above).

(*b*) Normally the Bank Reconciliation should contain nothing else but the four items (*a*), (*b*), (*c*) and (*d*) since all other adjustments should have been made *before* you reach the stage of preparing the Reconciliation. Occasionally, however, an examination problem will throw in a point regarding an item wrongly entered in the Current Account which should have appeared in the Deposit Account. Items such as this must be dealt with in the Reconciliation itself because they have no place in the Cash Book.

(*c*) Should the Bank Statement show an overdraft then, for convenience, alter the Reconciliation to read:

> *Overdraft* per Bank Statement   £
>   *Add:* Unpresented cheques
>
>   *Less:* Cheques not credited
>
> Balance (or overdraft) per Cash Book

16. Specimen question. Harrison's Cash Book showed a balance of £189 cash at the bank on 30th April. On checking with the Bank Statement it was found that cheques for £73 had not yet been presented and that an amount of £104 had been paid into the bank but not yet credited to his account in the bank's ledger. Bank Charges of £8 appeared in the Bank Statement but these had not been entered in Harrison's Cash Book. Prepare a Bank Reconciliation.

NOTE: There is no mention of the balance on the Bank Statement. We have first got to find what this amounted to.

SOLUTION:
Stage 1. The first task is to adjust the Cash Book, i.e., to enter the item of Bank Charges in order to show as the final balance the sum which we know must be the correct figure.

Cash Book

Apl. 30 Balance b/d	£189	Apl. 30 Bank Charges		£8
		Apl. 30 *Adjusted* balance c/d		181
	£189			£189
Apl. 30 Balance b/d	£181			

Stage 2. The next task is to adjust the Bank Statement

(a)   *Memorandum Bank Statement Account*

Apl. 30 Balance	?	Apl. 30 Balance	?

We do not know the amount of the balance nor do we know whether it is a debit or a credit balance. Therefore we will show a question mark on both sides for the moment.

We will now enter the unpresented cheques and those which the bank has not credited to Harrison's account

(b)   *Memorandum Bank Statement Account*

Apl. 30 Balance	?	Apl. 30 Balance	?
Apl. 30 Unpresented cheque	£73	Apl. 30 Cheques not credited	£104

The next step is to enter the *adjusted* balance which the Cash Book has produced, i.e., £181.

(*c*)   *Memorandum Bank Statement Account*

Apl. 30 Balance	?	Apl. 30 Balance	?
Apl. 30 Unpresented cheques	£73	Apl. 30 Cheques not credited	£104
Apl. 30 Balance, as ascertained on the Cash Book	181		
	£254		£104

By subtracting £104 from £254 we obtain the figure of £150 which, as has been shown, *must* have been the balance appearing on the proper Bank Statements, as standing to the credit of Harrison.

Finally the Bank Statement Account would appear as follows:

(*d*)   *Memorandum Bank Statement Account*

Apl. 30 Unpresented cheques	£73	Apl. 30 Balance	£150
Apl. 30 Balance c/d	181	Apl. 30 Cheques not credited	104
	£254		£254
		Apl. 30 Balance b/d	£181

Stage 3. Now using the balance of £150 for the Reconciliation we would proceed as follows:

Bank Reconciliation

Balance per Bank Statement	£150
Less: Unpresented cheques	73
	77
Add: Cheques not credited	104
Balance per Cash Book	£181

17. A more complicated specimen question. The balance on the Cash Book of James Emery & Co. showed an overdraft of £41 at 31st March. On checking the details with the Bank Statement it was found that the following items had been debited to the firm's account in the bank's ledger but that none of them appeared as payments on the credit side of the firm's Cash Book:

(*a*) A standing Order of £14 for the month of March in respect of a motor van being bought under a hire purchase agreement.

(*b*) Traders' credits (payments) totalling £30.

(*c*) Interest of £38 in respect of a special Bank Loan to the business.

In addition to these items one of the firm's customers had settled his account by means of a Trader's Credit; i.e., he had instructed his own banker to pay the money direct into Emery & Co.'s bank account. The customer had not notified Emery & Co. of his action. The sum involved was £245 and no entry had been made in the Cash Book.

Unpresented cheques amounted to £108, while an amount of £184 entered in the Cash Book and paid into bank had not been credited in the bank's ledger until 1st April.

Prepare a Bank Reconciliation as at 31st March.

SOLUTION:
Stage 1. Adjust the Cash Book as the first step.

Bank Account (Cash Book)

Mch. 31 Trader's Credit	£245	Mch. 31 Balance *overdrawn*		£41
		Mch. 31 Standing order		14
		Mch. 31 Traders' credits		30
		Mch. 31 Loan interest		38
				123
		Mch. 31 Balance, as *adjusted*		£122
	£245			£245
Mch. 31 Balance b/d	£122			

Stage 2. As the balance according to the Bank Statement has not been given we must now proceed to calculate what it amounted to and see whether it was in Emery's favour or not. We will adopt the same procedure as we did in the first example.

(*a*)   *Memorandum Bank Statement Account*

Mch. 31 Balance	?	Mch. 31 Balance	?

The second step is to enter the unpresented cheques and the cheques which have been paid into the bank but which have not yet been credited to the account of Emery & Co. in the bank's ledger.

(*b*)   *Memorandum Bank Statement Account*

Mch. 31 Balance	?	Mch. 31 Balance	?
Mch. 31 Unpresented cheques	£108	Mch. 31 Cheques not credited	£184

The third step is to enter the adjusted balance of £122 which we calculated on the Cash Book.

(*c*)   *Memorandum Bank Statement Account*

Mch. 31 Balance	?	Mch. 31 Balance	?
Mch. 31 Unpresented cheques	£108	Mch. 31 Cheques not credited	£184
Mch. 31 Balance, as ascertained on the Cash Book	122		
	£230		£184

By subtracting £184 from £230 we obtain a difference of £46 which *must* be the balance actually showing on the Bank Statement at 31st March, as standing to the credit of Emery & Co.

(d)   *Memorandum Bank Statement Account*

Mch. 31 Unpresented			Mch. 31 Balance	£46
cheques	£108		Mch. 31 Cheques not	
Mch. 31 Balance c/d	122		credited	184
	£230			£230
			Mch. 31 Balance b/d	£122

Stage 3. The Bank Reconciliation can now be constructed as follows:

Bank Reconciliation

Balance per Bank Statement	£46
Add: Cheques not credited	184
	230
Less: Unpresented cheques	108
Balance per Cash Book (as adjusted)	£122

NOTE: In this case the unpresented cheques have been brought in after the cheques not credited were added to the balance. The reason for this was that had the unpresented cheques, £108, been subtracted from the balance, £46, we would have shown an overdraft. This might have confused the student.

PROGRESS TEST 3

Theory

1. Explain the relationship between the entries in the Cash Book of a business and those in the bank's ledger relating to the firm. **(1, 2)**

2. What do you understand by the term "Bank Statement"? Explain its purpose. **(3)**

3. What is an "unpresented cheque"? **(5)**

4. Explain the meaning of the term "cheques not yet credited." **(6)**

5. Make a list of those items which may have been omitted temporarily from the Cash Book. **(7)**

Practice

6. What is meant by the phrase "Bank Reconciliation Statement"?

A trader's Cash Book has been made up, and it is then found:

(*a*) that two cheques for £100 and £50 respectively have not been cleared (they were both issued by the trader three days ago);

(*b*) that the trader's bank has paid out £20 on a Standing Order some days before this was expected to occur; no entry has been made in the Cash Book.

What will be the effect of these matters on the amount of the balance in the Cash Book? Give reasons for your answer.

(S.U.J.B.)

7. When J. Rogers received his Bank Statement for 31st December 19–4, he found that the balance therein differed from that in the Cash Book. A thorough check was then made of the Cash Book, the following items being raised for attention.

(*a*) The bank had wrongly debited a cheque for £25 which should have been placed against another customer's account.

(*b*) Cheques drawn up to 31st December 19–4, but not presented, totalled £1,060.

(*c*) Credit transfers which had been reported to Mr Rogers, but which had not been entered in the bank's ledger, totalled £545.

(*d*) Items in the Bank Account which had not been entered in the Cash Book were:

    (*i*) standing orders dealt with—£100
    (*ii*) bank interest and charges—£132

If the balance shown in Mr Rogers's Cash Book indicating the amount in the bank at 31st December 19–4 was £2,000, what was the balance shown in the Bank Statement?

(S.U.J.B.)

8. On 31st May B. Bee's Bank Statement showed that he had a balance at the bank of £230. On comparing the Statement with the Cash Book he found that the following entries on the Statement

had not been entered in his Cash Book: payment of insurance premium by Standing Order, £25; dividend on an investment paid direct to the bank, £15.

He also found the following entries in the Cash Book had not yet appeared on the Statement: cheques drawn up to 31st May, £616; cheques paid in on 31st May, £405.

Prepare a Bank Reconciliation Statement so as to show the Bank Balance according to the Cash Book on 31st May.

(N.J.E.C.)

9. On 31st December C. Courage's Bank Statement showed that he had an overdraft of £460. On comparing the Statement with his Cash Book he found that the following entries on the statement had not been entered in his Cash Book: payment of subscription by Standing Order, £10; Bank Charges for the half-year, £18.

He also found that the following entries in the Cash Book had not yet appeared on the Statement: cheques drawn up to 31st December, £308; cheques paid in on 30th and 31st December, £622.

Prepare a Bank Reconciliation Statement so as to show the Bank Balance according to the Cash Book on 31st December.

(N.J.E.C.)

10. A Trading and Profit and Loss Account for the year ended on 31st March prepared by F.V., a trader, showed a net profit of £4,128.

According to F.V.'s Cash Book the balance at the bank on 31st March was £832. You are informed that:

(*a*) Cheques from customers, amounting to £174, which were entered in F.V.'s Cash Book on 31st March were not credited by the bank until 1st April.

(*b*) Cheques drawn by F.V. on 30th March in favour of trade creditors, amounting to £259, were not paid by the bank until after 31st March.

(*c*) On 20th March a customer had paid £68 into F.V.'s Bank Account in full settlement of a debit balance of £70 in F.V.'s sales ledger, but no entries for this had been made in F.V.'s books.

(*d*) On 28th February the bank had paid, in accordance with standing instructions from F.V., the following:

(*i*) trade subscriptions, £6;

(*ii*) a monthly amount due under a hire-purchase agreement for the acquisition of household equipment for F.V.'s private house, £27.

No entries for these matters have been made in F.V.'s books.

You are required to prepare statements showing:

(a) The balance which should appear in the Cash Book on 31st March after making all the necessary corrections.

(b) A calculation of the balance shown on the Bank Statement by means of a Reconciliation Statement.

(c) F.V.'s correct profit for the year to 31st March.

(I.C.S.A.)

11. The following items appeared in the Bank Statement of Walter Russell & Co. for the month of June:

BANK STATEMENT

Date	Details	Dr	Cr	Balance
June		£	£	£
1	Balance			802 Cr
1	Sundries		127	
1	Myers	18		
2	Cash	25		
4	Parker	109		
7	Sundries		73	
10	Cash	25		
12	Richards	54		
15	Morgan	60		
16	Sundries		145	
17	Cash	25		
21	Harker	21		
22	Dillon	7		
24	Cash	25		
28	Bank charges	6		
29	Webster	14		
30	Sundries		84	
30	West	27		
30	Balance			815 Cr

The Cash Book of the firm had been written up during June from the Paying-in Book and the counterfoils in the cheque book, as follows:

CASH BOOK

June		£	June		£
1	Balance b/d	—	1	Petty cash	25
6	Sundries	73	7	Richards	54
15	Sundries	145	8	Morgan	60
29	Sundries	84	9	Petty cash	25
30	Sundries	139	14	West	27
			15	Porter	19
			16	Petty cash	25
			23	Webster	14
			23	Petty cash	25
			29	Forrester	108
			30	Woods	29

You are to assume that the amounts paid into the bank on one day are not credited by the bank to Russell and Co.'s Account until the next day.

(a) Ascertain the balance standing on the Cash Book at 1st June.
(b) Prepare a list of unpresented cheques at 30th June.
(c) Prepare a Bank Reconciliation at 30th June.

CHAPTER IV

The Journal

THE MAIN PURPOSE AND USES OF THE JOURNAL

1. The purpose of the "Day Books". We have already seen in *Basic Book-keeping* that "Day Books" or "Journals" are used to record the purchase or sale of goods on credit, or for recording the return of unsuitable goods to the source from which they originally came. The entries in these Day Books (also known as "Returns Books") are made from the original documents relating to particular transactions. Thus, if goods costing £75 are purchased from J. Snodgrass an invoice will normally be the original document and the details of date, name and amount will be the information to be recorded in the Purchase Day Book.

The purpose of these Day Books is to act as an "aide-memoire" to the person responsible for keeping the ledgers written up to date. That is to say, they are a form of daily diary in which will be recorded those transactions on credit which have taken place on a particular day. These diary entries are the basic information from which the double entry is made.

2. The Journal. In some businesses there still survives a book which has largely disappeared from the accounting scene. This book is called the "Journal". Sometimes it is spoken of as the "General Journal" or the "Private Journal".

Today, the Journal is used comparatively rarely in business but as it is a great favourite with many examiners students must make themselves familiar with it and its method of operation.

Although the name "Journal" has links with the various Day Books and although the rulings of the Journal are absolutely identical with the rulings found in the Day Books the use to which the rulings in the Journal are put are completely different.

3. The purpose of the Journal. The fundamental idea of a Journal entry is that it should tell us at a glance the two accounts in the ledger which are to be debited and credited respectively with the item under consideration.

EXAMPLE: By mistake the account of P. Evans in the Sales Ledger had been debited with a sale of £25. This should have been debited to the account of F. Evans. Show the Journal entry required to correct the error.

Looking first at the original entries (when the mistake was made) we see the following:

P. Evans Account

Sales A/c	£25	

Sales Account

	P. Evans A/c	£25

P. Evans is *not* a debtor since he has purchased nothing. It is F. Evans who should have been charged with the sum of £25 and so we must cancel the debit in the account of P. Evans and charge it to F. Evans. This will be done very simply by crediting the account of P. Evans and debiting that of F. Evans, as follows:

P. Evans Account

Sales A/c	£25	**F. Evans A/c**	**£25**

F. Evans Account

P. Evans A/c	**£25**	

The account of P. Evans has now been closed off and this, of course, is only right since nothing has been sold to him. F. Evans, on the other hand, has been properly charged with the sum of £25.

4. How the Journal is used. The rulings of the Journal, as was mentioned above, are exactly the same as the rulings of the various Day Books. The Day Books are used to serve as a reminder of the details of certain transactions, each of which must be posted daily to the personal account of the party concerned and, at the end of the month, the total of all the transactions will be entered in the appropriate nominal account, e.g., Sales Account, thus completing the double entry.

In the example given in **3** we showed how the items would appear in the ledger accounts. This was done so that the student could see what we may call the end-product: these entries in the ledger would normally only be made *after* the items had been entered in the Journal.

Now let us look at those same items in Journal form.

JOURNAL

			Fol	Dr	Cr
Date	F. Evans A/c	Dr		£25	
	To P. Evans A/c Correction of entry wrongly charged to P. Evans				£25

Attention is drawn to the following points. First of all, it must be noted that the account to be debited is always shown as the first entry and it is followed by the sign *Dr* indicating that this is the account which is to be debited. Next, look at the credit entry. This always bears the prefix "To." For emphasis it is inset a little from the margin of the date column. Finally the entries are followed by what is known as "the narration". This always used to start with the word "being" but today it is regarded as an archaic survival and is hardly ever used.

As can be seen the Journal entry is a kind of "shorthand" version of the entries which should appear in the respective ledger accounts.

5. The three basic uses of the Journal. Every single transaction which a business enters into *could* be translated into the terms of a Journal entry, but very few, in fact, are. So far as examinations are concerned, Journal entries are usually only required in three broad sets of circumstances. These are as follows.

    (*a*) The "opening" entries where:
        (*i*) a *new* business is starting, or;
        (*ii*) a new owner takes over an *existing* business.
    (*b*) The "closing" entries where:
        (*i*) a business is *ceasing* to trade or;
        (*ii*) an existing business has been *sold* to a new owner or;

(*iii*) circumstances are such that the "journalising" of certain items greatly assists and expedites the preparation of the accounts at the end of the financial year, e.g., where a business has a number of branches whose trading results have to be incorporated with those of the head office.

(*c*) For the purpose of correcting book-keeping errors (as illustrated in **3** above).

In the professional examinations, where a very high degree of knowledge is expected, we frequently encounter problems which require the candidate to work out a number of Journal entries. These questions appear so often that it is of paramount importance that students master this aspect of the subject. There is, of course, the additional personal satisfaction of knowing that one is equipping oneself with a greater degree of expertise. The examiner in these advanced examinations usually takes some kind of business transaction which requires *several* Journal entries. Often we find that such problems have no real bearing on the three major points referred to above; the object of the examiner is to test the ability of the student to think in terms of Journal entries generally. Far too many students try to answer such questions "in their head", so to speak, often with disastrous results. Students new to this subject are therefore recommended to train themselves along the lines set down in **9**.

JOURNALISING

6. Journalising the opening entries. Problems are often presented in an incomplete state so far as the position at the start of a period of trading is concerned. As a rule the pattern followed is identical. That is to say, all of the assets are stated in some detail: the amounts owing for goods and for services are also given; we are therefore left with the need to ascertain the amount of the "opening capital" which is, of course, the difference between the total of the assets and the total of the external liabilities, i.e., the amount owing to the various creditors.

The simplest way of dealing with this is to set out, in the form of a partial Journal entry, the information which is available, as stated in the question. This means that each item given as an asset must be placed in the *debit* column and, conversely, each liability should be placed in the *credit* column. The difference is the capital, the "unknown quantity".

EXAMPLE: The following are the assets and liabilities on 1st January of K. Swinfen who is intending to commence trading as a tobacconist. Stock £1,530; shop fittings, £415; bank, £280; cash in hand, £25; owing to Stringer & Co. for shop fittings, £200; owing to Blake for goods, £320.

Prepare a Journal entry setting out the opening position.

JOURNAL

19—		Fol	Dr	Cr
Jan. 1	Stock Dr		£1,530	
	Shop fittings		415	
	Bank		280	
	Cash		25	
			£2,250	
	To creditors:			
	Stringer			£200
	Blake			320
				520
	Capital = the difference			1,730
				£2,250
	Assets and liabilities at this date			

With this information journalised we now have a permanent record in Swinfen's Journal showing all of his assets and liabilities including his opening capital. Each item can now be transferred to its appropriate account, thus giving us a ledger which balances. It must be appreciated how important this is, for unless the books balance at the *start* of trading they will for ever remain in an "unbalanced" state.

7. Journalising closing entries. It is not usual for a business to pass entries through the Journal when dealing with the normal transfers to the Trading Account or Profit and Loss Account. Very often, however, professional accountants find it convenient to use Journal entries when dealing with adjustments which they deem necessary in the preparation of clients' accounts. In many cases the client does not have a proper set of books, let alone a Journal, and so the accountant is forced to make certain adjusting entries on what are called "working papers" which he retains on his file lest they may need to be referred to in the future.

EXAMPLE: J. Snodgrass, a retail trader, did not keep proper records and his accountant, when preparing his annual accounts, was forced to make estimates in relation to certain items. These he showed as Journal entries on the client's file.

Unrecorded cash drawing	£1,040
Goods taken from stock by Snodgrass for his own consumption	375
Petrol purchased by Snodgrass for the business out of his own pocket for which no receipts had been obtained	156

Make the Journal entries necessary to account for the above matters.

JOURNAL

19—		Fol	Dr	Cr
Dec. 31	Capital A/c (drawings) *Dr* To Sales A/c Estimate of money drawn from *cash takings* for own use (£20 per week)		£1,040	£1,040
	Capital A/c (drawings) *Dr* To Purchases A/c Estimate of goods taken from stock for own use		£375	£375
	Motor Expenses A/c *Dr* To Capital A/c Estimate of petrol purchased ex. own pocket (£3 per week)		£156	£156

TRAINING TECHNIQUE

8. Journal entries in examination questions. As was mentioned earlier in this chapter many examiners set problems requiring that the answer be given in the form of Journal entries. This applies not only to the more junior type of examination but also to the advanced examinations of the professional bodies. The reason for this is that by asking the student to show the appropriate Journal entries the examiner can readily assess the student's grasp of accounting principles. For this reason it is vitally important that this aspect of the use of the Journal should be studied with great diligence and every opportunity taken of working problems requiring the production of Journal entries in the answer.

Many of the problems are quite difficult, and in far too many cases students attempt to answer them in a very haphazard manner. Frequently they seem to have little idea as to how to set about their task; sometimes, however, one finds that the student has got the right idea but reverses the entries in the Journal, debiting what should appear as a credit, and vice versa. This is a particularly sad situation, since the examiner knows that the candidate is basically capable of solving the problem yet he cannot allow him any marks for his answer.

9. A suggested method of training. In the light of the remarks in **8**, it is important that students should be given some guidance. The first thing to be recognised is that Journal entries are a shortened form of ledger entries. That being so, the student should set himself to think, first of all, how the entries would appear if, in fact, they were entered in the appropriate ledger accounts. He should then go one step further and actually open ledger accounts ("T" accounts are quite sufficient for this purpose) and make the necessary entries therein. This practice, however, does present certain difficulties to the novice because even though he opens the ledger accounts he still finds that he is on unsure ground; he does not know exactly where to start making his entries or is, perhaps, uncertain as to which side of the account the entry should be made.

EXAMPLE: A cheque for £18 was received from A. Customer and paid into the bank. A week later it was returned by the bank marked "refer to drawer." Journalise this entry.

Here, by back-tracking one stage, we would find that goods

had originally been sold to A. Customer for £18. The sale and the receipt of his cheque would appear as below:

A. Customer Account

Sales A/c	£18	Bank A/c	£18

Bank Account

A. Customer A/c	£18		

When the cheque was *returned* the "status quo" would exist and the position would be:

A. Customer Account

Bank A/c (*cheque returned*)	£18		

Bank Account

		A. Customer A/c	£18

Thus we see A. Customer back to his previous condition, i.e., that of a debtor for £18.

The Journal entry can be easily picked out from the ledger accounts. The relevant entries are shown in italics above.

JOURNAL

		Dr	Cr
A. Customer A/c *Dr*		£18	
To Bank A/c			£18
Cheque returned marked R.D.			

EXAMPLES: A cheque for £25 received from S. Lewis was correctly entered in the Bank Account but was debited to Lewis's account. The difference in the books was entered temporarily in a Suspense Account. Make the Journal entries necessary to account for this.

The first thing to do is to ask oneself why it was that Lewis *paid* £25. The answer, obviously, is that he was paying for goods or services for that amount. Therefore let us take matters back one stage and show Lewis as a debtor for £25:

S. Lewis Account

Sales A/c	£25	

Clearly Lewis owes £25. When he pays this amount it is correctly entered in the Bank Account, i.e. *debited* therein. The corresponding credit should be to Lewis's account, but we are told that it was *debited* to Lewis's account. The position, therefore, now reads as follows:

S. Lewis Account

Sales A/c	£25	
Bank A/c	25	
	——	
	£50	

We have here reached a position whereby we can correctly conclude that £25 has been debited *twice*, once in the Bank Account and a second time in Lewis's account. This gives us a total of £50 debited in the books and *nothing* at all credited. This, of course, was the reason for the difference which, when a Trial Balance was extracted, was placed to the credit of the Suspense Account.

Suspense Account

	Difference on Trial Balance	£50

Since Lewis has, in fact, paid his debt he is a debtor no longer.

The correction is very simple. We debit the Suspense Account with £50 and credit the account of S. Lewis with £50. This closes off both accounts.

The question asks for the Journal entry. It would appear thus:

JOURNAL

		Dr	Dr
Suspense A/c	Dr	£50	
To S. Lewis A/c			£50
Correction of item wrongly posted			

From this Journal entry we would make the necessary postings to the appropriate ledger accounts as shown below:

S. Lewis Account

Sales A/c	£25	*Journal*	**£50**
Bank A/c	25		
	———		———
	£50		£50

Suspense Account

Journal	**£50**	Difference on Trial	
		Balance	£50

The postings *from* the Journal are shown in italics. When these have been completed the position is rectified and the accounts are automatically closed.

These two examples should be sufficient to indicate the way to set about these problems but it must again be emphasised that a great deal of practice is required in order to gain confidence and proficiency.

PROGRESS TEST 4

Theory

1. Describe the purpose of Day Books. **(1)**
2. What is the purpose of the General Journal? **(3)**
3. Describe the lay-out of a Journal entry drawing particular attention to the main features. **(4)**
4. What types of entries is the Journal mainly used for? **(5)**
5. What do you understand by the following terms (*a*) opening entries, (*b*) closing entries? **(6, 7)**

Practice

6. Prepare the opening Journal entries from the following information:

Herbert Aveling had paid rent in advance for three months, £90.
He was owed £207 by certain customers.

He owed £144 to his suppliers, £19 for electricity and £16 for telephone charges.

The business possessed shop equipment valued at £625, a delivery van worth £380 and stock at cost, £942.

7. The liabilities and assets of S. Keenan on 1st September are set out below. Prepare the Journal entries to open a set of books on that date and ascertain his capital. Post each item to the appropriate account in the ledger.

Liabilities		*Assets*	
Creditors for goods	£1,168	Land and buildings	£7,240
Creditors for expenses:		Shop fittings	1,329
Telephone	31	Shop equipment	576
Light and heat	27	Delivery van	440
Advertising	64	Stock	3,687
		Debtors	966
		Cash at bank	1,201
		Cash in hand	43

8. Enter the following transactions in the Journal of Bosworth, a builder:

Nov. 1   He bought a second-hand concrete mixer for £118, paying by cheque, and entered it under purchases of materials.

Nov. 7   An invoice for materials from Grant & Co. for £79 dated 17th October was discovered at the back of his desk. No entries had been made in the books.

Nov. 14   It was found that wages, amounting to £165, paid to some of his workmen who were building a garage for Bosworth at his private house, had been charged to the Wages Account.

Nov. 18   Bank charges of £14 had, by mistake been debited to the Insurance Account.

Nov. 23   It was found that the Purchase Day Book total for October had been undercast by £100, but an invoice for the same amount had not been posted to the account of Harley & Sons.

Nov. 26   Bosworth had received £45 in cash from A. Vance, a customer. He had not made any entry in the books and had used the money privately.

9. Fleetwood was the manager of a hotel which was owned by a brewery. He paid the brewers a rent of £2,000 per annum but took all the profits for the business. The hotel had a bar, a restaurant and a number of rooms which were let on a nightly basis. Each of the three sections were treated separately with regard to supplies and receipts.

Enter the following matters in Fleetwood's Journal:

June 4   A bill from the brewery, Hornbeams Ltd., for £1,560 for supplies, had not been entered in the books.

June 10 Receipts from hotel customers amounting to £127 for accommodation had been entered as bar sales receipts in the ledger.

June 15 Fleetwood was in the habit of taking cash from the bar sales till for his own use. On this day he took £30 but omitted to leave a note to this effect.

June 21 £12 was paid from the bar sales till to the stocktaker who visited the hotel at three-monthly intervals. No record of this had been made in the books.

10. The following balances were extracted from the books of G. Pennyfeather on 31st December:

Cash in hand	£23
Debtors	189
Stock at 31st December	487
Cash at bank	510
Fixtures	520
Premises	2,450
Creditors	617
Loans from D. Jones	430

The books were arithmetically correct, but certain errors were found.

Make the necessary adjustments by means of Journal entries and show the Balance Sheet as corrected.

(a) A cash sale of £16 had been posted to a creditor's account.

(b) J. Wilkins had bought goods to the value of £65 on 22nd December and on 27th December returned £15 worth. The returns were taken into stock on 31st December but the credit to Wilkins's account had not been entered in the books.

(*c*) Pennyfeather had drawn £75 for a week's holiday the previous August and had charged this in the Wages Account.

(*d*) Goods costing £88 had been delivered on 31st December, taken into stock but no entries had been made in the ledger.

11. David Cloncurrey was self-employed and acted as agent for a number of firms, being remunerated on a commission basis. On 4th June, he changed his car. He received the following invoice from Superior Motor Garages:

Vauxhall Cresta saloon (including tax)	£1,515.55
Automatic transmission	85.00
Reclining front seats	30.00
Supply and fit wing mirrors	5.74
Delivery charges	10.75
Road Fund Tax for 12 months	25.00
Comprehensive insurance	62.00
Number plates	5.75
Delivery petrol	1.37
	1,741.16
Less: Allowance on old Cresta	500.00
	£1,241.16

The old Cresta stood in the books at £542.00. Cloncurrey settled his account by cheque on 11th June.

Journalise the above matters including the settlement of the account with Superior Motor Garages.

12. On 31st October 19–4 Lomax Motors purchased a freehold property. Until that date the business had occupied part of the building at a rent of £840 per annum. The other part was occupied by McLintock & Co. at a rent, payable to the owner, of £252 per annum. All rates and repairs were payable by the owner. The tenancy of McLintock & Co. was continued, on the same terms as before, after 31st October 19–4.

The total amount paid by Lomax Motors in connection with the purchase of the property was £10,194. This represented the purchase price of the property, with additions or deductions in respect of the following.

(*a*) Rates for the five months to 31st March 19–5, paid by the vendor, £60.

(*b*) Water rate for the month of October 19–4, outstanding at 31st October, £1.

(*c*) Legal expenses relating to the purchase of the property, £317.

(*d*) Rent paid in advance to the vendor for the months of November and December 19–4:

(*i*) by Lomax Motors	£140
(*ii*) by McLintock & Co.	£42

You are required to:

(*a*) Show the entries for the above matters (including cash transactions) in the Journal of Lomax Motors.

(*b*) Show the amount at which the property should appear in the Balance Sheet of Lomax Motors as on the date of acquisition, 31st October 19–4.

(*I.C.S.A.*)

CHAPTER V

Suspense Accounts

INTRODUCTION

1. The Suspense Account is a temporary measure. When a Trial Balance is taken out it is by no means unusual to find that the two sides do not agree. We refer to this state of affairs as "having a difference on our Trial Balance" or "a difference in the books". Sometimes the urgency of the situation does not allow time to find the difference because the final accounts and Balance Sheet are needed urgently. In such circumstances the custom is to open a Suspense Account as a temporary measure and to prepare the final accounts and Balance Sheet before finding the difference.

2. The initial entry. Suppose the Trial Balance showed the following totals brought forward from the previous sheet:

	Debit	Credit
Brought forward	£27,194	£27,143

The next step would be to enter the difference in the Trial Balance and then to open a Suspense Account in the Private Ledger, placing the difference in the books on the same side as the entry made in the Trial Balance. The above Trial Balance would then read as follows:

	Debit	Credit
Brought forward	£27,194	£27,143
Difference in books		51
	£27,194	£27,194

In the Private Ledger we would open a Suspense Account as follows:

Suspense Account

	Difference in books	£51

SINGLE ENTRIES

3. The effect on a Trial Balance of a mistake in the book-keeping.
Having taken this emergency measure and placed the difference in
an account of its own we may now pause and consider what has
happened. We took out a Trial Balance and found that it did not
agree. What was the reason for this? In the process of recording our
business transactions under the double-entry system we must have
made one error at the very least. For the moment we are not
concerned with the type of mistake which has been made. What we
want to think about is the *effect* that the making of a mistake in the
double entry has upon the Trial Balance.

Two examples will help us to see and understand this effect.

4. A mistake in the additions. The first example shows the effect of
an error which has been made in the additions. In this instance the
error is shown to have been made in a subsidiary book, but the
same principle holds good no matter where a mistake in the additions occurs.

EXAMPLE: The Sales Day Book for the month of May has been
undercast by £100, i.e., the total sales for May appear to be
£2,800 instead of £2,900.

The effect of such an error is exactly the same as if an item of
£100 had been entered on the debit side of the ledger and
nothing at all entered on the credit side, i.e., a *single* entry.

Consider what has happened in detail. Each item which appeared in the Sales Day Book had been debited separately in the
personal account of the customer concerned. The total of these
debits amounted to £2,900. The corresponding entry for all these
debits is posted to the credit side of the Sales Account in one
lump sum, the Sales Day Book *total*, which had been wrongly
added up as £2,800. We thus have the following position:

Debits	*Credits*
in the customers' personal accounts	in one lump sum in the Sales Account
£2,900	£2,800

We can see at a glance that there is a shortage of £100 on the
credit side. Therefore if we open a Suspense Account as a tem-

porary measure and credit it with £100 we are, in essence, *completing* the double entry.

5. An error made when completing a double-entry posting. This example shows the effect that *a transposition of figures* has upon the balancing of the books.

EXAMPLE: A payment by cheque of £89 has been posted to the debit of the supplier's personal account in the Bought Ledger as £98.

Here it can be seen that £9 has been placed on the debit side of a ledger account for which there is no corresponding credit, i.e., £98 debited; £89 credited; difference, £9. The effect, once more, is that of a single entry for £9 on the debit side. If a Suspense Account is created to deal with this matter pending the finding of the mistake we would credit it with £9. The effect of this would simply be to *complete* the double entry. It must be clearly understood that this is done only as a temporary measure, until such time as the error is discovered.

OPENING A SUSPENSE ACCOUNT

6. The effect of a failure to complete the double-entry posting. The two examples above deal with errors made in the actual performance of the double entry. In the following example we show the effect of an omission to post the item to the *opposite* side of the ledger.

EXAMPLE: The following entries were made in a trader's books:

Capital Account				Bank Account			
		Bank	£250	Capital	£250	Purchases	£148
				Sales	72	Balance	174
					£322		£322

A. Customer Account				A. Supplier Account			
Sales	£190					Purchases	£60

Sales Account				Purchases Account			
		A. Customer	£190	Bank	£148		
				A. Supplier	60		
					208		

TRIAL BALANCE

	Dr	Cr
Capital		£250
Bank	£174	
A. Customer	190	
A. Supplier		60
Sales		190
Purchases	208	
	£572	£500

It is evident that the Trial Balance does not agree. What is the cause?

If we check the postings we find that the item of £72 for sales which has been debited in the Bank Account has not been credited *anywhere*. The cause of the difference then is a genuine single entry, for it is quite clear that we have debited the Bank Account with £72 and have not made a corresponding credit entry.

Let us imagine that we have no time to look for this difference at present. In such a case we should insert the difference in the Trial Balance under the heading "Suspense Account, £72" in the following manner:

TRIAL BALANCE

	Dr	Cr
Capital		£250
Bank	£174	
A. Customer	190	
A. Supplier		60
Sales		190
Purchases	208	
Suspense account— difference in books		72
	£572	£572

The Trial Balance now agrees, but it must be remembered that we still have a *single* entry in our ledger accounts. To correct this state of affairs we must open a Suspense Account and *credit* it with £72. That is to say, we will take the item of £72 which has been entered on the credit side of the Trial Balance and place it on the credit side of the Suspense Account. In this way we do, in fact, complete the double entry.

NOTE: The entry which is made in the Suspense Account must be on *the same side* as is the difference in the Trial Balance.

Suspense Account

	Difference in Trial Balance	£72

We have now completed the double entry in respect of the £72, i.e., the debit entry appears in the Bank Account and the credit entry in the Suspense Account.

7. The action to be taken when the difference is found. When it is discovered that the difference on the books arose through the failure to complete the double entry we must *debit* the Suspense Account with £72 and *credit* the Sales Account. That is to say, we enter the item finally on the credit side of the account to which it should have been credited in the first place. This action, of course, disposes of the balance on the Suspense Account.

Suspense Account

Sales A/c	£72	Difference in Trial Balance	£72

Sales Account

	Suspense A/c	£72

NOTE: When the mistake is found it is essential that we make a *double* entry to correct our books, for when we opened the Suspense Account we *completed* the original double entry by crediting the account with £72. It follows, therefore, that if we are going to make any further entries they must be *double* entries since the fundamental rule of book-keeping insists that every debit must have its corresponding credit.

8. Where a mistake is made in taking out the Trial Balance. Let us look now at another case where we have a difference on the Trial Balance.

EXAMPLE: The entries in the ledger accounts of a trader were as shown below:

Capital Account			P. Cleghorn Account		
	Bank	£425	Sales	£109	

Bank Account				Sales Account		
Capital	£425	Purchases	£81		P. Cleghorn	£109
Sales	46	B. Winters	95		Bank	46
		Balance c/d	295			
	£471		£471			£155
Balance b/d	£295					

Purchases Account			B. Winters Account		
Bank	£81		Bank	£95	Purchases	£195
B. Winters	195		Balance c/d	100		
	£276			£195		£195
					Balance b/d	£100

TRIAL BALANCE

	Dr	Cr
Capital		£425
Bank	£295	
Purchases	276	
P. Cleghorn	109	
Sales		155
	£680	£580

Here again we find a Trial Balance which does not agree, and again we must ask ourselves the reason for such lack of agreement. If we check the postings between the various accounts we find that they have all been correctly made; the *double* entry has been properly carried out. What, then, has gone wrong? The error arises through the *omission* of a balance of £100 (which has come about as a result of correctly carrying out the rules of double entry) in the Trial Balance. This is the £100 owing to B. Winters.

Let us imagine that we cannot locate the difference and that we show it in the Trial Balance as "Suspense Account—difference in books, £100". Having done this we should then open a Suspense Account and enter this *supposed* difference on the same side as it appears in the Trial Balance. Below is shown the detailed procedure:

TRIAL BALANCE

	Dr	*Cr*
Capital		£425
Bank	£295	
Purchases	276	
P. Cleghorn	109	
Sales		155
Suspense account—difference in books		100
	£680	£680

We now open a Suspense Account as follows:

Suspense Account

	Difference in books	£100

The entry which we have made in the Suspense Account is a *single* entry. It was made in the belief that a genuine mistake had occurred in the book-keeping. In fact, no such mistake had been made and so, when the Suspense Account was opened and credited with £100, this was, *in itself* a single entry. From the simplicity of the example given it is quite clear that the double entry had been carried out perfectly correctly. The error lay in the failure to include the full results of the double entry in the Trial Balance.

CLOSING THE SUSPENSE ACCOUNT

9. What happens when the difference is found? When the mistake is discovered all that is required is that we *cancel* the single entry in the Suspense Account by entering on the opposite side of that account the amount of the error. We thus *complete* the double entry. It must be clearly understood how very different is this second type of error from those shown in **4, 5** and **6**.

The Suspense Account would be completed and closed off as follows:

Suspense Account

Balance on creditor's account omitted from Trial Balance	£100	Difference in books	£100

When the Trial Balance was extracted part of the double entry which had been made correctly in the ledge was left out. As a temporary measure we made a single entry of **£100** on the credit side of the Suspense Account When we found our mistake all that was necessary was for the *double* entry to be completed. This was done by entering £100 on the debit side of the Suspense Account as shown above.

DEALING WITH EXAMINATION PROBLEMS

10. Specimen question. Let us now take a fairly simple problem and see how we might deal with it.

The Trial Balance for the year ended 31st December failed to agree. The errors which had caused the difference were as follows.

(*a*) An invoice for £172 from Falcon had been entered in the Bought Day Book correctly but had been posted as £271 in Falcon's account.

(*b*) The Sales Day Book additions for the month of December had been undercast by £10, i.e., the total was shown as £10 less than it should have been.

(*c*) The debit balance on the Motor Van Accounts, £120, had been omitted from the Trial Balance.

You are required to ascertain the amount of the original difference on the Trial Balance.

SUGGESTED SOLUTION: In the first place it is suggested that each mistake be treated in isolation, as though it were the *only* mistake. Then consider what effect these would have on the Trial Balance: which side of the Trial Balance would have the larger total?

Having worked this out (if necessary by setting out on paper what we think has happened) we can then see which side of the Trial Balance is in need of an additional amount to enable it to balance. As has been stated already we must, at this point, open a Suspense Account and enter in it, on the same side on which the Trial Balance is short, the amount which is required.

Taking each error on its own and applying the above suggestions we might, perhaps, argue along the following lines:

(*a*) The invoice for £172 has been entered correctly in the Bought Day Book. Therefore, the amount debited to the Purchases Account at the end of the month would be the correct figure, but it has been credited to the personal account of Falcon as a completely different amount, i.e., as £271. We have, as a result, this position:

Debits	Credits
£172	
	£271
99	
£271	£271

If this difference of £99 is taken in isolation the Trial Balance would show a total on the credit side which *exceeded* that on the debit side by £99. The Suspense Account which we now open will, therefore, have to be debited with £99. The entry in the Suspense Account will appear on the same side as the difference shown in the Trial Balance. The reason is clear. By making a credit entry of £271 against a debit of £172 we have been responsible for what amounts to a single entry to the extent of £99 on the credit side.

(*b*) The additions of the Sales Day Book were short of their proper total by £10 and as a result the Sales Account will be short on the credit side when the total is posted from the Day Book. The *individual* invoices which appear in the Sales Day Book will have been debited one by one to the personal accounts of the customers in the Sales Ledger. If we were to make a total of all these individual postings we would find that they come to £10 more than the corresponding credit in the Sales Account. Thus the effect is exactly the same as if a *single* entry of £10 had been made. It follows, therefore, that if this mistake was the only one the Trial Balance would have £10 more on the debit side than on the credit side and so, in order to balance, an amount of £10 would have to be inserted in the credit column of the Trial Balance. We would therefore have to place £10 on the credit side of the Suspense Account and in this way the double entry would be completed.

(*c*) The mistake here only concerns the Trial Balance and *not* the double entry. Once again we will assume that this error is the only one. The Trial Balance in this case is short on the debit side by £120. We therefore fill the gap by placing this amount in the debit column and make an entry of £120 in the Suspense Account *also* on the debit side.

Since the double entry has already been correctly made in the ledger accounts it follows that *this* entry in the Suspense Account must be a single entry. In other words, strictly speaking, it should never have been necessary to make it. The double entry had been carried out quite correctly; the carelessness arose when taking out the Trial Balance. The debit balance of £120 was there but that fact was completely overlooked.

Having decided upon the necessary entries, we will now make them in the Suspense Account.

Suspense Account (Part I)

Overcredit to Falcon's A/c in the Bought Ledger	£99	Error in the additions of the Sales Day Book (total being less than should have been)	£10
Omission of the balance on the Motor Van A/c from the Trial Balance	120	Difference c/d to Part II	209
	£219		£219

Having reached this point it is a matter of simple arithmetic to find the amount of the original difference in the Trial Balance;

£10 on the credit side subracted from £219 on the debit gives us a net difference of £209, which is the answer required. Since this is a debit figure, we would have needed to make an entry of £209 in the debit column of the Trial Balance in order to balance it. Thus, we would show a debit entry of £209 on the Suspense Account in order to have our books correctly balanced, temporarily. We therefore carry down the difference to the debit side of the second part of the Suspense Account as shown below:

Suspense Account (Part II)

Difference b/d	£209

Having succeeded in finding out what the original difference in the Trial Balance amounted to, we can now make the entries which would correct our books.

Taking the errors one by one, we find the following facts.

(*a*) Falcon's account has been *over*-credited by £99. It should therefore be *debited* with this amount in order to show the true position. A corresponding credit entry must, of course, be made in the Suspense Account.

(*b*) The Sales Account requires a further £10 on the *credit* side in order to show the true amount of sales. So we credit the Sales Account and *debit* the Suspense Account with £10.

(*c*) In this case the position is different. We had to make a *single* entry on the debit side of the Suspense Account amounting to £120. We now make the corresponding *credit* entry, again in the Suspense Account, thus cancelling the original single entry and, at the same time, completing the double entry.

Finally, the Suspense Account will be closed in the following manner:

Suspense Account (Part II)

Difference b/d	£209	Falcon's A/c	£99
Sales A/c	10	*Cancellation* of single entry in Suspense A/c (no longer required)	120
	£219		£219

WORKING TO A PLAN

11. Examination technique. Examination questions on this subject usually seek to test the student's knowledge of principles and, as a rule, the *amount* of the difference is not given. The ascertainment of this figure is normally the main point of the question.

The average student is notoriously weak in dealing with Suspense Account questions. It is therefore desirable to learn a technique or simplified method of dealing with the problem.

It is suggested that the following plan be followed:

(*a*) Take each point in the question and treat it as if it were the *only* mistake.

(*b*) Carefully consider what *effect* the error would have on the Trial Balance, e.g., does it leave the Trial Balance with a greater amount on the credit side than on the debit?

(*c*) Having decided which side of the Trial Balance is "short" then make an entry in the Suspense Account on the "short" side.

(*d*) Pass on to the next point and follow the same procedure until every point in the question has been dealt with. The Suspense Account will then have a surplus on one side or the other.

(*e*) Close off the Suspense Account by inserting the difference and then carry it down, as though it were a balance, to the *opposite* side.

Whatever corrections are required in the ledger accounts can then be made as was shown in the previous example.

12. Specimen question. A typical question taken from a recent professional examination is set out below.

The Trial Balance of a company for the year ended 30th June failed to agree and the difference was entered in a Suspense Account. Accounts were prepared on the basis of the Trial Balance and showed a net profit of £9,850.

The following errors were afterwards discovered:

(*a*) Discounts of £102 appearing on the debit side of the Cash Book had been posted to the wrong side of the Discounts Account.

(*b*) The Sales Day Book had been overcast by £15.

(*c*) Cash received from Brown, a customer (£87), entered correctly in the cash book, had been credited to the personal account as £78.

(d) A credit balance of £45 on the personal account of Smith in the Bought Ledger had been omitted from the Trial Balance.

(e) A credit note of £21 for goods returned by a customer had been entered twice in the Returns Inwards Book and credited twice to the personal account of the customer.

(f) A payment of £65 on 30th June for repairs to motor vans had been debited to the Motor Vans Account.

(g) Part of the company's premises had been let, as from 1st June, at a rate of £10 per calendar month. On 1st June the tenant paid three months' rent in advance. This amount had been entered in the Cash Book, but no other entry had been made in any other account.

After discovery of the above errors, the Suspense Account was closed and the Trading and Profit and Loss Account redrafted.

You are required to show the Suspense Account and to calculate the amount of the net profit as it would appear in the redrafted Profit and Loss Account.

(I.C.S.A.)

SOLUTION: Applying the technique suggested above the procedure should be along the following lines:

(a) The Discount Account has been *credited* with £102 instead of being *debited* with £102.

Result: The Trial Balance will thus have £102 too much on the credit side and £102 too little on the debit side; the net difference on the Trial Balance will therefore be an excess of £204 on the credit side. The Profit and Loss Account will have to be adjusted, the profit being reduced by £204.

(b) The Sales Account has been over-credited by £15.

Result: The Trial Balance will have an excess of £15 on the credit side. The Profit and Loss Account must be adjusted by reducing the profit by £15.

(c) Brown's personal account has been short-credited by £9.

Result: The Trial Balance has £9 more debit than it should have.

(d) An item has been omitted from the Trial Balance, i.e., a credit balance of £45.

Result: The Trial Balance has £45 more debit than it should have.

(e) The error in this case will have no effect on the Trial Balance. It will, however, affect the Profit and Loss Account and Balance Sheet, since £21 has been debited twice to the Sales Account, thereby reducing the Gross Profit by £21. Since the figure has also been credited twice in the customer's account, the final debit balance on his account will have to be increased by £21 in order to show the correct position.

(f) This error will have no effect on the Trial Balance. The Profit and Loss Account will have to be debited with £65 and the Motor Van Account credited with a like amount.

(g) The Rent Receivable Account has been short-credited by £10, i.e., for June. A single entry has been made on the debit side of the Cash Book for £30. This must be corrected through the Suspense Account.

Result: The Trial Balance will have £30 more on the debit side than on the credit side. The Profit and Loss Account will also be affected in that an adjustment will have to be made crediting that account with £10.

Dealing first of all with the items as they affect the Suspense Account, the following entries will be made:

Suspense Account (Part I)

Discounts	£204	Brown	£9
Sales	15	Smith	45
		Rent receivable	30
			84
		Difference c/d to	
		Part II	135
	£219		£219

Thus we build up the position until we finally ascertain the amount of the *original* difference in the Trial Balance, i.e., £135.

The next step is to close off the Suspense Account in the following manner:

Suspense Account (Part II)

	£		£
Difference b/d	135		
Correction:		Correction:	
Brown's A/c	9	Discounts A/c	204
Rent Receivable A/c	30	Sales A/c	15
Credit balance in			
Bought Ledger			
omitted from Trial			
Balance in error	45		
	——		——
	£219		£219

Finally, we come to the calculation of the correct net profit.

Profit and Loss Account

	£		£
Discounts	204	Net profit (original	9,850
Sales (adjustment)	15	Returns	21
Repairs to motor van	65	Rent receivable	10
Net profit as			
adjusted	9,597		
	——		——
	£9,881		£9,881

PROGRESS TEST 5

Theory

1. If your Trial Balance did not agree what action would you take as a temporary measure? **(1, 2)**

2. State what effect the following errors in book-keeping have on the Trial Balance (*a*) an error in the additions, (*b*) a posting error. **(3, 4, 5)**

3. What is the effect of failure to complete the double entry? **(6)**

4. If a posting has been made to a Suspense Account because the double entry was incomplete what action must be taken when the error is found? Give your reasons for such action. **(7)**

5. In what way will an entry in the Suspense Account be corrected when there was no original error in the books? **(8, 9)**

Practice

6. A firm's book-keeper was unable to agree the Trial Balance and he entered the amount by which it was out of balance in a Suspense Account.

The following errors were subsequently discovered.

(*a*) The debit side of the General Expenses Account had been overcast by £100.

(*b*) £600 paid for office furniture had been debited to the Office Expenses Account.

(*c*) The discounts received and allowed in the month of November amounted to £30 and £50 respectively and had been posted to the wrong sides of the Discount Account.

(*d*) Returns outwards amounting to £148 had been posted to the personal accounts only.

(*e*) A total in the Sales Day Book of £540 had been carried forward as £450.

Show the Journal entries which are necessary to correct the above errors. You should assume that Control Accounts have not been kept.

NOTE: Narrations are not required.

(R.S.A. II)

7. Using the particulars given in the previous question deal with the matters set out below.

(*a*) What was the full amount of the *original* difference on the Trial Balance?

(*b*) On which side of the Trial Balance would this difference have had to be entered in order that the Trial Balance totals agreed?

(*c*) Show in detail how the *original* difference was made up.

(*d*) Complete the postings from the Suspense Account in order to close it off and enable the books to be correctly balanced.

8. The Trial Balance of Snodgrass and Co. did not agree and a Suspense Account was opened as a temporary measure. The difference amounted to £90.14 too much credit. Subsequently, the entries in the books were checked and a number of errors were discovered and adjusted. The details were:

(a) A posting of £21.43 from the Returns Inwards Book had been entered on the wrong side of John Gunn's account.

(b) A typewriter had been purchased for cash, £101.50, but by mistake this item had not been posted to the Office Equipment account.

(c) A balance of £65.26 owed by Weedon and Co. had been omitted from the list of debtors.

(d) A sale of goods amounting to £346.68 had been entered in the Sales Day Book but had been posted as £352.38 to the acount of Kendall and Co. in the Sales Ledger.

(e) The total of one of the pages in the Purchases Day Book amounting to £745.68 had been carried forward to the next page as £773.74, and this error had not been rectified at the end of the year.

You are asked to write up the Suspense Account and to show clearly the effect which each adjustment would have on the various ledger accounts. When all the items have been dealt with in the Suspense Account there should be a difference of £90.14 on the account thus proving the correctness of your workings.

9. The difference on the books of a business was carried to a Suspense Account on 30th June 19–5. Subsequently, the following errors came to light in respect of the year ended on that date:

(a) The total (£15) of the Returns Inwards Book for February 19–5 had been posted to the debit of Returns Outwards Account

(b) A debit balance of £0.63 on a Bought Ledger Account had been listed as a credit balance of £63.

(c) No posting had been made to the personal account for interest at 5 per cent per annum on a bill receivable of £300 renewed for four months. The receipt of the bill itself had been properly recorded and interest posted to the Interest Receivable Account.

(d) The total of folio 170 in the Purchase Day Book, £307.95, had been carried forward to folio 171 as £309.75.

(e) The recovery of a bad debt previously written off (£13.30) had been posted to the customer's credit in that amount, but to the credit of the Bad Debts Account as £1.33.

(f) Sales delivered on 30th June 19–5 included an item of goods, £50, which also appeared in the stock figure at cost (£40) on that date.

(g) Goods sold subject to a trade discount of 17½ per cent had been entered at full list price in the Sales Day Book, and duly posted. Credit for the discount (£45.15) was given later in the customer's account only.

(*h*) On 30th June 19–5 no posting had been made from the Cash Book of bank deposit interest, £3.75.

After rectification of the above errors the books were in balance.

You are required:

(*a*) to state the effect of each error on the Trial Balance;

(*b*) to show the Suspense Account incorporating the necessary corrective entries.

CHAPTER VI

Bills of Exchange

THE USES OF BILLS OF EXCHANGE

1. Postponing the settlement of a debt. Sometimes it is not possible for a person or firm to pay for goods within the normal period of time allowed for credit. This must not be taken to mean that the debtor is a likely candidate for the Bankruptcy Court. It is much more likely to be due to purely temporary factors. For example, a business which uses as its raw material cotton from an overseas country may be forced to make a full year's purchases within a period of a few weeks. The producer of the cotton will obviously want to be paid within a comparatively short time of selling his goods. Equally obviously, the buyer will have to turn the raw cotton into finished goods before he, in turn, can sell them and receive payment. In such circumstances special arrangements will have to be made so that the purchase of the raw material may be financed.

A method whereby the actual payment is postponed yet where, at the same time, the creditor can obtain his money is by the use of what are known as "Bills of Exchange". People whose business lies in dealing with money, i.e., banks and finance houses, are usually prepared to step in and offer short-term financial accommodation in return for a suitable recompense in the form of interest.

2. Definition of a Bill of Exchange. The Bills of Exchange Act 1882 defines a Bill of Exchange in the following terms:

"A Bill of Exchange is *an unconditional order in writing addressed* by one person to another, *signed* by the person giving it, *requiring* the person to whom it is addressed *to pay* on demand, or at a fixed or determinable future time, *a sum certain in money* to or to the order of *a specified person* or to bearer."

By far the majority of Bills of Exchange are so drawn as to make them payable on a specific date in the future, e.g., three months after the date on which the Bill was drawn, i.e., written out and signed.

THE PARTIES TO A BILL OF EXCHANGE

3. The parties involved. Frequently only two people will be concerned in the dealings relating to Bills of Exchange. Sometimes, however, a third party may be named in the "instrument" (which is the name often given to a Bill of Exchange). The technical titles given to the parties are:

(*a*) the drawer
(*b*) the drawee or acceptor
(*c*) the payee

4. The drawer and acceptor of a Bill of Exchange. The drawer is the person who *issues* the bill. Normally, the drawer is owed money in respect of goods which he has sold. His debtor is called the drawee or acceptor.

EXAMPLE: J. Snodgrass sold goods for £300 to P. Cleghorn on 1st July. As Cleghorn was temporarily short of funds it was arranged that settlement should be made by means of a Bill of Exchange for £300 which would mature, i.e., become due for payment, in three months' time. The technical name for this is "a 3 months bill". Snodgrass drew, i.e., wrote out, the bill which was then sent to Cleghorn who duly accepted it by signing his name on it. By "acceptance" is meant that when Cleghorn writes across the face of the bill "Accepted—P. Cleghorn", he undertakes to ensure that there will be enough money in his bank account in three months' time to pay the bill when it matures. In other words he accepts *liability* for the Bill of Exchange. If he fails to ensure that sufficient funds are available the bill may be dishonoured, which could have serious repercussions for him.

5. A Bill of Exchange as a negotiable instrument. The Bill of Exchange drawn by Snodgrass in the above example would appear thus:

£300   1st July, 19—

Three months after date pay to me or my order the sum of three hundred pounds (£300), value received.

To P. Cleghorn   J. Snodgrass
    12 Friarsgate,
    Oldhamlet

In the form set out above, the Bill of Exchange is said to be a "draft" and in that state it is *not* a "negotiable" instrument. To turn the bill into a *negotiable* instrument, i.e., to make it an "acceptance", Cleghorn must indicate his agreement to make himself liable to pay the money concerned on the due date by signing across the face of the bill as was previously mentioned. Once it has been accepted the bill becomes negotiable. This means that it can be used by any person who has become the legal owner of the bill to settle his own debts. Thus Snodgrass could use it to pay one of his own creditors.

6. The payee of a Bill of Exchange. The *drawer* of a Bill of Exchange may make the bill payable either to himself or to somebody else. The person named in the bill as being the person who is to receive the money is known as the payee. Thus if Snodgrass owed £300 to F. Clutterbuck and worded the bill to read, "Three months after date pay to F. Clutterbuck the sum of £300," etc., then Clutterbuck would be the payee. In the example above Snodgrass wrote "pay to me". He was, therefore, both drawer and payee.

7. Days of grace. Formerly, when a bill reached maturity, three days (called "days of grace") were added before payment could be legally demanded. This concession was revoked *circa* 1973 when Saturday morning closure of the banks was introduced. The reasoning behind this decision was that much inconvenience would be avoided if the days of grace were no longer operative.

8. The two types of Bills of Exchange. Bills of Exchange fall into two clearly defined groups:

    (*a*) Bills Payable;
    (*b*) Bills Receivable.

These will be dealt with in the next section.

BILLS PAYABLE

9. The operation of Bills Payable. If we have purchased goods from a supplier and have agreed to accept a Bill of Exchange for settlement on a specified date some time in the future then the bill will appear in our books as a Bill Payable. That is to say, it must be regarded as a liability which we have undertaken to meet on some particular date in the future instead of following the normal prac-

tice of clearing our indebtedness by making an immediate payment
in cash or by cheque. The book-keeping entries are quite simple:
our creditor's personal account in the Bought Ledger will be debited and a fresh account, called the "Bills Payable Account", will be
opened in the Private Ledger and the corresponding credit entry
made therein. This last entry takes the place of a credit entry in the
Cash Book, of course. Since we have not paid out any money our
assets remain at the figure they were. On the liabilities side, however, we do have an alteration. The amount owing to creditors
has been reduced because we closed off the account of the supplier
when we accepted the Bill Payable. In the place of this creditor we
have, instead, a credit balance on the Bills Payable Account. Thus,
the *form* of our liabilities has changed but not the total.

EXAMPLE: H. Prodnose purchased goods from F. Wilkins at a
cost of £250 on 14th June. It was arranged that Prodnose would
accept a Bill of Exchange for this amount. It was to mature in
three months' time.

Under this arrangement Prodnose would have to have sufficient funds in his bank to meet the bill on 14th September, i.e.,
three months after the date of acceptance. The entries in the
books of Prodnose would be as follows:

Purchases Account

June 14 F. Wilkins A/c	£250	

F. Wilkins Account

June 14 **Bills Payable A/c**	**£250**	June 14 Purchases A/c	£250

Bills Payable Account

	June 14 F. Wilkins A/c **£250**

With the passage of time the date of maturity would be reached
and the bill would have to be met. What would happen, in fact,
is that the bank would simply charge Prodnose's Account with
£250 and advise him that they had done so in order that he could
make the necessary entries in his books. The entries would be:

Bank Account

| | Sept. 17 **Bills Payable** | |
| | A/c | **£250** |

Bills Payable Account

| Sept. 17 **Bank A/c** | **£250** | June 14 F. Wilkins A/c | £250 |

10. Discounting a Bill of Exchange. From the above example it can be seen that right from the start Wilkins did not appear as a creditor in the books of Prodnose. So far as he, Wilkins, was concerned his claim had been satisfied: he had a Bill of Exchange in his possession (a Bill Receivable from his point of view) which, if he so wished, he could discount at his bank. That is to say, he could obtain £250 in cash immediately, i.e., on 14th June, provided that he was prepared to pay a comparatively small charge to his bank for what is called "discounting" the bill. This process of discounting will depend on a number of things such as the credit-worthiness of Prodnose, the standing of Wilkins with his bank, the length of time during which the bill would be current, the rate of interest ruling at the time and possibly other matters besides.

The book-keeping process is straightforward. The amount charged by the bank for discounting the bill will be credited in the Bank Account in Wilkins's books when he receives the information and will then be debited to a new account called "Discounting Charges Account". It must be noted that this particular account is *in no way* connected with the Discount Allowed Account.

The status of both the drawer and the acceptor are important when application is being made to discount a bill. The bank or finance house will not part with money unless satisfied that payment may be expected to be made when the bill matures. The amount charged for discounting will depend upon current interest rates and the length of time for which the advance is to be made. Should the bill be dishonoured any charge which had been previously made for discounting it will be charged to the debtor, i.e., the person who *accepted* the bill in the first place.

11. Dealing with discounting charges. A word of warning is necessary as to the ledger entries relating to the discounting of a bill. A special account should be opened for this particular type of expense and headed "Discount on Bills Account" or "Discounting Charges Account". The discounting of a Bill of Exchange is a charge imposed by the bank or finance house for the *use* of the money.

BILLS RECEIVABLE

12. The operation of Bills Receivable. The manner in which Bills Receivable are operated is basically identical to that of Bills Payable. There is, however, an option open to the holder of a Bill Receivable which does not, in the nature of things, arise where Bills Payable are concerned. As explained in **10** the holder of a Bill Receivable may, if he so wishes, "discount" the bill which he holds, and thus obtain the use of the money (subject to a charge for discounting) at any time before the bill matures.

EXAMPLE: On 26th May C. Peters sold goods to G. Hughes for £500 and received a Bill of Exchange duly accepted by Hughes to mature in four months' time.

The entries recording the position on 26th May in Peters' books would be as follows:

Sales Account

	May 26 G. Hughes A/c £500

G. Hughes Account

May 26 Sales A/c	£500	May 26 **Bills Receivable** A/c	**£500**

Bills Receivable Account

May 26 **G. Hughes A/c £500**	

From the above entries we see that Hughes is no longer to be regarded as *a debtor*. This asset has now been replaced by an asset of a different kind, a Bill Receivable. This Bill of Exchange can, if so desired, be given to the bank which will, in most cases, be prepared to give Peters immediate credit of £500. In effect, it would be as though Peters had paid a cheque into his bank account. A few days later the bank will notify Peters of the discounting charge which he will enter on the payments side in his Cash Book debiting the Discontinuing Charges Account. If Peters decides to discount the bill the entries would be:

Bills Receivable Account

May 26 G. Hughes A/c £500	May 26 **Bank A/c** £500

Bank Account

May 26 **Bills Receivable** A/c £500	

DISHONOURING A BILL

13. The failure of an acceptor. When a bill matures and thus falls due for payment it sometimes happens that the acceptor cannot, for some reason, honour the obligation he has undertaken; he may, for example, not have received the funds which he had expected. If this happens the bill is said to "dishonoured". The person who is *the holder* of the bill at this date will, therefore, make his claim on the person who passed the bill to him. Who the holder happens to be will depend upon circumstances.

In the example in **12** Peters obtained the bill from Hughes in the first instance. He then discounted it with his bank and so the bank was the holder of the bill at the date of maturity. The bank will, therefore, refer to Peters for reimbursement, while Peters, in his turn, will apply to Hughes.

So far as Peters is concerned when he makes the appropriate entries in his books there is no real point in re-opening the Bills Receivable Account. The simple entries will be between the Bank Account and Hughes's Account. The effect of this will be to reduce the amount of money in the bank and make Hughes *a debtor* once again.

Bank Account

	Aug. 29 G. Hughes A/c £500

G. Hughes Account

Aug. 29 Bank A/c (bill receivable dis-honoured) £500	

14. Endorsing a Bill of Exchange. We sometimes find that a businessman will use a Bill of Exchange, that is, a Bill Receivable, which has been accepted by one of his own debtors, as a means of satisfying one of his own creditors. This is done by the holder (the businessman) *endorsing* the bill, i.e., signing his name on the back of it, and then passing it over to his own creditor in settlement of his indebtedness. As a result, the Bills Receivable Account will be credited and the creditor's account debited. Thus, an asset is lost but a liability of equal value also disappears.

A Bill of Exchange may be endorsed by any person who happens to be the holder of that bill. Thus A may endorse the bill to B; B may endorse it to C; C may endorse it to D, and so on. It is important to note, however, that each holder of a bill cannot obtain a better title to the bill than that held by his predecessor. Because of this, in the event of a bill becoming dishonoured every endorser will become liable for the value of the bill to the party to whom he endorsed it onwards, in settlement of his debt to that party.

EXAMPLE: Cole had purchased goods for £200 from Dickens, who agreed to accept a Bill of Exchange for £200 in settlement. Dickens duly drew the bill and passed it to Cole who signed his acceptance across it. It so happened that Dickens owed £200 to Gregory and so he endorsed the bill over to him.

Entries in Cole's Books

Purchases Account

Dickens A/c	£200		

Dickens Account

Bills Payable A/c	**£200**	Purchase A/c	£200

Bills Payable Account

	Dickens A/c	£200

We can see from the entries set out above how the shape of Cole's liability changes. Originally, Dickens appeared as a creditor in the Bought Ledger. This debt was settled by Cole's acceptance of the bill drawn by Dickens and the latter's account was closed by a debit entry, the corresponding credit being placed in the Bills Payable Account which now replaces the personal creditor (Dickens) as a liability.

Entries in Dickens's Books

Sales Account

	Cole A/c	£200

Cole Account

Sales A/c	£200	Bills Receivable A/c	£200

Bills Receivable Account

Cole A/c	£200	

Having received the accepted bill from Cole, Dickens now endorses it on to Gregory to whom he owes £200.

Bills Receivable Account

Cole A/c	£200	Gregory A/c	£200

Gregory Account

Bills Receivable A/c	£200	Balance b/d	£200

Entries in Gregory's Books

Dickens Account

Balance b/d	£200	

As can be seen, Dickens is a debtor for £200. When Gregory receives the bill endorsed by Dickens the account can be closed and he is left holding as an asset the Bills Receivable. He has the choice of two alternatives; either he can hold the bill until it matures, or he can discount it. In this example we will suppose that Gregory discounts the bill with his bank. First of all, however, let us record the receipt of the bill in Gregory's ledger.

Dickens Account

Balance b/d	£200	**Bills Receivable A/c**	**£200**

Bills Receivable Account

Dickens A/c	**£200**	

When Gregory puts into effect his decision to discount the bill his asset position alters since the bank will credit his account in its book, so giving him ready money in place of a document which, depending upon the length of time it had to run until maturity, he would have had to hold in his safe.

Bills Receivable Account

Dickens A/c	£200	**Bank A/c**	**£200**

Bank Account

Bills Receivable A/c	**£200**	

Now let us move on to the date when the bill matures (including the three days of grace). Let us also suppose that Cole's position has worsened considerably and that he has insufficient funds at his bank to meet the bill. The bank would, first of all, present the bill on Cole's bank and be informed that it could not be met. It then has the legal right to obtain reimbursement from

Gregory which it does. The entries in Gregory's books would then be:

Bank Account

Bills Receivable A/c	£200	Dickens A/c	£200

Dickens Account

Bank A/c— dishonoured bill	£200		

In this way we see that Dickens now reverts to his former position and once again becomes a debtor of Gregory. Dickens then proceeds to exercise his own rights and lays the burden on Cole, the entries being as follows:

Entries in Dickens's Books

Gregory Account

		Bills Receivable A/c	£200

Bills Receivable Account

Gregory A/c	£200		

These entries have now placed Dickens in his former position, i.e., Gregory once more becomes his creditor and he, Dickens, is the possessor of a Bill of Exchange. As this bill has been dishonoured it may well be worthless: not necessarily so, but the situation is undoubtedly an unhappy one for him. His action will, of course, be to cancel it as an asset and bring Cole back in his books as a debtor, for the time being, at least. Future events will decide whether or not the debt proves to be bad.

Bills Receivable Account

Gregory A/c	£200	Cole A/c	£200

Cole Account

Bills Receivable A/c	£200

As was mentioned earlier, any discounting charge made by the bank when Gregory discounted the bill would have appeared in a Discounting Charges Account in Gregory's books. He might well contend that Dickens should accept this charge but Dickens might contend that that was Gregory's affair since he discounted the bill with his bank for his own personal convenience. If, however, as a matter of policy, Dickens agreed to accept it as his responsibility it is likely that he, in his turn, would pass it on to Cole in the hope that he might ultimately recover it.

15. Contingent liabilities. When a Bill of Exchange is accepted by a debtor it becomes, as we know, a Bill Receivable in the hands of the creditor. He receives it in the expectation that it will be honoured on maturity and so he credits the debtor's account with the value of the bill. The person who receives the bill is now in a position to change it into money by discounting it with his banker and this is normally the end of the matter so far as he is concerned.

There is, however, always the possibility that the acceptor may be unable to meet his liability under the bill when it matures, i.e., he may not have enough money to pay it. If this is the case the bill will, in normal circumstances, be dishonoured. The holder at the time of dishonour will, providing he discounted the bill previously, have to repay his bank. His recourse against the debtor may be of no value since there is always the likelihood that the debtor is insolvent. There is thus always the necessity that where bills have been discounted for the original holder to consider how best the position should be shown in his balance sheet, if his financial year ends before the date on which discounted bills are due to mature. In such circumstances, a *contingent* liability is said to exist, because there is a possibility that the acceptor may default when the bill is due to be met. It must be understood that no book-keeping entries can be brought into being to deal with the position and, therefore, nothing can appear among the ordinary liabilities in the Balance Sheet.

Bills which have been discounted become what are called "contingent liabilities" until they have been paid on maturity. Once that has happened there is no possibility of dishonour and no claim by the bank remains as a potential threat. Until a bill under discount has been honoured, however, the contingency that it will not be met is always present and, as a result of this, it is customary for a note to be entered at the foot of the balance sheet that bills of a certain value are under discount at the date of the Balance Sheet and that a contingent liability exists.

16. Accommodation Bills. Occasionally, a person wishes to obtain funds and the only way by which he can do so is by drawing an "Accommodation Bill". In such a case the acceptor does not receive "valuable consideration", i.e., he is simply agreeing to *lend* the drawer money. As soon as the accommodation bill has been accepted the drawer is in a position to discount it and thus obtain the funds which he needs. His book-keeping entries will be to debit Bills Receivable Account and credit the acceptor's account. When he discounts the bill he will debit Bank Account and credit Bills Receivable Account. On maturity of the bill the acceptor will present it for payment and the drawer will debit his (the acceptor's) account and credit the Bank Account, thus closing the transaction. The entries in the books of the acceptor will be the reverse of those in the books of the drawer except that he will treat it as a Bill Payable and use that account instead of the Bills Receivable Account. Problems of this character cause students difficulty. If the two sets of accounts are kept quite separate and one set dealt with in its entirety before dealing with the other there should be very little trouble.

PROGRESS TEST 6

Theory

1. In what circumstances are Bills of Exchange normally used? **(1)**

2. Define a Bill of Exchange. **(2)**

3. How many parties are required to such a bill? What are the various parties called? **(3)**

4. Who writes out a Bill of Exchange in the first place? What is the next thing he must do? **(4)**

5. When a person accepts a Bill of Exchange, what happens? **(5)**

6. Where does the payee enter the proceedings? **(6)**

7. What types of Bills of Exchange do we find in business? **(8)**

8 What is meant by discounting a bill? **(10)**

9. What happens to dishonour a bill? **(13)**

Practice

10. On 1st January 19–2 Johnson drew and Williams accepted, a Bill at three months for £1,000. On 4th January, Johnson discounted the Bill at 6% per annum, and remitted half the proceeds to Williams. On 1st February, Williams drew and Johnson accepted a Bill at three months for £400. On 4th February, Williams discounted the Bill at 6 per cent per annum and remitted half the proceeds to Johnson. Johnson and Williams agreed to share the discounts equally. At maturity Johnson met his acceptance but Williams failed to meet his and recourse was had to Johnson. Johnson drew and Williams accepted a new Bill at three months for the amount of the original Bill, plus interest at 5 per cent per annum.

On 1st July 19–2, Williams became bankrupt. A first and final dividend of 50p in the £ was paid by his trustee in bankruptcy on 31st October 19–2, Williams obtained his discharge on 5th December 19–2, and agreed to pay Johnson the unsatisfied balance of his account. This was paid on 10th February 19–3.

Write up Williams' account in the books of Johnson. Calculations to be made in months.

11. On 1st July the following balances appeared in the ledger of Black:

Brown (debit)	£650
White (credit)	£740

On the same date Black drew a bill at three months on Brown for £400 and Brown accepted it.

On 5th July Brown endorsed over to Black a bill at three months for £175 which had been accepted by Grey on that day and, three days later, Black endorsed this bill over to White.

On 9th July Black accepted a bill at three months for £574 drawn by White in full settlement of his account, including interest. White immediately discounted this bill at his bank.

On 10th October White informed Black that Grey's acceptance had been dishonoured, and Black immediately sent White a cheque for £175. The other bills were paid on the due dates.

On 15th October Black received a cheque from Brown for the full amount due from him.

Show the entries for the above transactions in the ledger and Cash Book of Black.

(I.C.S.A.)

12. On 1st June Smith purchased goods from Brown for £860 and sold goods to Jones for £570.

On the same date Smith drew a bill (No. 1) at three months on Jones for £400 and Jones accepted it.

On 12th June Jones drew a bill (No. 2) at three months on Robinson for £150 which Robinson accepted.

On 14th June Jones endorsed bill No. 2 over to Smith and on 16th June Smith endorsed this bill over to Brown.

On 20th June Smith accepted a bill (No. 3) at three months for £720 drawn by Brown in full settlement of his account, including interest. On 23rd June Brown discounted bill No. 3 at his bank.

On 17th September Brown informed Smith that Robinson's acceptance had been dishonoured and Smith sent a cheque for £150 to Brown. The other bills were paid on the due dates.

On 20th September Smith received a cheque from Jones for half the amount due from him.

Show the entries to record these transactions in the ledger and Cash Book of Smith.

(*I.C.S.A.*)

13. Show, by means of Journal entries, how the following matters should be recorded.

(*a*) Barnes buys goods on credit from Simpson for £100.

(*b*) Barnes settles the transaction by accepting a Bill Payable in favour of Byers, who is a creditor of Simpson, payable in three months for £95.

(*c*) Barnes is informed that Byers has discounted the bill with the Northcountry Bank for £90.

(*d*) The Northcountry Bank presents the bill to Barnes but he arranges with them to substitute it with another bill which will become payable in a further three months' time for £100, in favour of the bank.

14. G. Connor commenced to trade on 1st March and he recorded the following transactions in his diary.

March 1 Bought goods from W. Reckitt for £250.
2 Sent Reckitt a cheque for £120 and accepted a bill drawn on him at one month for £100.
8 Sold goods to S. Pearce for £120.
9 Drew bill on Pearce for £120 at one month and discounted it at the bank for £118.
14 Bought goods from F. Kelly for £70 and paid him £40 on account.
23 Sold goods to H. Bradford for £50. Received cheque for £20 and a bill at one month for the balance.

26 Endorsed Bradford's bill and sent it to Reckitt in settlement of the open balance on his account.

April 4 Reckitt agreed to his bill for £100 being withdrawn; sent him a cheque for £60 and accepted another bill at one month for £40.

13 Pearce's bill for £120 was returned dishonoured.

18 Bradford returned goods which had been invoiced to him for £15.

20 Agreed with Pearce that he should return goods invoiced to him for £50 against a credit to him of £40. Agreed to accept 60 per cent of the balance of his account in full settlement if he paid by the end of June.

26 Bradford's bill was duly honoured.

Prepare the Personal Ledger Accounts recording the above transactions in Connor's books and also the Bills Receivable Account and the Bills Payable Account, bringing down any balances on 30th April.

15. Gold and Silver are in need of cash, and adopt the following course of action.

(a) Gold draws a bill for £1,500 on Silver who accepts it.

(b) Silver draws a bill for £2,000 on Gold who duly accepts it.

(c) Each party discounts the bill he holds with different bankers, the discounting charges being 5 per cent of the respective face value.

(d) Silver honours his acceptance at the due date.

(e) Gold cannot honour his acceptance. He arranges that his friend Pearl will pay Silver, which he does. Pearl takes Gold's acceptance at an agreed figure of £2,200 of which £200 is to be treated as interest.

Draw up the ledger accounts and the Cash Book which are kept by both Gold and by Silver respectively and then take out a Trial Balance.

Be *very careful* to separate the records of each party and to head each sheet with the name of the party keeping the relative books.

(*I.C.S.A.*)

CHAPTER VII

Control Accounts

TOTAL ACCOUNTS AS A MEANS OF CONTROL

1. Ensuring brevity in the Trial Balance. A Trial Balance consists of making a list in two columns of the various balances which appear in the ledger. As we know, the ledger is sub-divided into four basic sections, namely:

  (*a*) the Cash Book
  (*b*) the Bought Ledger
  (*c*) the Sales Ledger
  (*d*) the Private Ledger or General Ledger.

The individual balance on the account of each customer in the Sales Ledger is listed and *the total* of this list is put in the Trial Balance. This list is called "the schedule of debtors". As a result, only one figure occupying only one line in the Trial Balance will represent the many balances which appear on the individual accounts in the Sales Ledger. In the exercises worked in the earlier part of our studies we have been in the habit of entering each customer's balance as a separate item in the Trial Balance but this is not done in real life. If it were, the Trial Balance would, in most firms, then consist of pages and pages of these ledger balances and hardly anything else. In order to keep the Trial Balance as compact as possible this list of balances is extracted separately and *the total only* is entered in the Trial Balance.

Exactly the same procedure is followed with regard to the balances on the Bought Ledger.

2. The number of business transactions. Let us consider for a few moments the volume of entries which pass through the books before the Trial Balance is reached. As we know, the items appearing in the Trial Balance are merely the balances remaining on the various accounts in the four sections of the ledger and do not give any indication of *the number* of transactions which have passed through the accounts during the period of trading. Imagine a business which has, say, 1,000 customers and 200 suppliers of goods, all transactions being on credit. Suppose, also, that on the average there is one credit transaction on each of these 1,200 separate accounts every month. This, in turn, will mean that we may expect to have a settlement once each month for the transactions of the previous month which would mean that something in the region of 30,000 entries would be made in the Bought and Sales Ledgers in the course of a year's trading.

Next, consider how many transactions would pass through the Cash Book. The Cash Book entries will, of course, be linked directly with the entries in the ledgers, i.e., the record of each settlement. We may therefore expect to see something like 14,000 entries made in the Cash Book relating to the Bought and Sales Ledgers. In addition there will be other items which affect only the Private Ledger, e.g., wages. These other entries will, however, be comparatively few. For example, there will probably only be one item per month entered in the purchases account; twelve in the whole year. Again, on the rates account probably no more than two entries will be made during the year and perhaps only one on the insurance account. From consideration of these points it at once becomes evident that the vast majority of the transactions of many businesses will therefore be found in the Bought and Sales Ledgers.

The summary shown in the box on the following page will help to emphasise the point. This tabulated statement serves to show without any shadow of doubt that the main burden of traffic lies in the personal ledgers and the Cash Book.

The object of this statement and of the foregoing paragraphs is to bring to the notice of the student the fact that the number of entries in the Private Ledger is comparatively few. If, therefore, we can satisfy ourselves that the entries in the Sales Ledger, the Bought Ledger and the Cash Book are correct then any difference which may appear in the Trial Balance should not present much difficulty in finding, i.e., it must lie in the Private Ledger.

The question which we must now ask ourselves is "Can we be satisfied that the balances of any of these four sections, as they appear in the Trial Balance, are correct?" The answer to that question is "Yes, we can".

VERIFICATION

3. Verifying the bank balance. The balance at the bank as shown by the Cash Book can be verified with complete certainty by means of a *banker's certificate* supported by a reconciliation of the balance on the Bank Account (in the Cash Book) with the balance on the Bank Statement. In this way we can satisfy ourselves completely that the amount of cash at the bank which appears in the Trial Balance is correct. (For Bank Reconciliations see Chapter III.)

	Number of entries annually
Sales Ledger	
1,000 customers—one credit sale per month to each	12,000
Monthly settlement per Cash Book	12,000
Bought Ledger	
200 suppliers—one credit purchase per month from each	2,400
Monthly settlement per Cash Book	2,400
Cash Book	
Cheques from customers—monthly settlement	12,000
Payments to suppliers—monthly settlement	2,400
Payment for services—salaries, wages, rent and rates, light and heat, insurance, etc., say,	600
	43,800
Private Ledger	
Entries from Cash Book—payment for services	600
Total number of entries for the year	44,400

4. Verifying the cash in hand. A further balance involving cash is the balance of cash in hand standing on the Petty Cash Account (or Petty Cash Book). This can be verified by means of *an actual count* at any time. We can therefore say with absolute certainty that all the balances involving cash which appear in the Trial Balance are correct.

5. Verifying other balances in the Trial Balance. Now, if we can satisfy ourselves that the figure which represents *the total* of all the balances on the Sales Ledger (which appears in the Trial Balance) is correct and, similarly, verify *the total* of all the balances on the Bought Ledger, we shall be well on the way to having a Trial Balance which agrees because the only ledger left unverified will be the Private Ledger.

As we have already seen, most of the book-keeping entries made during a period of trading are made in the Cash Book, the Bought and the Sales Ledgers, with perhaps a few in the Petty Cash Book. It follows, therefore, that if there is a difference on our Trial Balance, it must be in the Private Ledger section *provided* that we can satisfy ourselves that the following balances (as they appear in the Trial Balance) are correct:

  (*a*) cash at bank;
  (*b*) cash in hand;
  (*c*) the debtors (on the Sales Ledger);
  (*d*) the creditors (on the Bought Ledger).

Thus, if we find that we have got a difference on our Trial Balance, and if we have verified the accuracy of the Bank and Cash Accounts as well as the totals of the balances on both the Bought and Sales Ledgers, we have only to check the Private Ledger figures in order to locate the difference. Since the number of entries made in the Private Ledger will be comparatively few, we can expect to agree the Trial Balance in a comparatively short time.

6. Memorandum accounts. Before studying an example the student must be introduced to what are known as "Memorandum Accounts". These accounts are *not* part of the double-entry system which, as we know, is extremely strict in its application. Nevertheless, they can be of immense use as an aid to the accountant. In proving the accuracy of the totals of both the Bought and Sales Ledger balances Memorandum Accounts are invaluable. In the context of Control or Total Accounts they are, quite literally, condensed versions of the Bought Ledger and Sales Ledger, respectively.

Basically, they consist of the *totals* obtained from the Day Books, Returns Books and Cash Book together with (when appropriate) certain isolated items which may have been passed through the Journal. The effect is to produce an account for each ledger separately, the contents comprising, in the form of *totals*, every single item which appears individually in the Bought Ledger and the Sales Ledger respectively.

The balance, i.e., the difference between the two sides, which emerges on each of the Memorandum Accounts should, therefore, equal precisely *the total* of the list of balances extracted from each of the two ledgers, i.e., the Bought Ledger and the Sales Ledger. It must be emphasised that these Memorandum Accounts which we call "Total Accounts" or "Control Accounts" are *not* part of the system of double entry—they are an extension of it.

PROOF

7. Proving the accuracy of the Personal Ledgers. Having discussed the advantages which may accrue if the Bought Ledger and Sales Ledger balances can be proved to be correct let us now show that, in fact, they can be so proved.

EXAMPLE

Double-entry postings		*Sales Day Book*		Fo. 41.	*Memorandum postings*
Details are posted to the debit of the Personal Account of Cleghorn as shown below. The total will be posted to the credit of Sales Account at the end of the month.			Sales Ledger folio		The total of £300 is posted to the debit of the "Sales Ledger Total Account" at the end of the month.
	Jan. 6	P. Cleghorn	C.23	£20	
	Jan. 12	P. Cleghorn	C.23	40	
	Jan. 18	P. Cleghorn	C.23	60	
	Jan. 24	P. Cleghorn	C.23	80	
	Jan. 31	P. Cleghorn	C.23	100	
				£300	

The double-entry postings from the Sales Day Book will be:

P. Cleghorn Account

Account No. C.23			
Jan. 6 Sales Day Book	41	£20	
Jan. 12 Sales Day Book	41	40	
Jan. 18 Sales Day Book	41	60	
Jan. 24 Sales Day Book	41	80	
Jan. 31 Sales Day Book	41	100	
		£300	

Sales Account

		S.D.B. folio	
Jan. 31 Sales Day Book		41	£300

It is clear from the illustration how the double entry is completed, i.e., in the personal account of P. Cleghorn each individual sale is dealt with as a *separate* transaction and is duly debited to Cleghorn's account. The corresponding credit entries are, for convenience, left until the end of the month when they are added together and then credited in *a lump sum* to the Sales Account.

Let us now suppose that Cleghorn makes two payments during the month of February and that in each case he takes (is allowed to deduct from his payment) a discount of 5 per cent. The first payment is in respect of the sale on the 6th and 12th January, amounting to £60, and the second for the sales on 18th and 24th January. We will assume that the sale on 31st January remains unpaid.

Folio 27   *Bank Account (in the Cash Book)*

	Dis-count all'd	Bank
Feb. 14 P. Cleghorn C.23	£3	£57
Feb. 27 P. Cleghorn C.23	£7	133
	£10	£190

The details are posted to the credit of the Personal Account of P. Cleghorn, while the totals are posted to the credit of the Sales Ledger Total Account (Memorandum).

P. Cleghorn Account

	S.D.B. folio			Cash book folio	
Jan. 6 Sales Day Book	41	£20	Feb. 14 Bank A/c	27	£57
Jan. 12 Sales Day Book	41	40	Feb. 14 Discount A/c	27	3
Jan. 18 Sales Day Book	41	60	Feb. 27 Bank A/c	27	133
Jan. 24 Sales Day Book	41	80	Feb. 27 Discount A/c	27	7
Jan. 31 Sales Day Book	41	100	Feb. 29 *Balance* c/d		100
		£300			£300
Mar. 1 Balance b/d		£100			

We can see from Cleghorn's account above how it is built up by a number of *detailed* entries. These details have come from two separate books, the Sales Day Book and the Cash Book.

Now it is possible to check the correctness of the *final* balance on Cleghorn's account by constructing what is called a

Total Account. To do this we take the various totals from the books concerned and set them out as follows:

Sales Ledger Total Account

Jan. 31 Sales Day Book (total) £300		Feb. 29 Bank A/c (total)	£190
		Feb. 29 Discount allowed column (total)	10
		Feb. 29 Balance c/d	100
	£300		£300

Mch. 1 Balance b/d   £100

NOTE: Although the Total Account has been set out in the form of a Ledger Account this is for convenience only. It is *not* part of the double entry. We refer to such accounts as Memorandum Accounts.

The example has been confined to the very simplest details and spread over the two months of January and February so that the principles may be grasped easily, and also for the student to realise that there is in fact a quite simple way of *proving* that the individual balances on a ledger are correct. *Total* Accounts are kept for this very reason. What is more, the balances thrown up by the Total Accounts are used in the Trial Balance (since the final balance on the Total Account should be the sum of all the balances on a particular ledger). In this way the Trial Balance can be extracted quickly without waiting for the detailed list of balances to be produced by the clerks in charge of the ledgers.

8. A further example. Let us now look at a further example to ensure that the principles are understood. This time we will deal with the Bought Ledger (i.e., the creditors' accounts) so that it can be seen that exactly the same principles apply.

EXAMPLE: On 1st May Wotherspoon was owed £25 and Raglan £30. During May the following goods were bought on credit and were entered in the Bought Day Book before being posted to the appropriate ledger accounts:

Bought Day Book	
May 4 Wotherspoon	£18
May 8 Dodds	6
May 12 Wotherspoon	45
May 16 Dodds	17
May 20 Wotherspoon	29
May 24 Raglan	70
May 28 Dodds	14
May 31 Raglan	56
	£255

Wotherspoon Account

May 1 Balance b/d £25	
May 4 Bought Day Book 18	
May 12 Bought Day Book 45	
May 20 Bought Day Book 29	
	117

Dodds Account

May 6 Bought Day Book £6	
May 16 Bought Day Book 17	
May 28 Bought Day Book 14	
	37

Raglan Account

May 1 Balance b/d £30	
May 24 Bought Day Book 70	
May 31 Bought Day Book 56	
	156

Goods as shown below were returned to suppliers:

Purchase Returns Book (Returns Outwards Day Book)		
May 13	Wotherspoon	£6
May 26	Raglan	11
		───
		£17

Wotherspoon Account

May 13 Returns Day Book	£6	May 1	Balance b/d	£25
		May 4	Bought Day Book	18
		May 12	Bought Day Book	45
		May 20	Bought Day Book	29

Raglan Account

May 26 Returns Day Book	£11	May 1	Balance b/d	£30
		May 24	Bought Day Book	70
		May 31	Bought Day Book	56

On 1st June Wotherspoon was paid £17 and Dodds £5, a discount of £1 being taken in each case. On 30th June further payments were made as follows:

Wotherspoon	£43 (£2 discount)
Dodds	£16 (£1 discount)
Raglan	£56 (£3 discount)

The credit side of the Cash Book would appear thus:

Bank Account (in the Cash Book)

		Discount Received	Bank
June 1	Wotherspoon	£1	£17
June 1	Dodds	1	5
June 30	Wotherspoon	2	43
June 30	Dodds	1	16
June 30	Raglan	3	56
		—	—
		8	137

When these items have been posted to the personal accounts concerned we would have the following position:

Wotherspoon Account

May 13 Returns Day Book	£6	May 1	Balance b/d	£25
June 1 Cash	17	May 4	Bought Day Book	18
June 1 Discount rec'd	1	May 12	Bought Day Book	45
June 30 Cash	43	May 20	Bought Day Book	29
June 30 Discount rec'd	2			
	69			
June 30 Balance c/d	48			
	£117			£117
			Balance b/d	£48

Dodds Account

June 1 Cash	£5	May 6	Bought Day Book	£6
June 1 Discount rec'd	1	May 16	Bought Day Book	17
June 30 Cash	16	May 28	Bought Day Book	14
June 30 Discount rec'd	1			
	23			
June 30 Balance c/d	14			
	£37			£37
			Balance b/d	£14

Raglan Account

May 26 Returns Day Book	£11	May 1 Balance b/d	£30
June 30 Cash	56	May 24 Bought Day Book	70
June 30 Discount rec'd	3	May 31 Bought Day Book	56
	70		
June 30 Balance c/d	86		
	£156		£156
		Balance b/d	£86

A list of the bought ledger balances at 30th June would appear thus:

Wotherspoon	£48
Dodds	14
Raglan	86
	£148

To obtain a check on the accuracy of this total we will now construct a "Bought Ledger Total Account" from the various totals concerned.

At the beginning of the ppriod, i.e., on 1st May, the following balances were owing to creditors:

Wotherspoon	£25
Raglan	30
	£55

To start with we must therefore show the total, £55, on the credit side of the Bought Ledger Total Accounts on 1st May and then place the totals obtained from the various columns of the other books in their appropriate positions, as follows:

Bought Ledger Total Account

May 31 Returns Outwards Day Book (p. 92)	£17	May 1 Balance b/d	£55	
June 30 Bank A/c (p. 93)	137	May 31 Bought Day Book (p. 84)	255	
June 30 Discount Rec'd A/c (p. 93)	8			
June 30 Balance c/d	148			
	£310		£310	
		Balance c/d	£148	

We thus see that the Total Account, or "Control Account," as it is more commonly called, has a final balance to the credit amounting to £148 which is precisely the total of the *list* of balances set out above at 30th June. This can be regarded as sufficient proof that the Bought Ledger balances are correct and may therefore be included in the Trial Balance with every confidence in their accuracy.

9. Dealing with Total Accounts. Many students find this part of their studies difficult to grasp, mainly, it would seem, because they have never seen the system operating in real life. It is an accepted fact that very many firms do employ some form of "Control Accounts" as a most important part of their book-keeping system. To help those students who may still have difficulty in understanding how the Total Account or Control Account is built up the following points should be noted.

(*a*) In the first place, do not think of the Total Accounts as some strange and frightening thing. Instead, imagine that you have only *one* customer and you want to make a summary of all the entries in his account during a particular month.

(*b*) So cross out the heading "Debtors Total Account" or "Creditors Total Account" and substitute a name, say, "J. Snodgrass Account."

(*c*) Then think of the various points given in the problem and decide in your own mind where each one would be placed in

Snodgrass's personal account if, in fact, you really had to enter all these details in his account.

If you can do this you will have solved the worst part of your problem. A simple example should help to make matters clear.

EXAMPLE: At 1st January various debtors owed £400. During the year credit sales amounted to £4,800 and cash received from debtors was £4,150. Returns inwards for the year were £52. Discounts of £150 were allowed to debtors in the course of the year.

First of all cross out the name of the account (i.e., Debtors Total Account) and in its place substitute J. Snodgrass Account.

Debtors Total Account but now called J. Snodgrass Account	

Jan 1 Balance
        b/d   £400
Dec. 31 Sales A/c 4,800
	Dec. 31 Cash A/c £4,150
	Dec. 31 Discounts A/c 150
	Dec. 31 Returns
	            Inwards A/c 52
	Dec. 31 Balance c/d 848

£5,200	£5,200
Balance b/d £848	

This idea is suggested to emphasise the basic simplicity of Control Accounts or Total Accounts which are simply built up from the *totals* of all the various items which appear (by means of the normal double entry) in all the various debtors' or creditors' accounts in the respective ledger.

NOTE: The Total Accounts are not—repeat *not*—a part of the *double entry*. They are Memorandum Accounts only.

10. The reasoning behind the use of Control Accounts. The amounts owing *to* suppliers or owing *by* customers are ascertained in the ordinary way. Each one of the many hundreds of personal accounts in the Sales Ledger and Bought Ledger has been built up by entering therein:

(*a*) each individual invoice which gives the details of the sale or purchase;

(*b*) each individual receipt of cash or payment of cash;

(*c*) each individual amount of discount allowed or received;

(*d*) each individual credit note which gives details of goods returned (inwards or outwards);

(*e*) The individual details of any other item which may affect the various personal accounts, *e.g.*, a cash refund to a customer who has overpaid;

(*f*) at the end of every month each personal account is balanced and ruled off, the balance (if any) being carried down ready to start the following month's transactions.

All of these balances are then listed, their respective totals representing the amounts owing *by* the firm's debtors and *to* the firm's creditors.

To obtain a check that the totals of all these balances are really correct a Debtor's Total Account and a Creditors Total Account are then built up, not from the thousands of details which go to make up the personal accounts, but from the *totals* of the various subsidiary books and/or columns.

These totals are obtained from the additions of the columns in the various subsidiary books which contain all the details used to construct the personal accounts. By putting all of these *totals* in their proper place in a Debtors Total Account we will, as a result, be in a position to strike a balance between the two sides.

If all the book-keeping has been properly carried out as to:

(*a*) correctly entering the details in the personal accounts;

(*b*) making the additions of all the subsidiary books correctly as well as those relevant columns in the Cash Book; and

(*c*) correctly casting each side of every personal account in the various ledgers;

then the balance found on the Debtors Total Account should be the same as the *total* of the *list* of debtors' balances. Since the total sum owed by customers has been reached by *two* completely different methods of calculation, and both totals have been found to be the same, it is not unreasonable to suppose that the figure is correct. In the same way the final balance on the Creditors Total Account will be found to agree with the total of the list of creditors' balances.

DEALING WITH EXAMINATION PROBLEMS

11. Introduction. By now a reasonably clear idea of the purpose of self-balancing ledgers and the broad manner in which the check is carried out should have been obtained by the student. Assuming this to be the case our final task will be to discuss certain matters which usually are to be found in examination problems on this subject.

12. Contra entries between Bought Ledger and Sales Ledger. It sometimes happens that a business will both buy goods from a firm and also sell goods to that same firm. In such cases it is usual to open two accounts for this firm, one in the Bought Ledger and one in the Sales Ledger. At the end of each month when all the debtors' and creditors' accounts are balanced off the practice is for the accounts of such a firm to be settled against the credit balance on the Bought Ledger. In this way a certain amount of time, trouble and expense is saved for both firms, for as a result of the set-off there remains only one account with a balance outstanding to be settled. The following examples should make the position clear.

EXAMPLE: Goods valued at £45 are sold on credit to Snodgrass on 3rd March while goods costing £71 are purchased from him on 17th March.

Entry in the **Sales** *Ledger*

J. Snodgrass Account

March 3 Sales Day Book £45	

Entry in the **Bought** *Ledger*

J. Snodgrass Account

	March 17 Bought Day Book £71

In order to determine where the liability for settlement lies we always begin by closing off the account which has the *smaller* balance. Therefore, in this case, we credit the Sales Ledger Account as the *first* entry and enter the corresponding debit in the Bought Ledger as our *second* entry. The final position would appear thus at 31st March:

Entry in the **Sales** *Ledger*

J. Snodgrass Account

March 3 Sales Day Book	£45	March 31 J. Snodgrass A/c in **Bought Ledger**	£45
	———		———
	£45		£45
	═══		═══

Entry in the **Bought** *Ledger*

J. Snodgrass Account

March 31 J. Snodgrass A/c in **Sales Ledger**	£45	March 17 Bought Day Book	£71

As a result of this part-settlement by *contra*, as it is called, a payment to Snodgrass of £26 will leave both accounts clear.

EXAMPLE: On 4th April goods to the value of £86 were sold on credit to Snodgrass, and on 22nd April goods costing £29 were bought from him on credit.

Entry in the **Sales** *Ledger*

J. Snodgrass Account

April 4 Sales Day Book	£86	

Entry in the **Bought** *Ledger*

J. Snodgrass Account

	April 22 Bought Day Book	£29

In this example we must start with the account in the Bought Ledger since the balance here is the smaller of the two. We therefore debit the Bought Ledger Account with £29 and credit the Sales Ledger Account with a similar amount. The final result at 30th April would be as follows:

Entry in the **Bought** *Ledger*

J. Snodgrass Account

April 30 **J. Snodgrass** **A/c (in** **Sales** **Ledger)**	**£29**	April 22 Bought Day Book		£29
	£29			£29

Entry in the Sales Ledger

J. Snodgrass Account

April 4 Sales Day Book	£86	April 30 **J. Snodgrass A/c** **(in Bought** **Ledger)**	**£29**

Comparing the two examples it will be observed that in both the book-keeping entries are on the same side, i.e., in each case the Bought Ledger Account is debited and the Sales Ledger Account is credited. A moment's thought will show us the reason. Settling accounts by contra means "*instead* of settling by cash". Because of this, contra entries will always appear in the respective ledgers *on the same side* as cash entries, since they take the place of cash.

It follows therefore that when dealing with such items in Total or Control Accounts we will enter these settlements by *contra* on the debit side of the Bought Ledger Total Account and on the credit side of the Sales Ledger Total Account, for it is on these sides of the respective ledgers that *cash* is entered.

13. Bills Receivable and Bills Payable. A favourite item for examiners to include in problems on Control Accounts relates to Bills of Exchange. It is most important for students to remember that:

(*a*) Bills Payable affect the Bought Ledger only;

(*b*) Bills Receivable affect the Sales Ledger only.

The points mentioned in examination questions often appear to be very confusing but are almost always quite simple. The important question to be determined is: should the item referred to go into the personal account of a customer in the Sales Ledger or should it go into a personal account in the Bought Ledger? If the answer is that the item is one that *should* be entered in the account of a customer or of a supplier then it must be included in one of the Total Accounts. The nature of the particular transaction will determine which of the Total Accounts is affected.

With regard to Bills Receivable in the Sales Ledger Total Account only two of the various items have to be considered. All the others may be disregarded entirely. The two items are:

(*a*) Bills Receivable *accepted* (sometimes referred to as "received"), which go on the credit side;

(*b*) Bills Receivable *dishonoured*, which go on the debit side.

No other items relating to Bills Receivable pass through the Sales Ledger Accounts and therefore they must *not* appear in the Sales Ledger Total Account.

With regard to the Bought Ledger Total Account the matter is even simpler:

(*a*) Bills payable *accepted* must be debited in the Bought Ledger Total Account;

(*b*) nothing else relating to Bills Payable affects the Bought Ledger Total Account unless, of course, a Bill is dishonoured. It is not usual for examiners to include such a contingency in a problem.

14. Interest charged on overdue accounts. This is a charge sometimes made by a supplier when a customer does not pay his account within a reasonable time. The customer's account is debited with the amount of the charge, thus *increasing* the debit balance and in such cases the Sales Ledger Total Account will therefore also have to be debited.

15. Refunds made to customers. If a customer overpays his account he may ask for a refund. If, on the other hand, he so wishes, the amount owing will be carried forward as a credit balance on his account. Should a refund be made the Bank Account will be credited and the customer's account debited. In that case, we must debit the Sales Ledger Total Account also.

16. A credit balance on a Sales Ledger Account. As indicated above we sometimes find that there is a *credit balance* standing on a Sales Ledger Account. In the Sales Ledger Total Account the following double entry must be made:

(a) enter the amount first of all on the *debit side* above the total;

(b) carry it down as a *credit balance* underneath the totals of the account.

Exactly the same treatment must be given in respect of any debit balances on the Bought Ledger Total Account. Remember, of course, that the first entry will be on the credit side *above the totals* and the other entry a debit *beneath* the totals of the account.

17. Specimen question. The following details were extracted from the books of John Jackson & Co. Ltd, relating to the transactions on the Sales Ledger for the month of May.

Debit balances on Sales Ledger at 1st May	£632
Credit balances on Sales Ledger at 1st May	11
Sales on credit during May	519
Sales returns	7
Cash received from debtors	467
Bad debts written off	4
Discounts allowed	21
Refunds to customers (by cheque)	3
Sales Ledger items settled by contra	7
Balance extracted from Sales Ledger at 31st May:	
Debit	640
Credit	3

You are required:

(a) to construct a Sales Ledger Total Account for the month of May;

(b) to indicate any circumstances that would give rise to a credit balance on a Sales Ledger Account.

SUGGESTED SOLUTION:

(a) Following the rules laid down in the preceding pages we would build up the Total Account as follows:

Sales Ledger Total Account

May 1 Balance b/d	£632	May 1 Balance b/d		£11
May 31 Sales Day Book	519	May 31 Returns Day Book		7
May 31 Bank (refunds to customers)	3	May 31 Bank		467
		May 31 Discounts		21
May 31 Balance c/d	3	May 31 Bad debts written off		4
		May 31 Contra with Bought Ledger		7
		May 31 Balance c/d		640
	£1,157			£1,157
June 1 Balance b/d	£640	June 1 Balance b/d		£3

(b) A credit balance on a Sales Ledger Account may arise when a customer has settled his account but later on returns goods for which he has already paid.

PROGRESS TEST 7

Theory

1. In what way are Control (or Total) Accounts of help in the preparation of a Trial Balance? **(1, 2)**

2. Certain items which appear in a Trial Balance can be verified with absolute accuracy. What are they? **(3, 4)**

3. There are other items which can be proved to be accurate, i.e., the totals of the balances on the debtors' and the creditors' ledgers. Which Trial Balance items cannot be so proved and where are they to be found? **(5)**

4. How is the accuracy of the personal ledgers proved? Detail briefly the system of accounting you would install to achieve this purpose. **(7)**

5. What is the reasoning underlying the use of Control Accounts? **(10)**

6. What do you understand by the expression "contra" in relation to accounts in the Bought Ledger and the Sales Ledger? Explain how such contras work. **(12)**

7. How is it that we sometimes find (a) our suppliers owing us money, (b) ourselves owing money to our own customers? How are such matters shown in the respective Control Accounts? **(14, 15)**

Practice

8. From the following particulars prepare

(a) The Bought Ledger Control Account.
(b) The Sales Ledger Control Account for 19–4.

Purchases	£19,000
Sales	40,000
Total creditors' balance on 1st January 19–4	7,000
Total debtors' balance on 1st January 19–4	6,000
Discounts received	210
Discounts allowed	400
Returns outwards	20
Returns inwards	300
Bills receivable	1,500
Cash paid	16,000
Cash received	35,000
Bad debts written off	500
Bills discounted with bank	1,000
(Note: discounting charge £40)	

(R.S.A. II)

9. When the balances on the books of Hyde & Park are extracted it is found that there is a difference of £10. In order to locate the difference, Total Accounts for the Purchases and Sales Ledgers are prepared and the necessary analysis gives the following figures:

19–4		
July 1	Balances on Purchases Ledger	£20,652
July 1	Balances on Sales Ledger	29,028
19–5		
June 30	Purchases during year	240,931
June 30	Sales during year	350,753
June 30	Purchases Returns during year	247
June 30	Sales Returns during year	473
June 30	Cash paid to suppliers	229,035
June 30	Cash received from customers	339,179
June 30	Discounts received	4,763
June 30	Discounts allowed	5,932

June 30 Bad debts written off	278
June 30 Purchases Ledger credits transferred to Sales Ledger	3,827
June 30 Purchases Ledger balances	23,701
June 30 Sales Ledger balances	30,092

Prepare the Total Accounts and state what they reveal.

(*R.S.A. II*)

10. The following information, relating to a complete year's trading, has been extracted from the books of XY & Co. All purchases and sales have been entered in personal accounts in the Bought Ledger and Sales Ledger respectively.

Sales-Ledger balances, 1st January: debit	£10,840
credit	34
Bought Ledger balances, 1st January: debit	15
credit	8,760
Payments to trade creditors	91,575
Receipts from customers, including net proceeds of discounted bills and a cheque for £385 (including £10 interest) from the acceptor of the dishonoured bill	118,600
Purchases	96,320
Sales	121,400
Bills Receivable in hand, 1st January	520
Bills Receivable accepted by customers	6,250
Bills Receivable discounted	6,770
Bankers' discounting charges	105
Bills Receivable dishonoured	375
Bad debts written off	227
Discounts allowed	2,780
Dsicounts received	1,930
Returns inwards	1,165
Returns outwards	218
Sales Ledger credit balances: 31st December	40
Bought Ledger debit balances: 31st December	63

During the year debit balances in the Sales Ledger amounting to £492 were transferred to the Bought Ledger.

You are required to prepare the Sales Ledger Control Account and the Bought Ledger Control Account for the year.

(*I.C.S.A.*)

11. Thornley Ltd. maintains control accounts for its Sales and Purchases Ledgers. Balances at 31st December 19–3 are:

	Debit	Credit
Sales ledger	£15,279	£133
Purchases ledger	216	12,491

Details of transactions during 19–4 are as follows:

Sales	£142,789
Purchases	96,241
Receipts from credit customers	136,182
Cash sales	99,046
Payments to suppliers for goods purchased on credit	93,438
Cash purchases	133
Returns inwards	1,016
Returns outwards	838
Bad debts written off	1,002
Refund to a credit customer for an overpayment	64

At 31st December 19–4, credit balances on the sales ledger amount to £184 and debit balances on the purchases ledger amount to £149.

Required:

Sales ledger control account and purchases ledger control account for 19–4.

(I.B.)

12. The balance on the Purchase Ledger Control Account in Cunningham's Books did not agree with the balances totalling £35,560 extracted from the purchase ledger at 31st December 19–2.

The following errors were found when the postings and additions were checked:

(a) The purchase returns day book had been overcast, an item for £300 having been misread as £500.

(b) A payment for advertising £360 had been analysed as a purchase of goods and posted to the account of a supplier in the Purchase Ledger. The balance on this account, £360, had been transferred to Advertising account in the Nominal Ledger, but no entry had been made in the Control Account.

(c) By agreement, Chadwick's account in the Sales Ledger was set off by contra against the credit balance of his account in the Purchase Ledger. Transfers of £900 had not been entered in the Control Account.

(*d*) The undermentioned balances which were in the purchase ledger had not been extracted to the list of balances:

Credits	£540
Debits	40

(*e*) The credit column on Holmes' account in the purchase ledger had been undercast by £20.

(*f*) An old debit balance of £2 on the purchase ledger had been written off as bad during the year, but no entry had been made in the Control Account.

(*g*) Discounts received for the month of March, £30, had been recorded in the cash book and posted to the correct accounts in the purchase ledger, but no entry had been made in the Control Account.

(*h*) Lee had been debited for goods returned to him, £80, without an entry having been made in the purchase returns day book.

(*i*) Credit balances of £70 in the purchase ledger had appeared as debit balances on the list of creditors.

(*j*) A payment of £240, to Snodgrass Brothers had been entered correctly in the Control Account but had not been posted to the purchase ledger account.

You are required to prepare:

(*a*) A statement reconciling the original net balances extracted from the purchase ledger with the adjusted final balance on the Purchase Ledger Control Account; and

(*b*) the Purchase Ledger Control Account showing the necessary adjustments and the balance on the account before these adjustments.

CHAPTER VIII

Manufacturing Accounts

THE BASIS OF THE MANUFACTURING ACCOUNT

1. Making goods to sell. In dealing with business accounts we have, so far, only considered the case of the *retail* trader, i.e., the shopkeeper. We must now give some thought to the accounts of those firms which actually make things; that is to say, those which purchase raw materials of one kind or another and then subject those materials to processes which alter them in some manner. For example, a business which manufactures cigarettes will have to buy, as its basic raw material, tobacco in the form of leaves. The leaves will first have to be stripped from the stalks and then shredded. Other processes will follow which will, ultimately, transform the leaves from something of little apparent value into a product which is widely recognised as a saleable commodity, i.e., cigarette or pipe tobacco. In the case of cigarettes a special type of paper must be purchased, cut to the required length and then, when the correct amount of tobacco has been placed on the paper, it must be rolled into a tube-like shape and a small quantity of adhesive added in order that it may retain its shape. When the cigarette is finally produced this does not end matters. It is a fragile article and needs some protective wrapping. This usually takes the form of a cardboard box or packet. Raw material again is needed and so cardboard, foil and cellophane must be bought and processed, the cigarettes inserted and the packet finally sealed. Only when these matters have been completed will the cigarettes be regarded as being in a condition fit for sale.

The question which now faces us is how are these matters to be dealt with in so far as accounting procedures are concerned? In the first place it must be recognised that we are *not* dealing with factors which differ in essence from those of an ordinary retail shopkeeper so far as double-entry book-keeping is concerned. That will go on as before. The main fact which we have to consider is that the business which manufactures things does so because it pays it to do so, i.e., it costs less to make the articles than it does to buy them in a complete and saleable form.

2. The Manufacturing Account. The basis of a Manufacturing Account is extremely simple. It consists of assembling all those expenses which comprise the *costs* of manufacture. These expenses consist primarily of the cost of materials consumed and the wages of the workers engaged in production. To these must be added the cost of all *factory* expenses such as rent and rates, power, lighting and heating, etc.

It must be emphasised at this point that *only* that part of these expenses which is strictly related to the factory—and *not* the part incurred by the administrative side of the business—will be debited in the Manufacturing Account. The sole objective of the Manufacturing Account is to ascertain the *cost of production.*

At the end of an accounting period the appropriate expense accounts (Nominal Accounts) will be closed off in the usual way, the corresponding debit being made in the Manufacturing Account. By this means all those items of expense which relate strictly to manufacture will be collected on the debit side of the Manufacturing Account and the total will, of course, be the cost of production, i.e., the amount of expense incurred in producing a supply of saleable goods.

PREPARING MANUFACTURING ACCOUNTS

3. Stocks. Before examining an example of a Manufacturing Account attention must be drawn to the matter of stocks. These fall into three categories:

(a) stocks of raw materials;
(b) stocks of work in progress;
(c) stocks of finished goods.

In the task of calculating the cost of production we are not concerned with the stocks of finished goods either at the beginning or at the end of the accounting period. Finished goods are saleable goods and therefore their place, quite properly, will be in the Trading Account. We are thus left with the raw material stock and the stock of work in progress as requiring inclusion in the Manufacturing Account.

4. Materials consumed. When preparing a Manufacturing Account it is customary to break it down into what may be called natural sections. The first of these is concerned with the ascertainment of the cost of goods which have been used up in the process of manufacture, i.e., the cost of materials consumed.

EXAMPLE: The following figures relating to production were extracted from the books of X Ltd and entered in the Manufacturing Account:

Manufacturing Account

Raw materials		
Opening stock	£5,640	
Purchases	71,265	
	———	
	76,905	
Less: Closing stock	6,175	
	———	
Raw materials consumed	£70,730	

WORK IN PROGRESS

5. Work in progress. The term "work in progress" is used to indicate *partly* manufactured goods, i.e., goods which have passed from the raw material stage but which have not yet reached the finished goods stage. These goods must, of course, appear in the Manufacturing Account. It must be appreciated that these goods are a form of *closing* stock at the end of a trading period and, therefore, a form of *opening* stock at the start of the following one. We must thus be prepared to meet with both opening *and* closing work in progress when dealing with problems relating to Manufacturing Accounts. It follows, therefore, that if work in progress at the beginning is debited to the Manufacturing Account and the amount at the end of the period credited the matter will be satisfactorily disposed of.

Modern presentation normally takes the form of showing everything on the debit side of the Manufacturing Account. This means that closing stocks of work in progress must be shown as a *deduction* instead of being entered as a credit. The final result would, of course, be the same if the closing stock of work in progress appeared as a credit. The idea behind this particular form of presentation is that the final cost of production will be the only item to appear on the credit side, thus closing off the account.

It is usual to find that both opening and closing amounts of work in progress are not dealt with until all the other items have been inserted in the Manufacturing Account. The reason for this is that work in progress usually includes a certain proportion of productive wages and, since it also includes some raw materials, the view is that this matter should be dealt with in isolation. The procedure is for the lesser amount (whether it be opening or closing work in progress) to be deducted from the greater. The result is either added to or deducted from the total of all the manufacturing expenses. The two following examples will clarify the situation.

EXAMPLE: The total of all the items of manufacturing expense incurred by X Ltd amounted to £10,000. Work in progress at the start of the period amounted to £1,800 and at the end to £1,400.

Total manufacturing expenses		£10,000
Work in progress *at start*	£1,800	
Less: Work in progress		
at end	1,400	
	Add £400 =	400
Cost of production		**£10,400**

EXAMPLE:

Total of all manufacturing expenses		£20,000
Work in progress at the start		3,450
Work in progress at the end		4,100
Total manufacturing expenses		£20,000
Work in progress *at the end*	£4,100	
Less: Work in progress at		
the start	3,450	
	Deduct £650 =	650
Cost of production		**£19,350**

FLEXIBILITY IN THE TREATMENT OF WAGES

6. Salaries and wages. Many students appear to have a fixed idea that wages must always be debited in the Trading Account while salaries are automatically a charge to the Profit and Loss Account. This is far from being the case. Broadly speaking, the term "salary" is taken to mean the payment to an employee for services rendered in an executive or administrative capacity in the conduct of a business, e.g., to the accountant, the chief buyer, the telephone switchboard operator, the wages clerk, the cashier, etc. Directors also are usually paid a salary as a part of their financial reward for serving a limited company. But this rigid distinction does not stand up to a closer examination. How are we to deal with the case of a director holding the position of Works Manager? This position is a most important one calling for great experience and technical knowledge in the field of production. This is an administrative post in the broad sense of the term but is mainly connected with manufacture, and, as a result, such a salary would be debited to the Manufacturing Account.

On the other hand wages are normally regarded as the financial reward for working by hand. That is to say, we tend to think of persons engaged on work of a productive nature as earning wages. This is true in a great many cases but by no means all. Consider the case of the man who sweeps out the factory yard, the office cleaners, the man who stokes the boilers, the night-watchman of the factory, the lift attendant at the main office, the man who sits at the enquiries desk or the doorkeeper. All these people are paid wages and not salaries. Are all of these expenses to be charged to the Manufacturing Account? Of course they are not. What is required is an analysis which will break them down into clear-cut grades of labour so that they may be debited to the appropriate section of the accounting system.

DIRECT FACTORY EXPENSES

7. Factory expenses. In order that an item may qualify as a factory expense and so be debited in the Manufacturing Account it must have some quite definite relationship to manufacture. Factory expenses fall into two groups:

(a) direct charges or expenses;
(b) indirect charges or expenses.

8. Direct charges or expenses. There are two types of direct charges:

(*a*) *Productive wages.* We speak of wages as being *productive* when they are paid to men who are actually engaged on work of a productive nature, i.e. making things. Examples would be the wages paid to a man who operates a machine pressing steel sheets into the shape of a motor-car body, or a miner who works at the coal-face. In cases such as these it is easy to see that these men are directly responsible for producing something which will ultimately have a selling value.

(*b*) *The cost of materials consumed.* The cost of materials used in manufacture is clearly a direct expense. Such materials can be definitely identified in the sense that when a quantity of raw material is purchased for the purpose of manufacture a specific price had to be paid for that quantity of goods. When a portion of those goods is used in the making of a certain product the actual cost of the quantity used can be ascertained and charged directly to the cost of making that product. Hence we use the term "*direct* charge" in relation to raw materials.

Occasionally, we meet with certain other items the cost of which is regarded as a direct expense. An example of this would be the cost of transporting raw material from its place of origin to our factory. Effectively, this is an additional direct cost because unless the raw material is available for our workmen to use we would have to close down. So this extra charge must be included in the direct charges.

PRIME COST

9. Prime cost. The ascertainment of the prime cost of manufacture is a matter of some importance to a manufacturing company. When dealing with examination problems requiring the production of a Manufacturing Account an answer showing "prime cost" will certainly score good marks if set out correctly and clearly. Prime cost consists of the following:

(*a*) direct materials consumed;
(*b*) direct wages;
(*c*) direct expenses.

EXAMPLE: Y Ltd is a company engaged on building a bridge. When the financial year ended the position was as follows:

Materials purchases	£25,000
Wages of workmen	64,000
Wages of foremen	8,000
Hire of special crane	2,000
Materials not yet used	3,700

Manufacturing Account

Raw materials		
Purchases	£25,000	
Less: Closing stock	3,700	
	———	
Raw materials consumed	21,300	
Productive wages		
Workmen	64,000	
Foremen	8,000	
	———	72,000
Direct expenses		
Hire of crane		2,000
		———
Prime cost		**£95,300**

This example shows the manner in which the first part of a Manufacturing Account should be set out and this lay-out should be memorised.

COMPLETING THE COST OF PRODUCTION

10. Indirect charges or expenses. These charges usually form a considerable part of the cost of production since they consist of those expenses necessary for the efficient running of a factory. Consider the following items

(*a*) Factory rent. Some part of this expense will, of necessity, enter into the manufacture of *every* item produced by the factory.

(*b*) Lighting and heating of the factory.

(*c*) The cost of motive power to drive the machines, e.g., electricity.

(*d*) Lubricants for the machines.

(*e*) The wages of storekeepers, timekeepers, toolsetters, boilermen, cleaners, etc.

The above list is simply a suggestion of the kind of expenses which cannot, by their very nature, be charged against any *specific* item of production. They are a varied selection but, it will be noted, not of an administrative character. Each one can be positively identified with manufacture.

11. Depreciation of machinery. Fixed assets lose their value by degrees as a result of being used or becoming obsolete. This loss of value, as we know, is called *depreciation*. Factory machines are no exception to this fact of business life and the charge for such depreciation must be included in the Manufacturing Account as one of the costs of production.

Depreciation of plant and machinery is regarded as being a factory expense of an indirect nature and must, therefore, be entered in the Manufacturing Account after the prime cost of production has been ascertained.

EXAMPLE: Z Ltd, a manufacturing company, produced the following figures from which a Manufacturing Account was to be constructed:

Raw materials at 1st January	£1,500
Finished goods at 1st January	4,875
Raw materials at 30th June	1,625
Finished goods at 30th June	5,760
Purchases of raw materials	7,200
Manufacturing wages	12,125
Electric power—factory	400
Light and heat—factory	700
Rent and rates—factory	2,000
Non-productive wages—factory	1,420
Depreciation of plant and machinery	1,000

Manufacturing Account for the six months ended 30th June

Raw materials		
Stock at 1st		
January	£1,500	
Purchases	7,200	
	8,700	
Less: Stock at		
30th June	1,625	
Raw materials		
consumed	7,075	
Manufacturing		
wages	12,125	
Prime cost	£19,200	
Factory expenses		
Electric power	400	
Light and heat	700	
Rent and rates	2,000	
Non-productive		
wages	1,420	
Depreciation of		
plant and		
machinery	1,000	
Factory cost of		
production	£24,720	

It will be observed that we have not shown either the opening or closing stocks of finished goods in the above Manufacturing Account. The reason for this is that the place of finished goods is in the Trading Account.

The Manufacturing Account tells us that *the cost* of producing a certain quantity of finished goods during these six months was £24,720. This figure must now be transferred to the Trading Account and so we close off the Manufacturing Account by crediting it with the factory cost of production (£24,720) and debiting the Trading Account.

Manufacturing Account

Factory cost of production (*as above*)	£24,720	**Transfer to Trading Account** (factory cost of production)	**£24,720**
	£24,720		£24,720

Trading Account

Stock of finished goods at 1st January	£4,875		
Finished goods produced (per Manufacturing Account)	**24,720**		
	29,595		
Less: Stock of finished goods at 30th June	5,760		
Cost of goods sold	£23,835		

This example should give the student a good idea as to how he should deal with a problem relating to a Manufacturing Account. The lay-out is most important and the information concerning the prime cost, the cost of production and the cost of sales are vital items. An examiner will be looking for all these points.

12. Specimen question.

Sudbury Ltd is a manufacturing company and the following details for the year 19–1 were extracted from its books:

Stock of raw materials, 1st January 19–1	£16,249
Stock of raw materials, 31st December 19–1	18,216
Stock of manufactured goods, 1st January 19–1	19,241
Stock of manufactured goods, 31st December 19–1	17,485
Work in progress, 1st January 19–1	22,706
Work in progress, 31st December 19–1	23,298
Purchases of raw materials	144,252
Manufacturing wages	88,264
Sales	366,487
Factory expenses	21,826
Rent, rates of factory	10,000
Rent, rates of office	4,500
General administration expenses	24,269
Salesmen's salaries	7,836
Motor expenses (for delivery to customers)	4,367
Other selling expenses	7,602
Depreciation of plant	9,000
Depreciation of motor vans	2,200

You are asked to prepare Sudbury's Manufacturing Account and a Trading and Profit and Loss Account for the year 19–1.

(*R.S.A. II*)

SUGGESTED SOLUTION:

Sudbury Ltd: Manufacturing, Trading and
Profit and Loss Account for the year 19–1

Raw materials consumed:			**Factory cost of pro-**	
Opening stock	£16,249		**duction** (transferred	
Purchases	144,252		to Trading	
	————		Account)	**£270,783**
	160,501			
Less: Closing				
stock	18,216			
	————			
	142,285			
Manufacturing				
wages	88,264			
	————			
Prime cost	230,549			
Factory expenses	21,826			
Factory rent	10,000			
Depreciation	9,000			
	————			
	271,375			
Add: Work in				
progress at				
start of year	22,706			
	————			
	294,081			
Less: Work in				
progress at				
end of year	23,298			
	————			
	£270,783			£270,783

Sudbury Ltd: Manufacturing, Trading and Profit and Loss Account for the year 19–1 (continued)

Stock of finished goods at start of year	£19,241	Sales	£366,487
Factory cost of production (transferred from Manufacturing Account)	**270,783**		
	290,024		
Less: Stock of finished goods at end of year	17,485		
Cost of sales	272,539		
Gross profit	93,948		
	£366,487		£366,487
Rent	£4,500	Gross Profit	£93,948
General administration expenses	24,269		
Salesmen's salaries	7,836		
Motor expenses	4,367		
Depreciation of motor vans	2,200		
Other selling expenses	7,602		
	50,774		
Net profit	43,174		
	£93,948		£93,948

PROGRESS TEST 8

Theory

1. What is the object of constructing a Manufacturing Account and what is the basis of its construction? **(1, 2)**

2. Into what categories do stocks of a manufacturing company fall? **(3)**

3. How would you calculate the value of materials consumed during a period of operation? **(4)**

4. Define "work in progress". **(5)**

5. How should work in progress be dealt with in a Manufacturing Account? **(5)**

6. Where should wages be charged in the annual accounts of a company? **(6, 10)**

7. What do you understand by (*a*) direct expenses, (*b*) indirect expenses? Give examples. **(8, 10)**

8. What broad classes of expenditure are included under "prime cost"? **(9)**

9. Set out a pro-forma Manufacturing Account showing (*a*) raw materials consumed, (*b*) prime cost, (*c*) factory cost of production. **(9, 10)**

Practice

10. Omega Ltd is a manufacturing company and the following details for the year 19–1 are extracted from their books:

Stock of raw materials, 1st January 19–1	£11,464
Stock of raw materials, 31st December 19–1	12,162
Stock of manufactured goods, 1st January 19–1	14,881
Stock of manufactured goods, 31st December 19–1	14,238
Work in progress, 1st January 19–1	18,294
Work in progress, 31st December 19–1	19,941
Purchases of raw materials	115,826
Manufacturing wages	71,242
Sales	284,369
Factory expenses	19,324
Rent, rates of factory	6,000
Rent, rates of office	3,000
General administration expenses	21,642
Salesmen's salaries	6,162
Motor expenses (for delivery to customers)	3,984
Other selling expenses	7046
Depreciation: Plant and machinery	8,000
Motor vans	1,800

You are asked to prepare a Manufacturing Account and a Trading and Profit and Loss Account for 19–1. You should indicate the significance of sub-totals and of balances carried down.

(R.S.A. II)

11. The following figures relating to the year 19–5 have been taken from the books of the Oldhamlet Manufacturing Company:

Sales	£145,600
Stock of materials, 1st January, at cost	3,315
Materials purchased	38,942
Stock of materials, 31st December, at cost	2,973
Manufacturing wages	52,681
Work in progress, 1st January, at factory cost	1,749
Work in progress, 31st December, at factory cost	1,894
Factory expenses	15,656
Office and administration expenses	7,450
Depreciation of plant and machinery	6,500
Depreciation of delivery vans	1,250
Stock of finished goods, 1st January, at factory cost	5,064
Stock of finished goods, 31st December, at factory cost	7,138
Factory power	3,670
Advertising	1,035
Delivery van running expenses	1,425
Salesmen's salaries and commission	4,630

You are required to prepare a Manufacturing Account, a Trading Account and a Profit and Loss Account for the year ended 31st December 19–5. The accounts should show prime cost, factory cost of goods completed during the year and factory cost of goods sold.

The factory cost of goods completed during the year is to be transferred from the Manufacturing Account to the Trading Account.

(I.C.S.A.)

12. On 31st December 19–4, the following balances were extracted from the books of the Toytown Manufacturing Company:

Stocks at 1st January 19–4:	
Raw materials	£5,415
Work in progress	4,920
Finished goods	7,245
Sales for the year	69,080
Purchases of raw materials	16,190
Manufacturing wages:	
Productive wages	19,260
Non-productive wages	5,830
Factory power and light	1,675
Factory rent, rates and insurance	1,560
Depreciation of machinery	2,750
Repairs to machines	600
Salary of works manager	5,200
Stocks at 31st December 19–4 were valued as follows:	
Raw materials	£5,910
Work in progress	5,230
Finished goods	7,970

Prepare a Manufacturing and Trading Account for the year ending 31st December 19–4 showing clearly the cost of raw materials consumed, the prime cost and the cost of factory production. Calculate the percentage of gross profit on sales to the nearest decimal point.

CHAPTER IX

Non-trading Concerns

INCOME AND EXPENDITURE ACCOUNTS

1. Introduction. Income and Expenditure Accounts are used mainly by sports clubs, social clubs, learned societies and the like; this type of organisation is not operated *primarily* with the object of making a profit as is the case with commercial concerns. For this reason the Final Account which sets out the financial results of the year's activities is not called a Profit and Loss Account but an Income and Expenditure Account. So far as accounting practice is concerned the difference is a difference in name only.

2. Important matters to be remembered when preparing an Income and Expenditure Account. The following points should be noted and committed to memory:

(*a*) An Income and Expenditure Account can be compared exactly with a Profit and Loss Account in its construction.

(*b*) Therefore, all items of Capital Expenditure must be *excluded* when preparing it.

(*c*) Accrued Expenses must be taken into consideration just as they are when a Profit and Loss Account is being prepared.

(*d*) The following items must be deducted when calculating the amount of any particular item to be included in an Income and Expenditure Account:

(*i*) payments made in advance;

(*ii*) money which has been received in advance.

When the Income and Expenditure Account has been completed a Balance Sheet must be drawn up in the usual way.

3. Receipts and Payments Accounts. Money received and payments made are recorded in the Cash Book of a business; in precisely the same way clubs and societies will record details of their income and out-goings. It is customary to refer to the Cash Book of a non-trading concern as a "Receipts and Payments Account" instead of a Bank Account or Cash Account.

EXAMPLE:

*The Silverstones Debating Society: Receipts and
Payments Account for year ended 31st December 19–1*

Balance b/d (at		Rent of premises	£1,000
1st January 19–1)	£71	Secretary's salary	500
Subscriptions	495	Repairs	76
Profit on refresh-		General expenses	99
ments and bar	1,548	Light and heat	385
		Balance c/d (at 31st	
		December 19–1)	54
	£2,114		£2,114

From this it can be seen that the above account is a *normal* Cash Book summary although it has been graced with the title "Receipts and Payments Account." It will play its part in the building up of an Income and Expenditure Account but it must never be confused with that account.

The following comparative table may help.

Clubs, etc.	*Businesses*
Income & Expenditure Account	= Profit & Loss Account
Receipts & Payments Account	= Bank Account (Cash Book)

4. Answering examination questions. The simple and elementary rules which follow should be observed when answering questions. The first is, perhaps, the most important.

(*a*) Before a start is made on the actual preparation of an Income and Expenditure Account it is absolutely vital that an opening statement be prepared to ensure that the total of all the assets is exactly equal to the total of all the liabilities. There will normally be an excess of assets over liabilities and the difference between the two sides of the statement must be inserted. This represents *the capital* of the concern. In the case of non-trading concerns we call this the "Capital Fund" or "Accumulated Fund" (instead of the "Capital Account" which is the term used for businesses).

(*b*) Open a Ledger Account for each balance on the Opening Statement and post thereto the appropriate amount, e.g., a debit entry of £460 for fixtures and fittings on the Opening Statement will be entered as a debit balance in the Fixtures and Fittings Account.

(c) Make a double entry for *every* transaction which has taken place during the period for which the account is being prepared.

(d) Enter all the closing balances in the respective accounts and carry them down.

(e) Take out a Trial Balance.

Provided that the rules are followed and the additions correctly made the Trial Balance must agree. From that point on the construction of an Income and Expenditure Account should present little difficulty.

SUBSCRIPTIONS

5. Annual subscriptions. It is the normal custom for clubs to charge each member an annual subscription. Dealing with subscriptions, especially in examination problems, can be a little difficult sometimes because they can fall into three different classes. These are:

(a) subscriptions for the current year;
(b) subscriptions received in advance;
(c) subscriptions in arrears.

6. Subscriptions for the current year. In the first place the Bank Account (or Receipts and Payments Account) will show on the debit side all the money received on account of subscriptions during the year, no matter *to which year* they relate. So long as the money is received it must be entered as a receipt. It follows therefore that subscriptions received which relate to the current year will be credited to a Subscriptions Account.

7. Arrears of subscriptions. If it is the practice to include those members whose subscriptions are in arrears as *debtors* at the end of any year, it is best to open a "Subscriptions in Arrears Account", and show the whole amount outstanding as a debtor. Any subscriptions *received* in the following period will therefore be debited in the Bank Account and credited to the Subscriptions in Arrears Account.

The accounting entries at the year-end are quite straightforward. Suppose that £47 was in arrears. The entries would be:

Subscriptions Account

	Subscriptions in Arrears A/c	£47

Subscriptions in Arrears Account

Subscriptions A/c	£47	

It must be noted that credit is taken in the Subscriptions Account. This would be added to any subscriptions which had actually been received, thus *increasing* the total which will ultimately be credited to the Income and Expenditure Account. Such treatment is open to question because it is by no means certain that any of those subscriptions will, in fact, ever be received. It would not be worthwhile for a club to sue for arrears. The remedy is to exclude the lapsed member from membership. In examination problems, however, examiners often include arrears of subscripions since it helps to make the question rather more complex.

In practice many clubs do not treat such arrears as debtors. The arrears are ignored when drawing up the year's accounts. This, of course, simplifies matters. Should any arrears be subsequently received from defaulting members they are simply treated as income of the year in which they are received, i.e., the Bank Account is debited and the Subscriptions Account credited.

8. Subscriptions received in advance. Some members will pay the following year's subscriptions in advance. This obviously must be recorded as a receipt in the Cash Book and will be credited to the Subscriptions Account. At the end of the year the simplest thing to do is to debit this sum in the Subscriptions Account and then to carry it down as a credit balance on this account. Alternatively, it could be credited to a "Subscriptions Received in Advance Account".

TRADING ACCOUNTS

9. Club Trading Accounts. Sometimes examination questions require the preparation of a Trading Account for some special activity carried on by the club, such as a bar or restaurant. Most clubs, whatever their nature, have a bar and it is usual for a Bar Trading Account to be prepared as a completely separate account from the Income and Expenditure Account and this will be con-

structed in the normal way. The gross profit will be transferred to
the credit of the Income and Expenditure Account.

A word of warning is needed here. Many students become confused when asked to prepare a Bar Trading Account. For the most
part they have no difficulty in dealing with the Trading Account
aspect but many do not transfer the gross profit to the Income and
Expenditure Account. The result of this, of course, is an inability to
balance the Balance Sheet. It is therefore of supreme importance
that students do realise that an Income and Expenditure Account
and a Bar Trading Account are complementary accounts and that
if the normal practices of double-entry book-keeping are followed
no difficulty should be experienced in balancing.

THE BALANCE SHEET

10. The Club Balance Sheet. The Balance Sheet will be prepared on
normal lines but a few special points will be dealt with in **11–15**
below, namely:

    (*a*) the Accumulated Fund;
    (*b*) Prize Funds;
    (*c*) entrance fees;
    (*d*) life members;
    (*e*) donations.

11. The Accumulated Fund. This is the equivalent of the Capital
Account in a commercial business. It is sometimes called the
"Capital Fund". Any excess of income over expenditure at the end
of the year will be added to the balance standing to the credit of the
Capital Fund, while any deficit will be deducted. The final balance
on this account will represent the net worth of the club since it will
amount to exactly the difference between the total value of all the
assets, on the one hand, and the amounts owed to outside creditors, on the other.

12. Prize Funds. It is not uncommon to find in club accounts that a
sum of money has been given to the club to be invested, and that
the yearly income from the investment is to be used to purchase a
prize to be awarded annually. When money is given to the club for
purposes such as these it will be debited in the Bank Account. The
corresponding credit will be made in a "Prize Fund Account".

    EXAMPLE. J. Snodgrass gave a donation of £500 to the Bunker
    Golf Club to provide a yearly income of £20 for the purchase of a

cup to be awarded to the winner of an annual competition to be named after him. The money was invested in 4% Government Stock.

The entries in the books of the golf club would be:

Bank Account

J. Snodgrass Prize Fund A/c	£500		

J. Snodgrass Prize Fund Account

		Bank A/c	£500

After the £500 has been invested by purchasing 4% Government Stock the accounts would appear as shown below:

Bank Account

J. Snodgrass Prize Fund A/c	£500	Prize Fund Investment A/c	£500

Prize Fund Investment Account

Bank A/c	£500		

J. Snodgrass Prize Fund Account

		Bank A/c	£500

The entries in the Balance Sheet would be:

**EXTRACT FROM THE BALANCE SHEET
OF THE BUNKER GOLF CLUB**

Liabilities		*Assets*	
J. Snodgrass prize fund	£500	Prize fund investments	£500

In due course the income from the investment will be received, debited in the Bank Account and credited to a "Prize Fund

Income Account". This income will be used up when the prize is purchased, the entries being a credit in the Bank Account and a debit in the "Prize Account". At the end of the year these accounts will be closed by transfer to the Income and Expenditure Account.

13. Entrance fees. Many clubs charge new members an entrance fee in the first year in addition to the annual subscription. This is simply a form of premium, i.e., a device for extracting more money from the new member than would otherwise be the case.

There is no fixed rule as to how the money received from entrance fees should be dealt with in the accounts. It can be credited to either the Income and Expenditure Account or else direct to the Accumulated Fund. Whichever method is used the final result will be the same because any surplus on the Income and Expenditure Account will ultimately be credited to the Accumulated Fund. If entrance fees have been credited to the Income and Expenditure Account this will mean that the surplus will be greater than otherwise would have been the case.

EXAMPLE: The Copper Beeches Golf Club had received £40 in entrance fees during the year. The Income and Expenditure Account showed a surplus of £435 before taking into account this item of £40. At the beginning of the year the Accumulated Fund showed a credit balance of £689.

The cash received in respect of entrance fees could be dealt with in either of the following ways.

(*a*) If the entrance fees are to be credited direct to the Accumulated Fund Account the entries would be:

Accumulated Fund

	Balance at start of period £689
	Surplus from Income and Expenditure Account 435
	Transfer from Entrance Fees Account 40
	————
	£1,164

(*b*) On the other hand if the money received from entrance fees is to be credited to the Income and Expenditure Account the position would appear thus:

Income and Expenditure Account

Transfer to Accumulated Fund Account	£475	Surplus of income over expenditure for the period (not including entrance fees)	£435
		Transfer from Entrance Fees Account	40
	£475		£475

Accumulated Fund

	Balance at start of period	£689
	Transfer from Income and Expenditure Account	475
		£1,164

Thus it makes no difference at all whichever method is adopted because, as can be seen, the total of the credit side of the Accumulated Fund, £1,164, is exactly the same whichever method is employed.

NOTE: The word "Account" is usually dispensed with when referring to the Accumulated Fund.

14. Life members. Most clubs will have an arrangement whereby any member who so wishes can become a member for life by paying a lump sum either when he joins or at any later date. For example, the annual subscription may be £1 but to become a life member may cost £10. In such cases the usual procedure is to capitalise the amount so paid and to create a "Life Membership Fund". The lump sum received from the life member is used to purchase an investment, the annual income from which will, at the end of the financial year, be credited to the Income and Expenditure Account.

The procedure then is an exact parallel with that of Prize Funds as illustrated above.

15. Donations. These are generally comparatively small amounts and are therefore credited to the Income and Expenditure Account in the year in which they are received.

16. Example. The following is a summary of the cash book of the Greenfingers' Club for the year ended 31st December 19–2.

Receipts and Payments Account

Balance at bank,		Restaurant and bar	
1st Jan. 19–2	£410	supplies	£6,250
Members' subscriptions:		Wages (restaurant and	
For year 19–1 185		bar)	340
For year 19–2 3,575		Postage and stationery	150
For year 19–3 200		General expenses	1,790
	3,960	New equipment	710
Restaurant and			
bar takings	7,500	Balance at bank,	
		31st Dec. 19–2	2,630
	£11,870		£11,870

On 31st December 19–1 the club equipment was valued at £3,590.

The following information is obtained:

	31 Dec. 19–1	31 Dec. 19–2
Freehold premises	£4,800	£4,800
Wages due but unpaid	35	30
Creditors for restaurant and bar		
supplies	630	555
Restaurant and bar stocks	725	740

During 19–1 the club treasurer had received £75 in respect of members' subscriptions for 19–2.

You are required to prepare:

(*a*) a Trading Account for the restaurant and bar for the year 19–2;

(*b*) an Income and Expenditure Account for the year 19–2;

(*c*) a Balance Sheet as on 31st December 19–2.

It is the practice to take no credit in the Annual Income and Expenditure Account for subscriptions in arrears at the end of the accounting period.

SOLUTION:
Stage 1
   List *all* balances at the start of the year.

	Dr	Cr
Bank	£410	
Freehold premises	4,800	
Wages due but not paid		£35
Creditors for supplies (*Restaurant and Bar Supplies Account*)	725	630
Stocks		
Subscriptions *received* in advance	3,590	75
Equipment		
		740
Accumulated Fund		?
	£9,525	

The Accumulated Fund is easily found by subtracting £740 from £9,525, i.e., £8,785.

Stage 2
   We now open Ledger Accounts for each of the above balances:

Freehold Premises Account

19–2	
Jun. 1 Balance b/d £4,800	

Wages Account

	19–2	
	Jan. 1 Balance b/d	£35

Restaurant and Bar Supplies Account

	19–2	
	Jan. 1 Balance b/d	£630

Equipment Account

19–2		
Jan. 1 Balance		
b/d £3,590		

Restaurant and Bar Stocks Account

19–2		
Jan. 1 Balance b/d £725		

Subscriptions Account

	19–2	
	Jan. 1 Balance b/d	£75

Bank Account

19–2		
Jan. 1 Balance b/d £410		

Accumulated Fund Account

	19–2	
	Jan. 1 Balance b/d	£8,785

If we check back we will be able to satisfy ourselves that we
have now got a ledger which agrees, i.e., the total of all debit
balances equals the total of all credit balances. In other words,
we have got a level platform, as it were, on which to operate the
transactions of the forthcoming year.

Stage 3

The next thing to do is to write up the details of the Bank
Account and post each item to the opposite side of the ledger in
the appropriate account.

Bank Account

19–2			19–2		
Jan. 1	Balance b/d	£410	Dec. 31	Restaurant and bar supplies	£6,250
Dec. 31	Members' subscriptions		Dec. 31	Wages	340
	For year 19–1 £185		Dec. 31	Postage and stationery	150
	For year 19–1 3,575		Dec. 31	General expenses	1,790
	For year 19–3 200		Dec. 31	New equipment	710
		3,960	Dec. 31	Balance c/d	2,630
Dec. 31	Restaurant and bar takings	7,500			
		£11,870			£11,870
19–3					
Jan. 1	Balance b/d	£2,630			

Dealing with the debit side of the Bank Account first we make the following entries:

Subscriptions Account

			19–2		
			Jan. 1	Balance b/d	£75
			Dec. 31	Bank Account:	
				For 19–1 £185	
19–2				For 19–2 3,575	
Dec. 31	Balance c/d	£200		For 19–3 200	
					3,960
					£4,035
			19–3		
			Jan. 1	Balance b/d	£200

Since we have had to credit the Subscriptions Account with £200 received in advance, i.e., for 19–3, we cannot take credit for it in the 19–2 Income and Expenditure Account. We must, therefore, reduce the total of the credit side (£4,035) by this £200 and bring it in as a liability, i.e., a credit balance.

Restaurant and Bar Takings Account

	19–2
	Dec. 31 Bank
	Account £7,500

Turning now to the entries on the credit side of the Bank Account the following postings must be made:

Restaurant and Bar Supplies Account

19–2	19–2
Dec. 31 Bank	Jan. 21 Balance b/d £630
Account £6,250	

Wages Account

19–2	19–2
Dec. 31 Bank	Jan. 1 Balance b/d £35
Account £340	

Postage and Stationery Account

19–2	
Dec. 31 Bank	
Account £150	

General Expenses Account

19–2	
Dec. 31 Bank	
Account £1,790	

Equipment Account

19–2		
Jan. 1	Balance b/d	£3,590
Dec. 31	Bank Account	710
		£4,300

Stage 4

In this stage two items concern us; the wages which have accrued due, £30, and the unpaid creditors for supplies, £555. Let us now make the necessary adjustments.

Wages Account

19–2			19–2		
Dec. 31	Bank Account	£340	Jan. 1	Balance b/d	£35
Dec. 31	**Balance c/d**	**30**			
		£370			
			19–3		
			Jan. 1	**Balance b/d**	**£30**

Restaurant and Bar Supplies Account

19–2			19–3		
Dec. 31	Bank Account	£6,250	Jan. 1	Balance b/d	£630
Dec. 31	**Balance c/d**	**555**			
		£6,805			
			19–3		
			Jan. 1	**Balance b/d**	**£555**

It can be seen that both the above accounts have been left in an unfinished state. The reason for this is that we want it to be perfectly clear which items are to be taken into the Trial Balance.

Stage 5

In building up the Trial Balance it will be necessary to refer to the accounts as they appear under *Stages 2, 3* and *4.*

TRIAL BALANCE AT 31ST DECEMBER 19–2

Account as at Stage		Dr	Cr
2	Freehold premises	£4,800	
2	Restaurant and bar stocks	725	
2	Accumulated Fund		£8,785
3	Bank	2,630	
4	Wages (£370 − £35)	335	
	Wages (accrued due)		30
4	Restaurant and bar supplies (£6,805 − £630)	6,175	
	Restaurant and bar supplies (owing to creditors)		555
3	Restaurant and bar takings		7,500
3	Postage and stationery	150	
3	General expenses	1,790	
3	Equipment	4,300	
3	Subscriptions (£4,035 − £200)		3,835
	Subscriptions (received in advance)		200
		£20,905	£20,905

Stage 6

Having agreed the Trial Balance we can now prepare the Trading Account for the restaurant and bar.

*Restaurant and Bar Trading Account for year
31st December 19–2*

Stock at 1st Jan. 19–2	725	Sales (takings)	7,500
Purchases (Suppliers Accounts)	6,175	Stock at 31st Dec. 19–2	740
Wages	335		
	7,235		
Gross profits **(transferred to Income and Expenditure A/c) 1,005**			
	£8,240		£8,240

Stage 7

It is doubtless unnecessary to give this word of warning but experience has shown that some students appear to be under the impression that it is still necessary to enter the purchase and sales again—this time in the Income and Expenditure Account. Surprising but true! All that is required, of course, is that we proceed in the normal way (as with a Profit and Loss Account) entering the gross profit from the Trading Account to the credit of the Income and Expenditure Account.

Income and Expenditure Account for year to 31st December 19–2

Postage and stationery	£150	Gross profit from Trading A/c	£1,005
General expenses	1,790	Subscriptions	3,835
	1,940		
Surplus, being *excess of income* over expenditure	**2,900**		
	£4,840		£4,840

Accumulated Fund Account

		19–2		
		Jan. 1	Balance b/d	£8,785
		Dec. 31	**Surplus**, transferred from Income and Expenditure Account	2,900
				£11,685

Stage 8

Finally, the Balance Sheet of the club must be drawn up.

BALANCE SHEET AS AT 31ST DECEMBER 19–2

Accumulated fund			*Fixed assets*		
Balance at 1st Jan. 19–2	£8,785		Freehold premises	£4,800	
Add: Surplus from Income & Expenditure Account	2,900		Equipment	4,300	9,100
		£11,685			
			Current assets		
			Stocks (bar and restaurant)	£740	
Current liabilities			Cash at bank	2,630	3,370
Creditors					
for supplies	555				
for wages	30				
for subscriptions received in advance	200	785			
		£12,470			£12,470

PROGRESS TEST 9

Theory

1. In what circumstances is it usual for an Income and Expenditure Account to be employed? **(1)**

2. What important points must be borne in mind when preparing an Income and Expenditure Account? **(2)**

3. What do you understand by the term "Receipts and Payments Account"? **(3)**

4. Tabulate the steps to be taken when preparing an Income and Expenditure Account. **(4)**

5. Into what categories can subscriptions fall? **(5)**

6. How should subscriptions in arrears be dealt with? **(7)**

7. How is any surplus or deficit on a club's working dealt with at the end of the year? **(11)**

8. Entrance fees sometimes present prroblems. Set out the alternative ways in which such fees may be dealt with. **(13)**

Practice

9. The accounts of a social club are made up annually at 31st December.

At 31st December 19–3, subscriptions in arrears amounted to £87 and subscriptions received in advance for the year 19–4 amounted to £71.

During 19–4 £1,214 was received in respect of subscriptions, including £87 arrears for 19–3 and £108 in advance for 19–5. At 31st December 19–4, subscriptions in arrears amounted to £53.

The annual Income and Expenditure Account is credited with all subscriptions in respect of the year to which the account relates, on the assumption that all arrears will be subsequently collected.

You are required to set out the Subscriptions Account for the year 19–4, making therein the appropriate adjustments for subscriptions in arrear and for subscriptions in advance at the beginning and at the end of the year.

(I.C.S.A.)

10. The Tynribbie Tennis Club makes up its accounts each year as at 30th September.

At 30th September 19–4, subscriptions in arrears amounted to £21 and subscriptions received in advance for the following year totalled £9.

During the year ended 30th September 19–5, the total of cash received for subscriptions amounted to £384. This sum included the arrears of £21 for the 19–3/4 season together with £12 in advance for the 19–4/5 season. Unpaid subscriptions for 19–4/5 were £15.

Every year the club's Income and Expenditure Account is credited with the total of subscriptions receivable for the year in question, on the assumption that all arrears will eventually be collected from the members.

Show the Subscription Account for the year ended 30th September 19–5.

11. The accounts of a social club are made up annually as at 31st December.

At 31st December 19–4, subscriptions in arrears amounted to £69 and subscriptions received in advance for the year 19–5 were £43.

During 19–5, £837 was received in respect of subscriptions; this included £69 arrears for 19–4 and £29 in advance for 19–6. At 31st December 19–5, subscriptions in arrears amounted to £76.

The annual income and expenditure account is credited with all subscriptions in respect of the year to which the account relates, on the basis that all arrears will afterwards be collected.

Show the subscriptions account for the year 19–5.

NOTE: There are no separate accounts for subscriptions in arrears or for subscriptions in advance.

(*I.O.B.*)

12. The following is a summary of the Cash Book of the Drifters Club for the year to 31st December 19–4.

Receipts and Payments Account

Balance at bank			Restaurant and bar	
1st Jan. 19–4	£360		supplies	£6,000
Members' subscriptions:			Wages	2,120
for year 19–3 £85			Printing, stationery	
for year 19–4 2,575			and postage	140
for year 19–5 100			New furniture	650
	——	2,760	General expenses	1,830
Restaurant and bar			Balance at bank	
takings	8,000		31st Dec. 19–4	380
	£11,120			£11,120

The following information is obtained:

	1st Jan. 19–4	31st Dec. 19–4
Freehold premises	£5,000	£5,000
Stock of restaurant and bar supplies	618	548
Creditors for restaurant and bar supplies	450	490
Wages accrued	25	30

At 31st December 19–3 the club furniture was valued at £3,620, and, during 19–3, £80 had been received in respect of members' subscriptions for the year 19–4.

You are required to prepare:

(a) a Trading Account for the restaurant and bar for the year 19–4;

(b) an Income and Expenditure Account for the year 19–4;

(c) a Balance Sheet as on 31st December 19–4.

The gross profit on the Restaurant and Bar Trading Account is to be transferred to the Income and Expenditure Account.

NOTES:

(a) It is the practice to take no credit in the Annual Income and Expenditure Account for subscriptions in arrears at the end of the accounting period.

(b) Wages are to be charged to the Income and Expenditure Account.

(c) Ignore depreciation of furniture.

13. The balance sheet of the Welcome Club at 31st December 19–4 is as follows:

Accumulated Fund		£48,420	Investments at cost	£24,600
Creditors:			Furniture and	
Bar			equipment at cost	
purchases	£2,040		less depreciation	15,200
Expenses	80		Bar Stocks	4,100
		2,120	Bank balance	6,640
		£50,540		£50,540

A summary of the club's bank account for 19–5 is as follows:

Balance at		Bar purchases	£40,380
Ast January 19–5	£6,640	Wages and salaries	8,420
Subscriptions received	6,200	Rent and rates	2,400
Bar sales	53,800	General expenses	2,680
Interest on		Cost of new	
investments	2,080	investments	13,000
		Balance at	
		31st December 19–5	1,840
	£68,720		£68,720

On 31st December 19–5 bar stocks were valued at £5,968 and £2,284 was owing for bar supplies: £124 was owing for expenses.

The owner of the building of which the club occupies a part proposes to sell it for £88,000; he has offered it to the trustees of the club and they are considering the proposal.

The investments held by the club could be sold for £40,160 and a member of the club has offered to lend £10,000 at 10 per cent per annum for five years; the secretary of the club has approached the bank to negotiate an overdraft for the balance needed to purchase the building; the bank has asked to see the 19–5 accounts and wishes to have an estimate of the amount that will be available annually for repayment.

Part of the building is occupied by a second organisation which pays its own rates and from which an annual rent of £800 is receivable. The club will remain liable for the rates on the part of the building it occupies, amounting to £900 per annum.

There are no subscriptions in arrears or in advance; depreciation should be charged on the furniture and equipment at the rate of 10 per cent per annum on the opening value.

Required:

(*a*) A Bar Trading Account and a Profit and Loss Account for 19–5 and a Balance Sheet at the end of that year.

(*b*) A calculation showing:

(*i*) the maximum amount to be borrowed on overdraft, as at 1st January 19–6, to meet the cost of the building, and

(*ii*) the annual surplus that will be available to meet the interest on the overdraft and for repayment on the assumption that the 19–5 results are repeated in each of the following five years.

NOTES:
  (a) Ignore income tax.
  (b) There was no capital expenditure in 19–5.

(*I.B.*)

14. The Woodgate Squash Club rents premises where certain facilities are available and it owns a quantity of equipment. On 1st January 19–7 the equipment was valued at £920. In addition, the club had £500 on deposit in a Savings Bank as well as £54 on current account at the bank. At the same time £74 was owing for one quarter's rent and there were also subscriptions paid in advance amounting to £90. During the year ended 31st December 19–7 interest of £12 was credited to the Savings Bank Account.

Prepare an Income and Expenditure Account for the year to 31st December 19–7 and a Balance Sheet at that date, after providing for depreciation of £140 on the equipment.

The following is the Receipts and Payments Account for the year:

Receipts		*Payments*	
Balances: 1st January 19–7		Rent Four quarters	
bank	£54	to 30th September	
cash	4	19–7	£296
Entrance Fees	22	Wages	416
Subscriptions	514	Repairs	20
Subscriptions in		Purchase of new	
advance	84	equipment	80
Withdrawn from		Sundry expenses	176
Savings Bank	100	Bank interest	4
Profit on		Cash in hand	
refreshments	150	31st December 19–7	6
Sale of surplus			
equipment	30		
Balance at bank (overdraft)			
at 31st December 19–7	40		
	£998		£998

CHAPTER X

Incomplete Records I

THE BRIDGE BETWEEN BOOK-KEEPING AND ACCOUNTING

1. Introduction. This section of the study of accounting is of such great importance that it is no exaggeration to say that unless it is mastered prospects of examination success will be seriously impaired. Furthermore, the student's long-term prospects as an accountant are likely to be jeopardised. An accountant's potential capacity can be seen to the full, and judged accordingly, by his ability to construct accounts from incomplete records. This warning is given in order to emphasise the immense importance of this aspect of study, but it should not be regarded as something to be feared. A sound knowledge of the principles of double-entry book-keeping plus a reasonable amount of common sense and, as always, plenty of practice on problems, should develop the ability required to deal with most of the problems which arise either in examination work or elsewhere.

2. The difference between practice and theory. Fundamentally, examination problems dealing with incomplete records differ very little from practical problems in business. When an accountant receives the books from a small trader he may well be handed nothing more than a pile of receipts and bills wrapped in brown paper or even newspaper. The information contained therein has to be extracted, sorted, checked and analysed before any attempt can be made to prepare the final accounts. This work is more often than not, both tedious and time-consuming, but it *has* to be done. In examination problems, on the other hand, all of this basic information is stated in the question. There are no lengthy preliminaries to be dealt with as there are in real-life situations and a start can be made immediately on working out the answer. Provided that the student has had plenty of experience in working problems of this type he should be able to produce the correct solution.

It is proposed, in this book, to deal only with the theoretical aspect of the problem. The normal type of examination problem will give all the basic information required for the student to

146

produce a correct answer. The information given, however, is only *partial* and is lacking in certain vital items of information. Thus the student must be trained to draw certain conclusions from a given amount of information. By so doing he is able to produce *complete* records from what were incomplete ones. It can be stated here that problems of this nature can be really fascinating and of absorbing interest for they provide a challenge which, when successfully overcome, gives one a solid sense of achievement. Furthermore, this tends to act as a great stimulant and invariably spurs the student on to pit his wits against further and more difficult problems.

3. What are incomplete records? The term "incomplete records" is usually applied to those cases where a full set of double-entry books is not kept. The reasons for not keeping a proper set of books can be many and varied but generally the trader has had no training in the art of book-keeping and is interested only in making as good a living as possible in whatever line of business he happens to be. Very often one finds that he has a very shrewd idea as to how much profit he has made and only engages the services of an accountant because the Department of Inland Revenue requires him to produce a set of accounts and a Balance Sheet, independently certified, in order to determine the amount of profit he has made and how much tax he must pay on that profit.

4. The bridge between book-keeping and accountancy. Accounting from incomplete records may reasonably be regarded as being the bridge between plain straightforward book-keeping, on the one hand, and accountancy on the other. The reason for saying this is because book-keeping, basically, is used to record business transactions in money terms according to a set pattern, i.e., by means of the double-entry method. Where this set pattern is only *partially* used, i.e., where the double-entry is *incomplete*, some other factor must, of necessity, be introduced if a reasonably accurate figure of trading profit is to be determined. In order to be able to do this the accountant has to call upon skills which are somewhat more advanced than simple book-keeping techniques.

5. Planning the work. Whether the problem be one of theory or of practice the student is advised to adhere to a strict *sequence* of work. By so doing he can keep a check on what he has done and is, as a result, far less likely to overlook any points. With this in mind a body of rules is set out below. These have a logical sequence and should be followed closely. It must be pointed out, however, that some problems of an advanced nature do not lend themselves entirely to this sequence but by the time the student reaches that level it is to be hoped that incomplete record accounting will no longer hold any terrors for him and he will be able to adjust his plan of attack according to the circumstances.

BASIC RULES FOR INCOMPLETE RECORD ACCOUNTING

6. Summary of the rules. Before proceeding to any illustrations a summary of the rules will be set out below in order to indicate the logical sequence of tasks to be undertaken. A simple example follows with suitable comments to clarify the various points.

(*a*) Make a list of the balances at the start of the trading period and calculate the amount of the *opening capital*.

(*b*) Open a separate ledger account ("T" Account) for each of the starting balances and post each asset or liability to its appropriate account.

(*c*) Write up the Bank Account (and/or Cash Account) in detail and carry down the closing balance.

(*d*) Post each item from the Bank Account (and/or Cash Account) to the opposite side of the appropriate account. It will almost certainly be necessary to open additional "T" accounts at this point to accommodate certain of the payments and receipts items.

(*e*) Enter the *closing* balances in the Trade Debtors Account (this will be given in the question) and carry this down as a debit balance.

(*f*) Enter the *missing item* (i.e., that *not* given in the question) from the debit side of the Trade Debtors Account and post it to the credit of the Sales Account.

(*g*) Enter the *closing* balance in the Trade Creditors Account (which will have been given in the question) and carry this down as a credit balance.

(*h*) Enter the *missing item* (i.e., that *not* given in the question) from the credit side of the Trade Creditors Account and post it to the debit of the Purchases Account.

(*i*) Enter the *closing* balance in the Expense Creditors Account (which will have been given in the question) and carry this down as a credit balance.

(*j*) Enter the *missing item* (i.e., that *not* given in the question) from the credit side of the Expense Creditors Account and post it to the debit of the Business Expenses Account (which must now be opened).

(*k*) Take out a Trial Balance.

(*l*) When the Trial Balance has been agreed prepare the Trading and Profit and Loss Account and Balance Sheet.

7. Some important points to note. It will have been noted that under rules (*c*), (*e*), (*g*) and (*j*) you are instructed to carry down the closing balances. The reason for this is to avoid their being overlooked when producing the Trial Balance. Students frequently fail to do this and regrettably they often fail to work to a Trial Balance. In consequence, they almost inevitably lose a great deal of time which, in an examination, could be fatal.

Another important point is an objection raised by students to working to the rules set out above. They claim that they will waste too much time by opening "T" accounts and making all the postings. There is some truth in this objection in that it does take a little longer to open and post all the accounts. Actually, with experience, it takes very little extra time. The big bonus to be obtained by opening all the accounts is that one can and should work to a Trial Balance. If this does not agree it is a comparatively simple matter to check each individual item and make quite sure that it has been *doubly* entered. The objection is also open to the criticism that in the event of the Balance Sheet *not* agreeing they are not likely to have much idea where the difference lies and one finds them frantically, and often, fruitlessly, searching for their errors. Finally, one can point to the fact that in practice no accountant would dream of preparing accounts from incomplete records without following the rules laid down above including the preparation of a Trial Balance.

8. Applying the rules. In order to expand upon the operation of the rules let us apply them to a simple problem. For convenience of explanation we will break the *question* element into a number of parts so that each part is, as it were, self-contained.

EXAMPLE—FIRST SECTION:

At 1st January 19–4 J. Snodgrass had the following assets and liabilities: cash at bank, £200; cash in hand, £110; trade debtors, £480; trade creditors, £515; fixtures and fittings, £148. Ascertain his opening capital and open the appropriate ledger accounts posting the balances thereto.

9. Apply rule (*a*). Read the question carefully and then prepare an Opening Statement in order to calculate J. Snodgrass's capital on 1st January 19–4.

At this stage of his studies the student should have no difficulty in carrying out the requirements of rule (*a*). Nonetheless, extreme care should be taken for it is from this opening Trial Balance that the capital of the business is calculated. It follows, therefore that if any of these opening balances are omitted the opening capital is bound to be wrong—and the final answer will also be wrong.

OPENING STATEMENT 1ST JANUARY 19–4

	Dr	Cr
Cash at bank	£200	
Cash in hand	110	
Trade debtors	480	
Trade creditors		£515
Shop fittings	148	
	938	515
Therefore the capital *must* be		423
	£938	£938

10. Apply rule (*b*). Enter *each* balance from the Opening Statement into a ledger account (debit balances on the debit side, of course, and credit balances on the credit side).

NOTE: It is not necessary to make elaborate accounts for this purpose; simple "T" accounts will do.

Bank Account	*Cash Account*
Balance £200		Balance £110	

Trade Debtors Account	*Trade Creditors Account*
Balance £480			Balance £515

Shop Fittings Account	*Capital Account*
Balance £148	Balance £423

We can see practically at a glance that the total of all the debit balances in the ledger agrees exactly with the total of the all the credit balances in the ledger. We thus have a *level platform* upon which we can build the double entry of all the transactions which take place afterwards.

NOTE: Experience has shown that some students try to make *double* entries for all the above balances. This is, of course, quite impossible. The balances which appear above came about as a result of the transactions which were entered into during an earlier period. We placed the assets in one column and the liabilities in another and then subtracted the lesser from the greater total and in that way calculated the amount of the capital. It follows that *no* double entry has to be made, for the balances are sufficient in themselves and taken collectively give us a ledger which is in balance.

11. Apply rule (*c*). Copy every item shown in the Bank Account from the question paper into your own "T" Bank Account which you have just opened. Insert the *closing* balance and carry it down to the opposite side of the account below the total lines.

EXAMPLE—SECOND SECTION: The details of the Bank Account of J. Snodgrass for the year 19–4 were as follows:

Summary of Bank Account for the year 19–4

Balance at 1st January 19–4	£200	Cash paid to trade creditors	£5,472
Cash received from trade debtors	8,400	General expenses	1,449
		Wages	1,280
		Rent	260
		Balance c/d at 31st December 19–4	139
	£8,600		£8,600
Balance b/d	£139		

The question will set out the details very much as shown above except that it will probably not bring the balance down. You must copy each item into your own Bank Account and bring the balance down, lest it be overlooked when extracting the Trial Balance.

12. Apply rule (*d*). Post, i.e., transfer, each item from the Bank Account (except the opening and closing balances) to the opposite side of the ledger account concerned, thus completing the double entry. It will be necessary, of course, to open certain additional accounts, e.g., a Wages Account.

Trade Debtors Account			*Trade Creditors Account*		
Balance b/d £480	Bank A/c £8,400		Bank A/c £5,472	Balance b/d £515	

The additional accounts should be opened, posting thereto the appropriate payments, as follows:

General Expenses Account		*Wages Account*	
Bank A/c £1,449		Bank A/c £1,280	

Rent Account	
Bank A/c £260	

Having ascertained the opening capital and then opened the various ledger accounts we proceeded to post each item from the Bank Account to the opposite side of the appropriate account concerned, opening any additional ones which were necessary. In theory our ledger, at this stage, should be in balance, so let us take out a Trial Balance to see if, in fact, this is the case.

FIRST TRIAL BALANCE

	Dr	Cr
Bank A/c	£139	
Cash A/c	110	
Trade Debtors A/c	480	£8,400
Trade Creditors A/c	5,472	515
Fixtures and Fittings A/c	148	
Capital A/c		423
General Expenses A/c	1,449	
Wages A/c	1,280	
Rent A/c	260	
	£9,338	£9,338

ASCERTAINMENT OF THE UNKNOWNS

13. The unknown quantities. The next stage is of immense importance for it is now that we come, for the first time, face to face with the problem of ascertaining *unknown* quantities; figures which are vital to the solution but which have not been given in the question.

14. Finding the sales (rules (*e*) and (*f*)). The problem set does not give us any hint as to the amount of the sales. On the debit side of the Bank Account, however, we find the item "Cash received from trade debtors, £8,400" which has already been posted to the credit of the Trade Debtors Account. In addition, information is given (see below) stating how much was owing by trade debtors, i.e., customers, at the end of the year. This Trade Debtors Account is actually a *summary* containing in bulk form all the details of the transactions with every customer during the trading period.

Rule (e). The amount owing by the various debtors at the end of the period will be given in the question. This information must be entered in its proper place in the Debtors Account. Remember to carry this balance down to the debit side underneath the total lines as it will be required for the final Trial Balance.

EXAMPLE—THIRD SECTION: The following information was obtained from various sources relating to J. Snodgrass's business.

Debtors (i.e., amounts owing from customers) at 1st January 19–4	£480
Cash received from debtors during the year 19–4	£8,400
Debtors at 31st December 19–4	£750

We would arrange the first two items of the above information in
the ledger account as shown below. This has, in fact, already
been done under rule (*d*).

Trade Debtors Account

19–4		19–4	
Jan. 1 Balance b/d	£480	Dec. 31 Bank A/c	£8,400

Next we enter the closing balance, i.e., the amount owing by the
debtors, carrying it down.

Trade Debtors Account

19–4		19–4	
Jan. 1 Balance b/d	£480	Dec. 31 Bank A/c	£8,400
		Dec. 31 Balance c/d	750
	——		£9,150
	═══		═══
19–5			
Jan. 1 Balance b/d	£750		

It is quite clear from the above account that it is not complete.
The information which was available has been placed, item by
item, each in its proper place but there is, clearly, a *gap* in our
knowledge which we must now proceed to fill. Before we enter
the missing figure we should ask ourselves "What is the nature of
the item we are seeking?" The answer to that question is not
difficult. It is the *sales* for the year.

Rule (*f*). Enter the *missing* amount required on the debit side
of the Trade Debtors Account and post it to the credit side of the
Sales Account.

In problems of this type the student is expected to know that
he must *complete* the construction of the account which, as can

be seen, is not a difficult matter. All that is required is that the lesser total be subtracted from the greater and the *remainder* inserted on the debit side. The figure thus ascertained represents the sales on credit and this must, of course, be posted to the credit side of the Sales Account in order to complete the double entry.

The final position would appear as set out below.

Trade Debtors Account

19–4			19–4		
Jan. 1	Balance b/d	£480	Dec. 31	Bank A/c	£8,400
Dec. 31	**Sales A/c**	**8,670**	Dec. 31	Balance c/d	750
		£9,150			£9,150
Jan. 1	Balance b/d	£750			

Sales Account

	19–4	
	Dec. 31	**Trade Debtors A/c** **£8,670**

15. Finding the amount of goods purchased (rules (g) and (h)). Here we are faced with a similar problem. *Some* information is given but not all of it. The missing item has to be calculated.

Rule (g). The amount owing to the various suppliers of goods at the end of the period is given in the question (see below). This information must now be entered in its proper place in the Trade Creditors Account. This balance must be carried down to the credit side of the account underneath the total rulings.

EXAMPLE—FOURTH SECTION:

On 1st January 19–4 J. Snodgrass owed his suppliers £515. During the year 19–4 he paid them £5,472. On 31st December 19–4 he owed them £801.

Assuming that we have already opened an account for the creditors and entered the balance owing to them at 1st January 19–4 and later on posted the cash paid to them from the Bank Account, the Creditors Account would then read:

Trade Creditors Account

19–4		19–4	
Dec. 31 Bank A/c £5,472		Jan. 1 Balance b/d	£515

We now enter the amount owing to the suppliers at the end of the period in the following manner:

Trade Creditors Account

19–4		19–4	
Dec. 31 Bank A/c £5,472		Jan. 1 Balance b/d	£515
Dec. 31 Balance c/d 801			
	£6,273		
		19–5	
		Jan. 1 Balance b/d	£801

Once again, as with the Debtors Account, we have constructed an account which will ultimately help us to determine the cost of goods purchased. We have placed the *known* quantities in their correct positions in the account and can now draw our conclusion, i.e., that the difference between the two sides is the value of the purchases that have been made on credit during 19–4.

Rule (*h*). Enter the missing amount required on the credit side of the Creditors Account and post it to the debit side of the Purchases Account.

The final position would appear thus:

Trade Creditors Account

19 4		19–4	
Dec. 31 Bank A/c £5,472		Jan. 1 Balance b/d	£515
Dec. 31 Balance c/d 801		Dec. 31 **Purchases A/c 5,758**	
	£6,273		£6,273
		19–5	
		Jan. 1 Balance b/d	£801

Purchases Account

19–4	
Dec. 31 **Trade Creditors**	
A/c **£5,758**	

16. Outstanding expenses (rules (*j*) and (*k*)). Most problems will be so designed as to include certain expenses of a revenue nature, e.g., salaries, rent, light and heat, insurance, etc. One or more of these items will need to be adjusted for an outstanding amount, i.e., an accrued expense or a prepayment. In the present example we have made use of an all-embracing "General Expenses Account", but often the question requires that the various items of expenditure be treated *individually*, necessitating the opening of a separate account for each head of expense.

Rule (j). Enter the *closing* balance in the account concerned and carry it down to the opposite side below the totals.

EXAMPLE—FIFTH SECTION: During 19–4 J. Snodgrass paid £1,449 in respect of general expenses. At 31st December 19–4 there was £63 due but unpaid.

Under Rule (*d*) we showed the General Expenses Account debited with the cash paid. If we now enter the closing balance the position is as follows.

General Expenses Account

19–4			
Dec. 31 Bank A/c	£1,449		
Dec. 31 Balance c/d	63		
	£1,512		
		19–5	
		Jan. 1 Balance b/d	£63

Rule (k). Complete the General Expenses Account by crediting it with the figure of £1,512. Then debit the same amount to a Sundry Expenses Account (which should now be opened) to complete the double entry.

NOTE: In this particular problem nothing was outstanding for business expenses at the beginning of the year. Had there been we would have opened an account called "Creditors for General Expenses" and the outstanding amount would have been credited to it in exactly the same way that the Trade Creditors Account was credited with the opening balance owing. The parallel between these two accounts is *exact* and both are closed by transfers to the debit of some other account. In the case of the Trade Creditors Account the transfer will be made to the Purchases Account: in the case of the Creditors for General Expenses Account the transfer will be to the General Expenses Account.

This method ensures that a missing item is not overlooked and, equally importantly, that the two items which relate to General Expenses, i.e., the closing credit balance as well as the amount which is to be written off to the Profit and Loss Account, are both clearly visible and there will be no risk of their not being picked up when the Trial Balance is being extracted.

From this we can see that when we extract a Trial Balance we must place £1,512 in the debit column as the total amount of expenditure *incurred* during the year, and £63 in the credit column representing the sum owing.

17. The Trial Balance (rule (*l*)). When preparing accounts from incomplete records we must remember that we are building up to a basis of double entry and so the following rule *must* be carried out:

Rule (l). Extract a Trial Balance.

Although this is the shortest "rule" of all it is a most important one. Students should *never* attempt the preparation of the Trading and Profit and Loss Account or the Balance Sheet until they are satisfied that the books are in balance. Hence the necessity of taking out and agreeing a Trial Balance at this point. We ensured that the opening position was one of being in balance by inserting the missing figure of capital. Furthermore, we made certain that for every *subsequent* transaction a double entry was made. As a result, we should have no difficulty in agreeing the Trial Balance.

If the Trial Balance does not agree then it will be necessary to check the ledger entries. All the accounts are there; all the entries should have been made; thus a check should soon establish where any error lies. It is important to make sure that the *correct* amounts have been entered in the Trial Balance and, also, that they are on the *correct* side.

The Trial Balance would appear as follows.

TRIAL BALANCE

	Dr	Cr
Bank	£139	
Cash	110	
Debtors	750	
Sales		£8,670
Creditors		801
Purchases	5,758	
Fixtures and fittings	148	
Capital		423
General expenses	1,512	
Creditor for general expenses		63
Wages	1,280	
Rent	260	
	£9,957	£9,957

We can now see that everything has been properly recorded and it is only a very small step from here to the preparation of the Trading and Profit and Loss Account and the Balance sheet (rule (*m*)).

18. Dealing with difficult points. We have now seen what the basic pattern looks like but must not run away with the idea that that is the whole story. Complications may be introduced into the problem. They can be many and varied. Suppose, for example, that in the illustration which we have been working, it was stated that discounts received had amounted to £139 and that returns outward were £95. How would such matters be dealt with and what would be the effect on our answer?

In each of the cases mentioned a *double* entry is required. For the first item we would debit the Creditors Account and credit the Discounts Received Account, while for the second we would again debit the Creditors Account and credit the Purchases Returns Account. Remember, therefore, *always* to make a double entry.

In order that this matter may be impressed on the student's mind we will now show the accounts concerned. Pay particular attention to the effect which the making of these adjustments has upon the figure of *purchases*.

Creditors Account

19–4			19–4		
Dec. 31	Bank A/c	£5,472	Jan. 1	Balance b/d	£515
Dec. 31	**Discount**		Dec. 31	**Purchases A/c**	**5,992**
	Received A/c	139			
Dec. 31	**Purchase**				
	Returns A/c	**95**			
Dec. 31	Balance c/d	801			
		£6,507			£6,507
			19–5		
			Jan. 1	Balance b/d	801

Discount Received Account

		19–4		
		Dec. 31	**Creditors A/c**	**£139**

Purchase Returns Account

		19–4		
		Dec. 31	**Creditors A/c**	**£95**

Purchase Account

19–4				
Dec. 31	**Creditors A/c**	**£5,992**		

NOTE: Reference to the Purchases Account on p. 156 shows that the total of the "purchases" was £5,758. As a result of the adjustments for discounts and returns the purchases show an increase of £234.

19. A brief recapitulation of the rules. To sum up the position so far, let us make a brief recapitulation of the rules.

(*a*) List the opening balances and find the "capital".

(*b*) Open a Ledger Account for each of the opening balances.

(*c*) Write up the Bank Account in detail.

(*d*) Post each item from the Bank Account to the opposite side of the appropriate account.

(*e*) Enter closing balances in the Trade Debtors Account.

(*f*) Enter the missing item on the debit side of the Trade Debtors Account.

(*g*) Enter the closing balance on the Trade Creditors Account.

(*h*) Enter the missing item on the credit side of the Trade Creditors Account and post it to the debit of the Purchases Account.

(*i*) Enter the closing balance in the Expense Creditors Account.

(*j*) Post the missing item to the debit side of the Business

Expenses Account.

(*k*) Extract a Trial Balance.

(*l*) Prepare final accounts and a Balance Sheet.

Let us now work through a simple problem to make certain that all the points have been properly understood.

EXAMPLE: B. Hopkins had the following assets and liabilities at 1st January 19–4:

Shop equipment	£300
Debtors	490
Creditors	410
Stock	352

Summary of Bank Account for the year 19–4

Balance at 1st Jan. 19–4	£418	Paid to creditors	£5,294
		Wages	604
Received from debtors	6,970	General expenses	757
		New motor van	406
Balance at 31st Dec. 19–4	193	Drawings	520
	£7,581		£7,581

At 31st December 19–4 the stock was £385; debtors, £531; creditors, £448; equipment remained at £300.

Prepare a Trading and Profit and Loss Account for the year ended 31st December 19–4 and a Balance Sheet as on 31st December 19–4.

(*a*) *Opening Statement at 1st January 19–4:*

Shop equipment	£300	
Bank	418	
Debtors	490	
Creditors		£410
Stock	352	
	1,560	410
Therefore the capital *must* be		**1,150**
	£1,560	£1,560

(b)

Shop Equipment Account		Bank Account	
Balance £300		Balance £418	

Debtors Account		Creditors Account	
Balance £490			Balance £410

Stock Account		Capital Account	
Balance £352			Balance £1,150

(c)   Bank Account

19–4			19–4		
Jan. 1 Balance b/d	£418		Dec. 31 Paid to creditors		£5,294
Dec. 31 Received from debtors	6,970		Dec. 31 Wages		604
Dec. 31 Balance c/d	193		Dec. 31 General expenses		757
			Dec. 31 New motor van		406
			Dec. 31 Drawings		520
	£7,581				£7,581
			Jan. 1 Balance b/d		£193

(d) Debtors Account

Debtors Account		Creditors Account	
Balance £490	Bank A/c **£6,970**	Bank A/c **£5,294**	Balance £410

Wages Account		General Expenses Account	
Bank A/c **£604**		Bank A/c **£757**	

Motor Van Account		Drawings Account	
Bank A/c **£406**		Bank A/c **£520**	

NOTE: The postings from the Bank Account have been shown in heavy type in the appropriate ledger accounts so that they may be more easily distinguished.

(e) and (f)   *Debtors Account*

Balance	£490	Bank A/c	£6,970
Sales A/c	**7,011**	Balance c/d	531
	£7,501		£7,501
Balance b/d	£531		

Sales Account

	Debtors A/c	**£7,011**

(g) and (h)   *Creditors Account*

Bank A/c	£5,294	Balance b/d	£410
Balance c/d	448	**Purchases A/c**	**£5,332**
	£5,742		£5,742
		Balance b/d	£448

Purchases Account

Creditors A/c	**£5,332**	

When extracting the Trial Balance it will be found simpler if we work backwards, starting with the *most recent* ledger account shown, i.e., the Purchases Account. The reason for working this way is because both the Debtors and the Creditors Accounts each appear three times in the workings shown above. The final state of each account is the *most recent* and therefore the earlier ones are to be ignored:

TRIAL BALANCES AT 31ST DECEMBER 19–4

	Dr	Cr
Purchases	£5,332	
Creditors		£448
Sales		7,011
Debtors	531	
Drawings	520	
Motor van	406	
General expenses	757	
Wages	604	
Bank		193
Capital		1,150
Stock	352	
Shop equipment	300	
	£8,802	£8,802

Trading and Profit and Loss Account
for the year ended 31st December 19–4

Stock at 1st Jan 19–4	£352	Sales	£7,011
Purchases	5,332	Stock at 31st Dec. 19–4	385
Gross profit	1,712		
	£7,396		£7,396
Wages	604	Gross profit	1,712
General expenses	757		
Net profit:	351		
	£1,712		£1,712

BALANCE SHEET AS AT 31ST DECEMBER 19–4

Capital			Shop equipment	£300
Balance at			Motor van	406
1st Jan.	£1,150		Stock	385
Add Net			Debtors	531
Profit	351			
	1,501			
Less				
drawings	520			
		£981		
Creditors		448		
Bank overdraft		193		
		£1,622		£1,622

PROGRESS TEST 10

Theory

1. What do you understand by the term "incomplete records" when applied to accountancy? **(3)**

2. Make a list of the rules to be followed when constructing accounts from incomplete records. **(6)**

3. Why is it important to carry down closing balances on certain accounts? **(7)**

4. When solving a problem in incomplete records it is most important that the opening capital be ascertained. Why is this so and what effect would the omission of one or more of the opening balances have? **(8)**

5. How should the entries in the cash book be dealt with? **(6, 11, 12)**

6. What do you understand by the "unknown quantities"? **(13, 14, 15, 16)**

7. Describe the action you would take to ascertain these unknowns. **(13, 14, 15, 16)**

Practice

8. Debtors at 1st January 19–5   £840
    Cash received from debtors during 19–5   5,609
    Debtors at 31st December 19–5   917

State the amount of the sales on credit during 19–5.

9. Debtors at 1st February 19–5   £674
    Sales to credit customers during the year ended 31st
        January 19–6   4,949
    Debtors at 31st January 19–6   628

Show the sum of money received from credit customers during the year ended 31st January 19–6.

10. Debtors at 1st March 19–5   £2,105
    Sales on credit for the twelve months to 28th
        February 19–6   23,741
    Cash received from debtors in year ended 28th
        February 19–6   22,993

Ascertain the figure of debtors at 28th February 19–6.

11. Credit sales for the year ended 31st March 19–6 £16,486
    Cash received from debtors during year ended 31st
        March 19–6   15,801
    Debtors at 31st March 19–6   3,229

How much was owing by debtors at 1st April 19–5?

12. Amounts owing to various creditors for general
        expenses at 1st May 19–5   147
    Cash paid to "expense" creditors during year en-
        ded 30th April 19–6   922
    Amount owing to various creditors for general
        expenses at 30th April 19–6   135

Calculate the amount of expenditure incurred on general expenses during year ended 30th April 19–6.

13. The amount owing to the Electricity Supply
        Company at 1st June 19–5 was   £24
    During the year ended 31st May 19–6 the amount
        paid to the electricity company was   105
    At 31st May 19–6 there was owing to the electricity
        company   27

What amount of expense was incurred in respect of electricity during the year to 31st May 19–6?

14. Barton purchased an existing business for £5,000 which included stock valued at £1,250, fixtures and fittings at £675 and the balance was the cost of the goodwill.

He opened a bank account in the name of the business, Richard Barton & Co., and paid in £5,200 from his private funds. His only records were a notebook in which he entered the daily cash takings and certain payments in cash, surplus cash being banked weekly. He kept bills and receipts on a file.

A summary of the business Bank Statements at the end of the first year of trading was as follows:

Bank Account

Cash paid in			Purchase of business	£5,000
1st January 19–4	£5,200		Rent, 15 months to	
Cash Account	39,480		31st March 19–6	1,500
			Rates, 9 months to	
			30th October 19–5	300
			Electricity	167
			Hire of equipment	125
			Goods from suppliers	31,978
			Cheques for private	
			items	1,790
			Balance at	
			31st December 19–4	3,820
	£44,680			£44,680

Payments in cash recorded in the notebook were:

Purchase for resale	£2,310
Wages	1,517
General expenses	274
Cash drawings	764

On 31st December 19–4, stock valued at cost amounted to £1,860; amounts due to suppliers, £371; amounts owing by customers, £95; cash in hand, £108. Depreciation is to be ignored. £58 was owing for electricity, and unpaid rates amounted to £100.

You are asked to prepare Barton's Trading and Profit and Loss Account for the year ended 31st December 19–4, and a Balance Sheet as on that date.

15. Bobbin agreed to buy the goodwill and fittings of an existing business for £2,500, plus stock at valuation. Fittings included in the price had an agreed value of £500. The owner of the premises agreed to grant Bobbin a new lease for seven years at £400 per annum, payable quarterly in arrears.

Bobbin opened a Bank Account for the business with £6,000, paid the vendor the amount due for the business including the stock, and commenced business on 1st April 19–4.

The only record he kept was a note-book in which he recorded cash payments made out of takings, before paying them into the bank. The following payments were extracted from the books for the year ended 31st March 19–5: wages, £597; cash purchases for resale, £158; sundry shop expenses, £104; and his drawings, £624.

A summary of his Bank Account for the year ended 31st March 19–5 showed the following:

Deposits		Withdrawals	
Cash introduced	£6,000	Vendor	£3,750
Shop bankings	12,050	Purchases for resale	10,000
		Rent	300
		Rates	196
		Electricity	49
		Additional fittings (purchased 1st April 19–4)	100

On 31st March 19–5 stock on hand (at cost) was valued at £1,456; cash on hand amounted to £112; and amounts owing to trade creditors were £268 and for electricity £17. Depreciation on fittings is to be provided at a rate of 10 per cent per annum.

You are required to prepare Bobbin's Trading and Profit and Loss Accounts for the year ended 31st March 19–5 and a Balance Sheet as on that date.   (A.C.A.)

16. On 1st June 19–4 a fire occurred at the premises of R. Honeybone resulting in the loss of a considerable amount of stock.

From the details set out below you are asked to calculate the amount of the loss in order to submit a claim to the insurance company.

Stock at cost on 1st January 19–4	£2,086
Sales from 1st January to 31st May 19–4	10,560
Purchases from 1st January to 31st May 19–4	8,608
Stock (at cost) salvaged from the fire	604

Honeybone estimates that the rate of gross profit on sales amounts to 20 per cent.

17. During 19–4, Philip Stevens, a shopkeeper, drew £2,506 in cash for his personal use from the Business Bank Account. When his accounts and Balance Sheets were produced for the year 19–4 it was found that his assets had increased by £176 from what they had been one year earlier, and that his liabilities had decreased by £99 during the same period.

Calculate Stevens's net profit for the year 19–4.

CHAPTER XI

Incomplete Records II

CONSTRUCTING A BANK ACCOUNT

1. The need for flexibility in approaching problems. In the previous chapter we discussed the basic principles to be followed when building up accounts from information which, in itself, is incomplete; that is to say, where certain details are not given, but where there is sufficient information available enabling us to place in their correct positions those items which have been given. In such cases we build up the particular account and are then able to calculate arithmetically the amount of the missing item. Experience will normally tell us the nature of this item, e.g., in a Total Debtors Account, if the opening and closing debtors are given as well as the cash received from them during the period, reason tells us that the missing figure must be the value of the sales. We know, too, that when we have ascertained both the amount and the nature of the missing item it must be made the subject of a double entry.

Generally speaking, students learn the fundamental rules set out in the last chapter very readily and become quickly capable of solving simple problems. However, it is frequently the case that when they meet a problem which does *not* conform to the pattern they find themselves in some difficulty. Almost certainly, the reason for this is their lack of experience. It is fair to say that if they are capable of solving problems of the basic type then they should be able to solve those problems where the approach has to be made from an unusual angle, but it must be recognised that they will need plenty of practice in order to become competent. This can only come with experience. Much hard work is needed on the practical side in working problems, but even more important is the thought that is often required to see around and through a problem, i.e., the appreciation that it cannot be solved in the conventional way and that a radically different approach is required.

RECEIPTS AND PAYMENT OF CASH

2. Calculating the amount of cash received from debtors. A common type of problem in incomplete records which does not conform to the basic pattern is the one in which no Bank Account is given. The question will contain all the basic information for the construction of the Bank Account but it will be given in an indirect way. For example, with regard to the amount of cash received from debtors there will be no mention whatever of this figure, but sufficient information will be given to enable the student to construct a Total Debtors Account on the same lines as laid down in the last chapter. The difference will be in the details which are given. In the earlier case it was said that the opening and closing debtors would be stated as well as the cash received from debtors, thus enabling us to calculate the total of the sales on credit. In the present case the opening and closing debtors will still be given but not the cash received. In its place we will be given the total sales on credit and will have to work out the missing item which must, of course, be the amount of cash received.

Having ascertained the amount required we must then make it the subject of a double entry, i.e., we will have to credit the Total Debtors Account and debit the Bank Account (or Cash Account, as the case may be).

EXAMPLE: On 1st January 19–4 S. Green's debtors owed him £624. During 19–4 he sold goods on credit totalling £10,471 and on 31st December 19–4 the total of debtors stood at £783.

Notice that no mention is made of any cash received from debtors. From the information given above the Total Debtors Account would appear as follows:

Total Debtors Account

19–4			19–4		
Jan. 1	Balance b/d	£624	Dec. 31 Balance c/d		£783
Dec. 31	Sales A/c	10,471			
		£11,095			
19–5					
Jan. 1	Balance b/d	£783			

Our next step is to subtract the present credit total (£783) from the debit total of £11,095, the remainder being £10,312. This sum must be regarded as being the amount of cash received from the debtors.

NOTE: For the sake of clarity the illustration has been kept as simple as possible. If any further items were involved such as discounts allowed to debtors, returns inwards, etc., information concerning these would be stated in the question and we would still be left with only one missing item to find. In other words, we know the *nature* of the item we are seeking, i.e., the cash received from customers.

EXAMPLE: J. Robinson's debtors on 1st January 19–4 stood at £1,402 and on 31st December 19–4 amounted to £1,549. During the year sales on credit amounted to £18,191 and returns inwards were £645. Discounts allowed to customers were £203 and bills receivable to the value of £1,000 had been accepted by one customer.

Once again the problem makes no mention of the amount of money which was received from customers during 19–4. However, by placing each of the known items in its proper position in the Total Debtors Account we can calculate the unknown figure—that of the cash received.

Total Debtors Account

19–4			19–4		
Jan. 1	Balance		Dec. 31	Returns	
	b/d	£1,402		Inwards A/c	£645
Dec. 31	Sales A/c	18,191	Dec. 31	Discounts	
				Allowed A/c	203
			Dec. 31	Bill Receivable	
				A/c	1,000
			Dec. 31	Balance c/d	1,549
		———			———
		═══			═══
19–5					
Jan. 1	Balance				
	b/d	£1,549			

There is a greater amount of detail to be entered in the Total Debtors Account than in the previous illustration but the principle remains exactly the same, i.e., we place *each* item in its proper position in the account. We know what we are looking for—the missing figure of cash received—and so, having placed all the known items in their correct places the task of ascertaining the value of the unknown becomes a very simple matter. We therefore add up both the debit and the credit columns as set out above and find that they amount to £19,593 and £3,397 respectively. The subtraction of one from the other leaves us with the sum of £16,196 which we conclude is the figure of cash received for the year.

Our next step would be to credit the Total Debtors Account with £16,196 and enter the corresponding debit in the Bank Account, thus completing the double entry and, at the same time, taking the first step towards building up the Bank Account.

Total Debtors Account

19–4			19–4		
Jan. 1	Balance b/d	£1,402	Dec. 31	Returns Inwards A/c	£645
Dec. 31	Sales A/c	18,191	Dec. 31	Discounts Allowed A/c	203
			Dec. 31	Bills Receivable A/c	1,000
			Dec. 31	**Bank A/c**	**16,196**
			Dec. 31	Balance c/d	1,549
		£19,593			£19,593
19–5					
Jan. 1	Balance b/d	£1,549			

Bank Account

1974		
Dec. 31	**Total Debtors A/c**	**£16,196**

3. Cash paid to creditors. Continuing to deal with the problem of building up the Bank Account, let us now turn our attention to the credit side of that account, i.e., the side on which payments appear.

The main payment item will undoubtedly be the amount of money which has been paid to creditors for goods purchased. Once more the procedure will be the same as when ascertaining the amount received from debtors and an illustration should make the matter clear.

EXAMPLE: **B.** Robson owed £746 to various suppliers for goods at 1st January 19–4. During 19–4 he purchased further goods on credit for the sum of £6,984. He was allowed £279 by way of discount and during the year he returned goods which had cost him £563. At 31st December 19–4 he owed £813 to his creditors.

Here, again, no payment of any money is mentioned and so our common sense should tell us that this must be the item we are seeking.

Total Creditors Account

19–4			19–4		
Dec. 31 Discount Received A/c		£279	Jan. 1 Balance b/d		£746
Dec. 31 Returns Outward A/c		563	Dec. 31 Purchases A/c		6,984
Dec. 31 Balance c/d		813			
		———			———
		≡≡≡			≡≡≡
			19–5		
			Jan. 1 Balance b/d		£813

The total of the known debit items amounts to £1,655 so we must subtract this from the credit total of £7,730. The result of this will give us the sum of £6,075 which is, of course, the amount of cash which has been paid to creditors for goods supplied. This amount will, therefore, be debited in the Total Creditors Account and credited in the Bank Account as follows:

Total Creditors Account

19–4		19–4		
Dec. 31 Discount		Jan. 1 Balance b/d		£746
Received A/c	£279	Dec. 31 Purchases A/c		6,984
Dec. 31 Returns				
Outwards A/c	563			
Dec. 31 **Bank A/c**	**6,075**			
Dec. 31 Balance c/d	813			
	£7,730			£7,730
		19–5		
		Jan. 1 Balance b/d		£813

Bank Account

	19–4		
	Dec. 31 **Total Creditors**		
	A/c		**£6,075**

4. Cash paid for general expenses. Under the heading of "general expenses" we may group all of those items which cover the supply of services of any kind, e.g., telephone, insurance, advertising, rent, rates, gas, electricity, etc. It is probable that the majority of such items of expense will have an outstanding balance on the respective accounts both at the beginning and at the end of a trading period.

Examination problems dealing with incomplete records frequently lump together expense items of varied kinds and show them under one account heading called "General Expenses Account". The reason for this is simply that sometimes the examiner may not consider it necessary to test the candidate on too many points of detail and that it will be sufficient if he shows a reasonable knowledge of the principles. In other cases, however, the test may be much more searching and the ability to cope with every type of problem must be acquired. This can only come by practice.

Our first example in this context will deal with the general type of Expenses Account.

EXAMPLE: At 1st January 19–4 C. Rhodes was owing £63 in respect of expenses incurred during the year ended 31st December 19–3. The total expenditure *incurred* during 19–4 amounted to £1,484. At 31st December 19–4 he had still not paid £39 of these expenses.

In order to find the amount of cash paid during the year to these expense creditors, as they are called, let us open an account for them:

Expense Creditors Account

19–4		19–4		
Dec. 31 **Bank A/c**	**£1,508**	Jan. 1 Balance b/d		£63
Dec. 31 Balance c/d	39	Dec. 31 General		
			expenses A/c	1,484
	£1,547			£1,547
		19–5		
		Jan. 1 Balance b/d		£39

Here, the missing item of cash *paid* is found by deducting £39 from £1,547, which leaves £1,508. This sum would then be entered in the Bank Account as a payment and debited to the Expense Creditors Account.

Bank Account

	19–4	
	Dec. 31 **Expense**	
	Creditors A/c	**£1,508**

5. Example. When the following exercise and its answer has been read through it should be worked independently. Students should, as a result, feel satisfied that they need have no fears of their ability to cope with a problem of this type in an examination.

The following figures have been taken from the books of P. Cleghorn, a trader:

Creditors for goods, 1st January 19–4	£1,260
Debtors at 1st January 19–4	1,480
Purchases on credit for year 19–4	14,400
Sales on credit for year 19–4	18,900

Discounts allowed	520
Balance at bank at 1st January 19–4	2,700
Creditors for goods, 31st December 19–4	1,530
Debtors 31st December 19–4	1,660
General Expenses unpaid at 1st January 19–4	140
General Expenses incurred during 19–4	1,500
Amount owing for General Expenses at 31st December 19–4	175
Drawings (for Cleghorn's private use) during 19–4	3,130

There were no returns inwards; no discounts were received from creditors but bad debts written off during the year amounted to £124 and returns outwards were £218.

Cleghorn paid all receipts into the Business Bank Account and all payments were made by cheque.

Prepare a summary of Cleghorn's Bank Account for the year 19–4.

NOTE: There were no entries in Cleghorn's Bank Account other than those which can be ascertained from the information given above.

SUGGESTED SOLUTION: The first thing to note is that only two pieces of positive information directly connected with the Bank Account have been given in the question. The first is the balance at 1st January 19–4 of £2,700, and the second is the fact that Cleghorn drew £3,130 from the bank for his own use. From the wording it is quite clear that we are to assume that this amount was withdrawn from the Bank Account. (If the intention was otherwise we may rest assured that we would be given full information.)

We will now open the Bank Account and enter therein what direct information has been given.

Stage 1

Bank Account

19–4			19–4		
Jan. 1	Balance b/d	£2,700	Dec. 31	Drawings A/c	£3,130

Note especially the dates here. It must be appreciated that we are simply summarising the details of the whole year and that at present we have insufficient information to enter anything other than the two items shown.

Stage 2

Building up the Total Debtors Account we will obtain the figure of cash *realised* from debtors in respect of sales on credit.

Total Debtors Account

19–4			19–4		
(*1*) Jan. 1			Dec. 31 ?		?
Balance b/d	£1,480		Dec. 31 Discount		
(*2*) Dec. 31			Allowed A/c		£520 (*3*)
Sales A/c	18,900		Dec. 31 Bad Debts		
			A/c		124 (*4*)
			Dec. 31 *Balance*		
			c/d		1,660 (*5*)
	£20,380				
19–5					
Jan. 1 Balance					
b/d	£1,660				

It will be noted that the entries have each been given a number indicating the sequence which has been followed in building the account up. The next thing which has to be done (after making sure that there are no other items which have to be entered) is to find the difference between the two sides. The debit total amounts to £20,380 while the credit total (*at present*) amounts to £2,304. The difference between these two figures is £18,076 and this sum will represent the amount of cash which has been received from debtors and paid into the bank. The Bank Account will therefore be debited with £18,076 and the corresponding credit entry placed in the Total Debtors Account, i.e., as the first entry.

The Bank Account will now appear as follows.

Bank Account

19–4			19–4	
Jan. 1 Balance			Dec. 31 Drawings	
b/d	£2,700		A/c	£3,130
Dec. 31 **Total**				
Debtors A/c	18,076			

Stage 3
In this stage we will build up the Total Creditors Account.

Total Creditors Account

19–4			19–4		
Dec. 31 Returns			Jan. 1 Balance		
Outwards A/c	£218 **(3)**		b/d		£1,260 **(1)**
Dec. 31 Balance			Dec. 31 Purchases		
c/d	1,530 **(4)**		A/c		14,400 **(2)**
	1,748				
					£15,660
			19–5		
			Jan. 1 Balance		
			b/d		£1,530

To find the total sum paid to the creditors we simply deduct £1,748 from £15,660 which gives us £13,912. So the **Bank** Account will now appear as follows:

Bank Account

19–4		19–4	
Jan. 1 Balance		Dec. 31 Drawings	
b/d	£2,700	A/c	£3,130
Dec. 31 Total		Dec. 31 **Total**	
Debtors A/c	18,076	**Creditors A/c**	**13,912**

Stage 4
It only remains for the amount which has been paid for general expenses to be ascertained and from the information given we will now construct an account which we will call the "Creditors for Expenses Account".

Creditors for Expenses Account

19–4			19–4		
Dec. 31			Jan. 1 Balance b/d		£140
Dec. 31 Balance c/d	£175		Dec. 31 General		
			Expenses		1,500
					£1,640
			19–5		
			Jan. 1 Balance b/d		£175

Having written up the General Expenses Account we are, once again, in a position of having to do no more than a simple subtraction sum in order to find out the amount which has been paid for general expenses. £175 deducted from £1,640 leaves £1,465 and so this will be entered on the debit side of the Creditors for Expenses Account and credited in the Bank Account.

Bank Account

19–4			19–4		
Jan. 1 Balance			Dec. 31 Drawings		
b/d	£2,700		A/c		£3,130
Dec. 31 Total			Dec. 31 Total		
Debtors A/c	18,076		Creditors A/c		13,912
			Dec. 31 **Creditors for**		
			Expenses A/c		**1,465**
					18,507
	£20,776				

In this way we build up the Bank Account. One thing only is now needed to complete matters: the striking of the balance at 31st December 19–4. This is easily done. The debit total amounts to £20,776 and the credits to £18,507. The difference then is £2,269 which is of course the *balance at the bank*.

THE VITAL IMPORTANCE OF DOUBLE ENTRY

6. The double-entry aspect in incomplete records. In the present chapter emphasis has been laid on the technique required for ascertaining amounts of money which have been received or spent (when this information has not been given directly) and the gradual build-up of the Bank Account. What has *not* been concentrated on, however, is the double-entry aspect of the situation. It has been demonstrated but not emphasised. The examples have been removed from the context of examination questions and have been used simply to show how the information given can be made to yield fresh information. It is on this *fresh* information that emphasis must be laid, i.e., that when we discover a figure which has relevance to the solution of the problem that figure must be given full double-entry treatment. This may, therefore, be regarded as being a suitable point for a re-statement of the basic principles to be employed.

(*a*) At the start make certain that both assets and liabilities form a level platform. By this we mean that in almost every case the student will have to calculate the amount of opening capital and introduce it on the liabilities side. This is normally the first test set by the examiner.

(*b*) Open up rough ledger accounts ("T" accounts are quite sufficient) and enter all the opening balances therein including, of course, the Capital Account.

(*c*) Write up the Bank Account and/or Cash Account in detail so that you may post each payment or receipt to the opposite side of the appropriate account, thus completing the double entry for every item. This process is especially recommended for beginners; it is excellent training and has the additional virtue of making checking easier.

(*d*) Remember, finally, that it is vital always to work to a Trial Balance before attempting the final accounts and Balance Sheet.

7. Variations in examination questions. Having digested these two chapters dealing with incomplete records and having understood the general principles a student may feel reasonably satisfied that he will be able to cope adequately with most examination problems. It will be well for him to heed a word of warning at this point.

Problems falling under the heading of incomplete records can

have a surprising number of variations and the student must not
become over-confident simply because he thinks he has mastered
the basic techniques. Quite often one finds a student completely
stranded because of some little point introduced by the examiner
with which he is not familiar. He cannot see round it and as a
result gets worried. The more worried he gets the less he tends to
remember about his basic principles and the final result is, very
often, disastrous. What is more, he realises that he has made a
mess of a question which he feels he ought to have had at his
fingertips and this knowledge sometimes has a bad effect upon
the rest of his answers to that paper. Have a healthy respect for
these problems and do not treat them in too casual a manner.

8. Specimen question. The following is the Balance Sheet of
Rawson, a trader, as on 30th April 19–5.

BALANCE SHEET AS ON 30TH APRIL 19–5

Capital	£7,205	Furniture and fittings	£850
Trade creditors	4,425	Stock	7,340
		Trade Debtors	290
		Cash in hand	185
		Balance at bank	2,965
	£11,630		£11,630

During the year to 30th April 19–6 all takings were paid into
the bank with the exception of:

(*a*) £8,400 which was applied in paying wages (£7,270), general
expenses (£130) and Rawson's drawings (£1,000).
(*b*) The takings of 30th April 19–6.

During the night of 30th April 19–6 the Cash Book was destroyed in a fire. The cash on the premises, representing the business takings of 30th April and certain monies held by Rawson on
behalf of a club of which he was treasurer, was saved, but there
was no record to show how much represented the day's takings.
   The entries in the other books for the year to 30th April 19–6,
had been completed before the fire and, from these books, the
following information is obtained:

Cash and credit sales	£62,750
Purchases	43,580
General expenses paid by cheque	5,810
Discounts received	965
Trade creditors, 30th April 19–6	5,235
Drawn from bank for private purposes	2,000
Trade debtors, 30th April 19–6	410
Balance at bank, 30th April 19–6	7,545
Stock at 30th April 19–6	4,970

No discounts were allowed to customers

You are required to prepare:

(a) A statement showing your calculation of the cash in hand at 30th April 19–6, i.e., the takings of that day.

(b) A Trading and Profit and Loss Account for the year to 30th April 19–6 and a Balance Sheet as on 30th April 19–6.

(I.C.S.A.)

SUGGESTED SOLUTION: As has been stressed earlier you must work to a plan. Follow as far as is possible the pattern of rules already laid down.

You have been given the opening capital and so you do not have to bother with rule (a). Proceed then to rule (b) which states that you should open Ledger Accounts for each of the opening balances. Open, therefore, seven Ledger Accounts, one for each balance as it appears in the Balance Sheet in the question. For the present we are concerned only with four of them, namely the Cash Account, Bank Account, Debtors Account and Creditors Account.

Stage 1

We will begin with the Debtors Account which shows a debit balance of £290. To this figure we will add the sales which are given in the problem. Note carefully that we take the full amount of cash and credit sales and treat it as though it all goes through the Debtors Account. In a case such as this we have no choice since no split is given. However, it is only a means to an end and the student must not be too worried about it. We also enter the closing balance on the Debtors Account which enables us to calculate the total amount of money received from customers.

Debtors Account

19–5			19–6		
May 1	Balance b/d	£290	Apl. 30		
19–6			Apl. 30	Balance c/d	£410
Apl. 30	Sales A/c	62,750			
		———			———
		£63,040			
		═══			═══
19–6					
May 1	Balance b/d	£410			

From this we can see that the amount of money received is the difference between £63,040 and £410, i.e., £62,630.

This sum then will be credited to the Debtors Account and debited in the Cash Account.

Cash Account

19–5				
May 1	Balance b/d	£185		
19–6				
Apl. 30	Debtors			
	A/c	62,630		

The reason for debiting this money in the Cash Account instead of the Bank Account is that the problem states that all takings were paid into the bank except £8,400. It therefore follows that if the total amount received was £62,630 the amount to be debited in the Bank Account is to be £8,400 less than that figure. So we enter the larger amount in the Cash Account in the first place and later on transfer to the Bank Account the proper figure which was actually paid into the bank.

Stage 2

The next matter to be dealt with is the Creditors Account so that we may ascertain the sum paid for goods purchased.

Creditors Account

19–6			19–5		
Apl. 30 Discounts			May 1 Balance b/d		£4,425
Received A/c		£965	19–6		
Apl. 30 Balance c/d		5,235	Apl. 30 Purchases		
			A/c		43,580
					£48,005
			19–6		
			May 1 Balance b/d		£5,235

The total of the debit side amounts to £6,200. Subtracting this from the credit side we find a difference of £41,805 which represents the amount paid for purchases. In this case (since there are no other complications to be considered) we will make the double entry direct to the Bank Account as follows:

Bank Account

19–6			19–6		
May 1 Balance			Apl. 30 **Creditors**		
b/d		£2,965	A/c		**£41,805**

Stage 3

You may now decide that the time has come to complete the Cash Account. In that case you will proceed to enter those items which you have been told were paid out of takings.

Cash Account

19–5			19–6		
May 1 Balance b/d		£185	Apl. 30 Wages A/c		£7,270
19–6			Apl. 30 General		
Apl. 30 Debtors			Expenses A/c		130
A/c		62,630	Apl. 30 Drawings A/c		1,000
					8,400
		£62,815			

From this we conclude that the amount to be treated as paid into the bank is £54,415. We now make the necessary entries for this and then complete the construction of the Bank Account from the other details given in the problem, i.e., the amounts paid out for Drawings and General Expenses. Finally we enter the balance at the bank of £7,545 on 30th April 19–6 (also given in the question).

Bank Account

19–5			19–6		
May 1 Balance			Apl. 30 Creditors		
b/d		£2,965	A/c		£41,805
19–6			Apl. 30 Drawings A/c		2,000
Apl. 30 **Cash A/c**		**54,415**	Apl. 30 General		
			Expenses A/c		5,810
			Apl. 30 Balance c/d		7,545
		£57,380			£57,160

Now, we would expect to find that the totals of each side agree since we have been given the closing balance at the bank, but on totalling up we see that the debits amount to £57,380 and the credits to £57,160, i.e. a shortage on the credit side of £220 or, alternatively, an excess on the debit side of £220.

Since the Bank Account must be regarded as the sheet anchor in this type of problem it will have to be adjusted. The only figure which is available for any adjustment is the amount of £54,415 from the Cash Account and so we will reduce this by £220 and make the amount paid in £54,195. Of course, this will mean a corresponding adjustment in the Cash Account on the credit side, and so our revised Cash Account would appear as follows:

Cash Account (revised)

19–5			19–6		
May 1 Balance b/d	£185		Apl. 30 Wages A/c	£7,270	
19–6			Apl. 30 General		
Apl. 30 Debtors			Expenses A/c	130	
A/c	62,630		Apl. 30 Drawings A/c	1,000	
				8,400	
			Apl. 30 Bank A/c		
			(revised figure)	**54,195**	
				62,595	
		£62,815			

We have now established the difference of £220 in the Cash Account. This must represent that part of the cash on the premises which relates to the takings of 30th April, i.e., cash sales for that day which have not yet been banked. For the purpose of these accounts, then, we must regard it as the *balance* on the Cash Account; which, if you refer to the examiner's requirements at the end of the question, you will find to be the first thing asked for. The final stage of the Cash Account would therefore appear as follows:

Cash Account

19–6		19–6	
Apl. 30 Total brought		Apl. 30 Total brought	
forward as		forward (as	
above)	£62,815	above)	£62,595
		Apl. 30 *Balance* c/d	220
	£62,815		£62,815
19–6			
May 1 Balance b/d	**£220**		

NOTE: Remember that the question tells us that "the entries in the other books, for the year to 30th April 19–6 had been completed *before* the fire, and, from these books, the following information is obtained: . . ." Then follows a list of balances.

This completes the really difficult part of the problem so we will proceed to the next stage with a feeling of something accomplished and with the end now in sight.

Stage 4

As was stressed in the last chapter we should always work to a Trial Balance in this type of problem.

Whatever happens do not lose sight of the fact that a certain amount of double entry has to be made as a result of your building up of the Cash Account, Bank Account, Debtors Account and Creditors Account. The general situation is set out below in the shape of a number of "T" accounts and is followed by a Trial Balance.

Capital Account	*Furniture Account*
Balance £7,205	Balance £850
Stock Account	*Sales Account*
Balance £7,340	Debtors A/c £62,750
Purchases Account	*Wages Account*
Creditors A/c £43,580	Cash £7,270
General Expenses Account	*Drawings Account*
Cash A/c £130 Bank A/c 5,810 _____ 5,940	Cash A/c £1,000 Bank A/c 2,000 _____ 3,000

Creditors Account		*Debtors Account*	
	Balance £5,235	Balance £410	

Cash Account		*Bank Account*	
Balance £220		Balance £7,545	

Discounts Received Account	
	Creditors A/c £965

TRIAL BALANCE 30TH APRIL 19–6

Capital		£7,205
Stock	£7,340	
Sales		62,750
Purchases	43,580	
Wages	7,270	
General expenses	5,940	
Drawings	3,000	
Furniture	850	
Cash	220	
Bank	7,545	
Discounts received		965
Creditors		5,235
Debtors	410	
	£76,155	£76,155

The second matter the examiner requires is final accounts and Balance Sheet; but you may rest assured that you will have already earned the bulk of the marks for this question by solving the first requirement.

Trading Account

Stock	£7,340	Sales	£62,750
Purchases	43,580	Closing stock	4,970
Gross profit	16,800		
	£67,720		£67,720

Profit and Loss Account

Wages	£7,270	Gross profit	£16,800
General expenses	5,940	Discounts received	965
Net profit	4,555		
	£17,765		£17,765

BALANCE SHEET AS ON 30TH APRIL 19–6

Capital Account				
Balance			Furniture and fittings	£850
1st May 19–5	£7,205		Stock	4,970
Add: Profit	4,555		Debtors	410
			Bank	7,545
	11,760		Cash	220
Less: Drawings	3,000			
	8,760			
Creditors	5,235			
	£13,995			£13,995

PROGRESS TEST 11

Theory

1. How would you set about determining how much money had been received from customers, assuming that the question did not provide the normal information in the form of a summarised Bank Account? **(2)**

2. In the event of no Bank Account being given in a question, describe the steps you would take to ascertain the amounts paid to (a) creditors for goods, and (b) creditors for services. **(3, 4)**

3. What basic information would you need to be given in order to build up a Bank Account? **(1, 2, 3, 4)**

4. How much importance do you attach to double-entry book-keeping in the solution of incomplete records problems? **(6)**

Practice

5. The following figures, relating to the year 19–5, have been extracted from the books of Hastings, a trader:

Balance at bank at 1st January	£685
Furniture and fittings at 1st January	925
Loss on sale of furniture	108
Trade creditors at 1st January	1,660
Trade debtors at 1st January	1,490
Purchases	18,500
Sales	24,750
Discounts allowed	530
Discounts received	775
Trade creditors at 31st December	1,725
Trade debtors at 31st December	1,580
Drawn from bank for private purposes	2,198
General expenses paid in advance at 1st January	17
General expenses paid during the year	843
General expenses outstanding at 31st December	14
Stock in trade at 1st January	1,248
Stock in trade at 31st December	1,367
Wages paid	2,472

The furniture which was sold stood in the books at 1st January at £130.

Hastings paid all business receipts into the bank and all business payments were made by cheque.

There were no transactions other than those which can be ascertained from the information given above.

You are required to prepare:

(*a*) a summary of Hastings's Bank Account for the year 19–5;

(*b*) a Trading and Profit and Loss Account for the year 19–5 and a Balance Sheet as on 31st December 19–5.

(I.C.S.A.)

6. James Snelling owned a flourishing tobacconist and confectionery shop. His records consisted of a Cash Book and a file which contained his invoices and receipts. All his sales were for cash but he purchases all his goods from wholesalers who allowed him one month's credit.

On 1st January 19–5 he held a cash float of change amounting to £15 and his shop fittings were valued at £527. During the year 19–5 he paid the following business expenses out of his cash takings and retained £3,460 for himself:

Wages of assistant	£724
General expenses	627

A summary of his Bank Account disclosed the following:

Balance at bank at 1st January	£1,291
Business takings paid into bank	14,614
Payments to trade creditors	11,487
Rent of shop	750
Light, heat and insurance	198

His stock in trade at 1st January 19–5 amounted to £1,302, while at 31st December 19–5 it amounted to £1,421.

At 1st January 19–5 he owed £1,777 to trade creditors and at 31st December 19–5, £1,898. His cash float at this date was £19.

His suppliers allowed him £293 in discount during 1975.

Prepare Snelling's Trading and Profit and Loss Account for the year 19–5 and a Balance Sheet as on 31st December 19–5.

7. Edward Jackson commenced business on 1st May 19–5, paying £3,000 into a Business Bank Account. He bought shop fittings and equipment costing £640, paying for these items by cheque from the Business Bank Account. Jackson decided that he would prepare accounts at 31st December 19–5, so that his future accounts might be prepared annually on 31st December. The results of his first eight months' trading were as follows:

Credit sales amounted to £14,208.

All purchases had been made on credit and amounted to £11,206.

The following business expenses had been paid by cheque.

(a) Rent, £30 per month payable in advance.

(b) Rates had been paid up to 31st March 19–6 in two instalments as follows: five months to 30th September 19–5, £147; six months to 31st March 19–6, £162.

(c) Light and heat, £108.

(d) Telephone, £43.

(e) General expenses, £572.

(f) Insurances, £144.

He drew £2,680 for his personal needs.

Payments to trade creditors amounted to £8,979.

Receipts from debtors were £12,675.

On 31st December 19–5 the following matters had not been dealt with:

Insurance paid in advance, £48.

General business expenses outstanding, £72.

£32 was to be written off shop fittings.

You are required (a) to prepare a Bank Account and to calculate the value of the stock in trade (at cost) on 31st December 19–5, and also the amounts of the debtors and the creditors; (b) to prepare Jackson's Trading and Profit and Loss Account for the eight months ending on 31st December 19–5 and a Balance Sheet as on that date. The gross profit on sales was 40.29 per cent.

NOTE: All payments were made by cheque and all receipts were paid into the bank.

CHAPTER XII

Single Entry

STATEMENTS OF PROFIT

1. When a Statement of Profit is required. The traditional title given to this aspect of accounting is a courtesy title only and is not meant to suggest a system of book-keeping. All that it is intended to convey is that the double-entry system of book-keeping is *not* in operation.

It is comparatively rarely in actual practice that one is confronted with the need to produce a Statement of Profit from the sketchy information beloved by some examiners. It does occasionally happen, however, that an Inspector of Taxes, not satisfied with information as to profits or income given by a taxpayer, will himself produce a statement which he contends shows that person's income or profit earned during a particular period. The term "single-entry book-keeping" is applied to such productions as these and it is, of course, then up to the taxpayer to prove the Inspector wrong, if he can.

2. What is the origin of profit? Before we consider the manner in which the profit for a period of trading would be calculated by this method let us ask the question: "What constitutes profit?" The simple answer is: *Profit can only arise as a result of trading.* If one thinks about this statement one realises the truth of it and it is of the greatest importance that one keeps it in mind when solving single-entry problems.

3. Measuring the amount of profit. In normal circumstances we calculate the amount of profit made during a period of trading by dealing systematically with each business transaction and by making a double entry in the ledger accounts in every case.

EXAMPLE: Suppose P. Cleghorn invests £100 in a business and buys goods for £80; he sells them all for £115 and then withdraws £12 from the business for his own personal needs.

The transaction would be recorded as follows.

P. Cleghorn: Capital Account

Bank (drawings)	£12	Bank	£100

Bank Account

Capital	£100	Purchases	£80
Sales	115	Drawings (Capital A/c)	12
		Balance c/d	123
	£215		£215
Balance b/d	£123		

Purchases Account

Bank	£80		

Sales Account

		Bank	£115

Trading Account

Purchases	£80	Sales	£115
Gross profit	35		
	£115		£115

So by means of double-entry book-keeping we calculate the profit to be £35. This sum will, of course, be credited to the Capital Account to complete the double entry and so the final position of that account would appear as set out below.

P. Cleghorn: Capital Account

Bank (drawings)	£12	Bank	£100
Balance c/d	123	Gross profit	35
	£135		£135
		Balance b/d	£123

From inspection of the Capital Account as shown in its final form we may now correctly conclude that the profit made during a period of trading can be measured, fundamentally, in terms of the amount by which the owner's capital has *increased* by the end of the period.

What are the facts shown in the example?

At the start £100 was invested by Cleghorn and this was credited to his Capital Account. When trading ceased the balance on this account had increased to £123, i.e., a net increase of £23 over the starting figure. *In addition* to this net increase of £23, however, Cleghorn had withdrawn £12 from the business, i.e., he had reduced his original investment of £100 by £12 to a net figure of £88. So we find that there must have been a *gross increase* of £35 to bring the Capital Account balance at the end to £123. This, of course, is the amount of the profit which we originally proved by double entry.

Summarising the position we have the following:

Original sum invested in the business and credited to the Capital Account	£100
Deduct: Cash withdrawn for own private use	12
	88
Add: Amount required to increase the balance of the Capital Account to £123	35
Closing balance on Capital Account	£123

Thus, the profit for the period is confirmed as being £35.

NET WORTH

4. The meaning of "net worth". The net worth of a business at any time may be defined as being the difference between the value of the assets and the amount which is owed to outside creditors, i.e., *not including* the amount owed to the proprietor of the business.

Consider the following Balance Sheet.

BALANCE SHEET AS AT 31ST DECEMBER

Capital	£7,219	Freehold building	£2,250
		Fixtures and fittings	415
Creditors			
Supplies	£3,482	Motor van	340
Accrued			
expenses	167	Stock	2,617
		Debtors	5,301
Bank		Cash in hand	34
overdraft	89		
	3,738		
	£10,957		£10,957

What is the net worth of the business according to the definition stated above?

The total value of the assets is	£10,957
The amount owing to outside creditors is	3,738
Therefore, the net worth is	£7,219

By looking again at the Balance Sheet we see immediately that the net worth of the business is *precisely* the sum owed by the business to the owner, i.e., the balance on his Capital Account. This is true for every business.

5. An increase in the net worth. If there is an increase in the net worth of a business between two dates which is *due to trading* then a profit has been made. We must, however, appreciate that merely to set the balance of the Capital Account at the end of a trading period against the balance at the start is not necessarily going to tell us the amount of the profit. If we look back to the example of P. Cleghorn in **3** we find that the closing balance on his capital account was £123 whereas the opening balance was £100, a difference of £23. But we know that the profit was £35. If we set out the Capital Account as shown below we can, perhaps, see the true position more clearly.

Opening capital	£100
Less: Drawings	12
	——
	88
Add: Net profit on trading	35
	——
Closing capital	£123

This has been set out in the above manner to show that where we have ascertained both the opening and the closing balances on the Capital Account and when we know the amount of the drawings, we can deduce the profit.

Suppose we set out a part of the above results once again as follows:

Opening capital	£100
Less: Drawings	12
	——
	£88

We know that the closing balance on the Capital Account is £123, and that by subtracting £88 from £123 we obtain the result of £35. This is the amount of the profit which we have obtained already by means of double entry. Thus we may feel satisfied that we can safely apply the above method to calculate the profit where it is impossible to use the normal double-entry method owing to lack of information.

6. Calculating the true profit. From this it is clear that in order to calculate the true profit we must:

(*a*) subtract from the opening balance on the Capital Account the amount of the owner's drawings.

(*b*) subtract the result so obtained from the closing balance on the Capital Account.

ADDITIONAL CAPITAL INTRODUCED

7. Introducing additional capital. The same principle must be applied in those cases where the owner invests *additional* capital

XII. SINGLE ENTRY 199

during a period of trading. If this happens the effect will be the opposite to that of withdrawing money from the business.

EXAMPLE: J. Snodgrass starts his business by investing £500. He pays this into a Business Bank Account. He then buys goods costing £475, selling them for £560. He invests *a further* £300 and buys goods for £750, all of which are sold for £915. He takes £40 out of the business for his personal use.

In this instance the following entries would be made if proper double-entry book-keeping was being operated:

J. Snodgrass: Capital Account

Bank A/c (drawings)	£40	Bank A/c	£500
		Bank A/c	300

Bank Account

J. Snodgrass:		Purchases A/c	£475
Capital A/c	£500	Purchases A/c	750
Sales A/c	560	Drawings (Capital A/c)	40
J. Snodgrass:		Balance c/d	1,010
Capital A/c	300		
Sales A/c	915		
	————		————
	£2,275		£2,275
	=====		=====
Balance b/d	£1,010		

Purchases Account

Bank A/c	£475
Bank A/c	750
	————
	£1,225

Sales Account

		Bank A/c	£560
		Bank A/c	915
			————
			£1,475

Trading Account

Purchases	£1,225	Sales	£1,475
Gross profit	250		
	£1,475		£1,475

The true gross profit is £250 and this would be credited to the Capital Account (since in this simple illustration we have nothing to enter in the Profit and Loss Account). We would then have the following details on that account:

J. Snodgrass: Capital Account

Bank A/c (drawings)	£40	Bank A/c	£500
Balance c/d	1,010	Bank A/c	300
		Trading A/c (gross profit)	250
	£1,050		£1,050
		Balance b/d	£1,010

If we used the tabular form of setting out the Capital Account we should set it out in the following manner:

Opening capital	£500
Add: Additional cash paid in	300
	800
Less: Drawings	40
	760
Add: Profit for the period	250
Closing capital	£1,010

8. Introducing additional assets. If additional capital is invested it is usually in the form of money. It must be understood, however, that sometimes an owner will put *assets* into the business instead of money; for example, the proprietor may privately own a motor vehicle which he decides could be employed in the business. In such a case, naturally enough, a cash value will be given to the vehicle, the Capital Account being credited and the Motor Vehicle Account debited (if normal double entry was being carried out).

When calculating profit by means of the single-entry method we must simply consider the value of the asset introduced as being an addition to the owner's capital invested in the business. That is to say, we treat it in exactly the same way we would treat an addition of further capital in cash. If, in the last example, instead of introducing further capital of £300 in the form of cash, the owner gave to the business a motor van which he valued at £300, the effect on his Capital Account would be precisely the same. Therefore, when dealing with single-entry problems any assets introduced will be dealt with by adding them to the owner's opening capital.

RULES FOR SINGLE-ENTRY PROBLEMS

9. How to recognise single-entry problems. It is obviously of great importance that a student is capable of recognising the nature of a question. To judge by answers submitted in examinations there is no doubt that many students do not recognise a single-entry problem when they see one. They try to solve it by applying the "build-up" method of accounting which is appropriate only to incomplete record problems. The treatment required for these two aspects of accounting differs radically and unless the type is recognised the wrong treatment may well be applied. It is, therefore, vital that a student is able to distinguish between the two kinds of problem. The following "recognition signals" may help.

(*a*) *Single entry.* The question will normally ask for the preparation of a Statement of Profit. If so, use the single-entry technique to be described shortly.

(*b*) *Incomplete records.* When the question asks for.

(*i*) the preparation of a Trading and Profit and Loss Account with a Balance Sheet; and

(*ii*) where a summarised Bank Account (or Cash Account) is given,

then the incomplete records technique is called for, i.e., the "build-up" of all the ledger accounts.

NOTE: It is most important that the Bank Account features in the question because without it one could not build up the accounts into full double entry. This note is given as a warning since there is one special type of single-entry problem which does ask for a Trading and Profit and Loss Account. But this type of question never gives the detailed Bank Account. It will be dealt with in section **15**.

10. Three simple rules. There are only three simple rules to be observed when working out the solution to a problem of single entry. These are as follows.

(*a*) Ascertain the opening capital of the owner at the start of the period. This will, in the majority of cases, call for the construction of an *opening* Balance Sheet.

(*b*) Build up a closing Balance Sheet from the assets and liabilities given in the question. The difference between the two sides will be the owner's *closing capital.*

(*c*) Construct a Capital Account for the owner in normal double-entry fashion. Insert on the credit side the balance of opening capital. Below this add any *additional* capital contributed either in the form of cash or other assets. On the debit side enter all drawings either of cash or of goods. Finally, enter the closing balance of capital obtained from the Balance Sheet constructed at the end of the period. The difference between the two sides of the Capital Account will be the profit or loss for the period.

NOTE: When preparing the closing Balance Sheet it is most important that every asset and every liability is included. Many students fail to include some or all of the fixed assets and long-term liabilities. Almost certainly the reason for this is that the question gives details of the closing current assets and current liabilities but makes no mention of the fixtures and fittings, motor vans, long-term loans, etc. which appeared in the opening Balance Sheet. These, obviously, must be brought in at the end of the period. If the student fails to do this his closing capital figure will be sadly astray.

11. Solving a single-entry problem. A problem on single-entry accounting would be stated broadly on the following lines.

The first part of the problem would give enough detail to enable us to construct the opening position but no details of the *trading* transactions would be given. There would only be mention of some of the closing balances (almost certainly some would be left to the student to deduce). Details of any additions of a capital nature i.e., assets, and the introduction of any fresh capital (either in cash or equipment, etc.) would certainly be given. Finally, a note as to drawings would be added.

EXAMPLE: J. Snodgrass started business on 1st December 19–1 with fixtures and fittings, £1,000; stock, £1,500; and £500 cash at the bank. At 31st May 19–2 his balance at the bank stood at £2,155. During this six months the business had bought fittings costing £180 and Snodgrass had given to it an old car he owned and which he valued at £215. His personal drawings amounted to £250 during the period.

Prepare a statement showing his profit for the period after taking into consideration the additional information given at Stage 2 below.

Such a problem should be tackled in the following manner

Stage 1

The opening capital must be calculated. This, of course, is a simple matter.

OPENING STATEMENT 1ST DECEMBER 19–1

	Dr	*Cr*
Fixtures and fittings	£1,000	
Stock	1,500	
Cash at bank	500	
Capital is therefore		£3,000
	£3,000	£3,000

Stage 2

We must prepare a closing statement or Balance Sheet in order to ascertain his capital at the end of the period. The only items to be shown are the assets at their final values, i.e., *after* deducting depreciation, provision for bad debts, etc. Suppose, as an example, there were debtors valued at £600 but we were told that a provision for doubtful debts of £20 must be made. In our Closing Statement we would show the debtors at their *final* value, i.e., £580.

CLOSING STATEMENT 31ST MAY 19–2

	Dr	Cr
Cash at bank	£2,155	
Fixtures and fittings:		
At 1st December		
19–1 £1,000		
Additions 180		
	1,180	
Motor car	215	
Capital is therefore		£3,550
	£3,550	£3,550

Stage 3

The last matter to be dealt with is the ascertainment of the profit. To do this we construct a Capital Account *in ordinary double-entry form* from the information given in the question and facts which we have deduced from the Opening and Closing Statements.

Capital Account

Drawings	£250	Cash and assets per opening statement	£3,000
		Motor car introduced at valuation	215
			3,215
Balance, ascertained from the Closing Statement	3,550	Net profit	?
	£3,800		£3,800

The net profit is found by the simple process of subtracting £3,215 from £3,800, i.e., £585.

This method of ascertaining net profit by the construction of a Capital Account on ordinary double-entry lines has the twin virtues of great simplicity and the certainty that the answer is the correct one. It is yet another example of *using* information. Certain facts and figures are given or are capable of being calculated. These are then fitted into their proper places (in this case, in the Capital Account) with the result that we are left with only one *unknown* factor and by the simple process of subtracting one total from another we obtain the answer.

12. Depreciation. As has been mentioned already, questions relating to single entry are frequently asked in examinations and can be made to appear very complex indeed, but if the method set out above is employed to solve them the student can rest assured that the solution can be found very quickly. As an example, a question may state that depreciation of motor vans amounted to a certain sum and that a provision for doubtful debts was required. No real problem arises in such cases. The difficulty is only an apparent one.

EXAMPLE: In the example in **11** suppose we were told that £40 had to be provided for depreciation on the motor van. We do not have to worry about debiting a Profit and Loss Account for it must be remembered that here we are thinking in terms of single entry.

All that we have to do is to adjust the value of the motor car on the Closing Statement. The automatic effect of this is that the total value of the assets is diminished by the amount of depreciation deducted from the motor car. This in its turn automatically *reduces* the amount of the closing capital and as an immediate consequence the profit is reduced by the amount of the depreciation. The result immediately becomes apparent if we reconstruct the Closing Statement (shown on p. 204) after making the adjustment for the £40 depreciation.

CLOSING STATEMENT RECONSTRUCTED

		Dr	Cr
Cash at bank		£2,155	
Fixtures and fittings:			
At 1st December 19–1	£1,000		
Additions	180		
	———	1,180	
Motor car:			
At 1st December 19–1	215		
Less: Depreciation	40		
	———	175	
Capital is therefore			**£3,510**
		———	———
		£3,510	£3,510
		═══	═══

It will be necessary, of course, to reconstruct the Capital Account also since the closing balance is now different:

Capital Account

Drawings	£250	Cash and assets contributed	£3,000
		Motor car introduced	215
			3,215
Balance (ascertained from the Closing Statement)	3,510	Net profit *now* becomes	545
	£3,760		£3,760

13. Increase in the capital invested. The important point is that the amount by which the capital invested has increased as a result of *trading* is the measure of the profit, subject, of course, to the amount of drawings. This point should be quite clear from the two examples, for in the second case the *closing* balance of capital is less than it was in the first by precisely the amount by which the profit has been reduced by the amount of depreciation, i.e., in the first Capital Account the closing balance was £3,550 whereas in the second one it was £3,510, a reduction of £40 which was the amount of the depreciation.

From this it is easy to see how important it is that the *closing* balance of capital be correctly calculated. Thus, if we are told that a certain amount of depreciation must be written off an asset, then in the Closing Statement the reduced balance of Closing Capital must be entered and this, in its turn, gives a reduced figure of profit.

14. Specimen question. As this aspect of accounting studies is so imperfectly understood it is felt that an example based on a recent professional examination should be shown at this point. The question would carry about 18 marks. By applying the principles laid down above it can be worked out very speedily thus giving the candidate a large proportion of the marks required to pass as well as giving him a bonus of time which he could spend on other questions, a matter of very great importance in an examination.

The Balance Sheet of Peter Puffin as on 31st December 19–1 was as under:

BALANCE SHEET

Capital	£4,355	Furniture and	
Trade creditors	3,845	equipment	£1,400
Loan from		Stock-in-trade	3,800
Freeman £1,000		Trade debtors	2,950
Interest accrued 50		Cash at bank	1,100
	1,050		
	£9,250		£9,250

You are given the following information:

(a) During 19–2 Puffin purchased new furniture for £80.

(b) On 1st January 19–2 Puffin borrowed a further £1,000 from Freeman. This loan and the earlier loan of £1,000 both carried interest at 5 per cent per annum. During 19–2 Puffin made no repayments of the loan capital but he did pay off the interest outstanding at 31st December 19–1.

(c) During 19–2 Puffin's drawings amounted to £1,200.

(d) At 31st December 19–2 Puffin's stock was valued at £2,290 and debtors amounted to £2,440. Creditors were £3,360 and his Bank Account was overdrawn by £75.

(e) Puffin took goods from the business for his own use. The cost of these was £268.

(f) 5 per cent depreciation was to be written off the furniture and equipment.

You are required to prepare a statement showing Puffin's net profit or loss for the year 19–2 and his Balance Sheet as on 31st December 19–2.

SOLUTION:

Stage 1

The opening balance on the Capital Account per rule (a). This is given to us in the question in the opening balance sheet.

Stage 2

The production of a Closing Balance Sheet which enables us to calculate the closing capital, per rule (b).

BALANCE SHEET AT 31ST DECEMBER 19–2

Capital	?	Furniture and equipment balance at 31st Dec. 19–1	£1,400	
		Additions during year	80	
			1,480	
Creditors	£3,360	Less: 5% depreciation	74	
				1,406
Bank overdraft	75	Stock		2,290
Loan A/c: Freeman— Balance at 31st Dec. 19–1 including interest	£1,050	Debtors		2,440
Add: Further amount borrowed	1,000			
	2,050			
Less: Interest paid	50			
	2,000			
Loan interest accrued	100			
				£6,136

NOTE: The total of the liabilities side has been deliberately omitted at this point to indicate that something is missing.

The liabilities as listed above must be subtracted from the assets total in order to give us the figure of closing capital. That is to say, £5,535 deducted from £6,136 = £601.

Stage 3

The construction of a Capital Account on double-entry lines, per rule (c).

Peter Puffin: Capital Account

19–2			19–2		
Dec. 31 Drawings:			Jan. 1 Balance at		
	Cash	£1,200		start	£4,355
	Goods	268			
Dec. 31 Loss for year		?			
Dec. 31 Balance					
	at end	601			
					£4,355

The total of the debit side set out above amounts to £2,069. Deducting this from the credit total of £4,355 we have a difference of £2,286. This figure must be inserted on the debit side in order to make the two sides equal.

We know from our study of book-keeping that any loss incurred as a result of trading must be debited in the owner's Capital Account. We are therefore entitled to conclude that a *loss of £2,286* has been incurred during the year 19–2.

15. The exception to the rule. Mention was made at the end of **9** that there is one type of question which comes within the sphere of single entry where a Trading and Profit and Loss Account may be asked for. In this chapter we have shown how the profit can be ascertained in a straightforward manner. It must be understood that it is the *net profit* that we so obtain. Provided that we are given information regarding the total amount of the expenses which must be debited to the Profit and Loss Account, not forgetting to include any charge for depreciation, we can build up the debit side in full. The total of all the debits (*including* the net profit) will be equal to the figure of the gross profit which will be inserted, thus closing off the Profit and Loss Account.

The gross profit, of course, comes from the debit side of the Trading Account. We will be told what percentage of gross profit to sales is made by the business so we can thus calculate the sales. Opening and closing stocks are given in the question, so by placing these items in their respective positions we are left with the one further figure needed for completion, i.e., the purchases. By totalling up both sides and subtracting the debits from the credits we obtain the missing figure.

210   XII. SINGLE ENTRY

The following example will show how this type of problem should be dealt with.

EXAMPLE: The assets and liabilities of Baxter, a shopkeeper, at 31st December 19–1 were as follows:

Land and buildings	£5,000
Furniture and fittings	900
Stock-in-trade	6,275
Trade debtors	4,820
Bank overdraft	307
Trade creditors	3,648
Loan from Scott	2,000
Wages outstanding	54

In March 19–2 Baxter won £1,500 in a football pool, and paid the entire sum into the Business Bank Account.

On 30th June 19–2 he paid £1,050 to Scott, representing £50 interest and £1,000 in repayment of the loan.

Baxter's current assets at 31st December 19–2 were:

Balance at bank	£231
Stock-in-trade	7,100
Trade debtors	4,163

His trade creditors on the same date amounted to £4,319. No fixed assets were bought or sold in 19–2. Baxter's drawings during 19–2 were £3,000.

The expenses charged in the Profit and Loss Account for the year to 31st December 19–2 amounted to £8,279 made up as follows:

Wages and general expenses (all paid by the end of 19–2)	£8,114
Depreciation of furniture and fittings	90
Interest on loan (of which £25 was outstanding at 31st December 19–2)	75

Baxter's gross profit is at the rate of 20 per cent of the selling price for all goods.

You are required:

(a) to calculate the net profit for the year 19–2;
(b) to set out a summary of the Trading and Profit and Loss Account for the year 19–2.

Stage 1

OPENING BALANCE SHEET

Loan	£2,000	Land & buildings	£5,000
Trade creditors	3,648	Furniture & fittings	900
Wages owing	54	Stock-in-trade	6,275
Bank overdraft	307	Trade debtors	4,820
	6,009		
The **difference** =			
the capital	10,986		
	£16,995		£16,995

Stage 2

CLOSING BALANCE SHEET

Loan	£1,000	Land and buildings		£5,000
Add: Interest				
accrued	25	Furniture and		
	1,025	fittings		
		Balance at		
		31st Dec.		
Trade creditors	4,319	19–1	900	
		Less		
	5,344	Depreciation	90	
The difference =				810
the capital	11,960	Stock-in-trade		7,100
		Trade debtors		4,163
		Bank		231
	£17,304			£17,304

Stage 3

Capital Account

Drawings	£3,000	Opening balance b/d	£10,986
Closing balance		Cash paid in from	
c/d	11,960	pools win	1,500
			12,486
	£14,960		

Subtracting £12,486 from £14,960 we obtain the *net* profit which amounts to £2,474.

Stage 4

The question asks for a summary of the Trading and Profit and Loss Account. In this type of question we have to *start at the end*, i.e., with the net profit, and *work back* to the Trading Account.

Profit and Loss Account

Wages and general		
expenses	£8,114	
Depreciation	90	
Loan interest	75	
	8,279	
Net profit	2,474	
	£10,753	

The total of the debit side, £10,753, must also be the total of the credit side. As we have no information regarding any items to be credited in the Profit and Loss Account we are forced to conclude that the gross profit must amount to £10,753 and so enter it on the credit side, thus completing the account.

The gross profit will be debited in the Trading Account in the normal way. The question tells us that the gross profit percentage on sales is 20 per cent, i.e., one-fifth. Multiplying £10,753 by 5 we obtain the amount of sales, £53,765.

From the two Balance Sheets we ascertain the opening and closing stock figures and are left with the purchases as the only unknown item.

Trading Account

Opening stock	£6,275	Sales	£53,675
Purchases	?	Closing stock	7,100
Gross profit	10,753		
	£60,775		£60,775

A simple exercise in arithmetic will tell us that the missing figure of purchases is £43,747.

PROGRESS TEST 12

Theory

1. How does profit arise? **(2)**
2. State how you would measure the amount of profit earned during a period of trading. **(3)**
3. What do you understand by the expression "net worth"? **(4)**
4. In what way can the net worth of a business be increased? **(5)**
5. How would you distinguish a single-entry problem from a question requiring incomplete records treatment? **(9)**
6. Set out the rules for dealing with single-entry problems. **(10)**

Practice

7. Albert Munn's business position on 1st January 19–4 was as follows:

Stock	£2,000
Cash at bank	400
Creditors	1,800
Debtors	3,200

By 31st December 19–4 the situation had altered to:

Stock	£4,750
Cash at bank	1,875
Creditors	6,150
Debtors	3,625

During 19–4 he had taken £5,000 out of the business for his own use, but on 30th December 19–4 he paid £250 from his private funds into the Business Bank Account.

Ascertain Munn's profit for the year ended 31st December 19–4.

8. On 1st January 19–5 L. Speed's fixed assets amounted to £4,725; his current assets stood at £5,482 and he owed £2,229 to his creditors.

During the year 19–5 Speed paid £500 from his private funds into his Business Bank Account and a motor vehicle costing £1,260 was purchased by the business. Speed took £180 per month out of the Business Bank Account for himself.

On 31st December 19–5 current assets amounted to £6,864; sundry creditors were owed £2,579 and the Bank Account of the business was overdrawn by £318.

Prepare a statement to ascertain Speed's net profit for the year 19–5 after depreciating the fixed assets by £475 and the motor vehicle by 20 per cent of its cost.

9. Alan Woodford's assets at 31st December 19–4 were as follows:

Shop fittings	£794
Stock	991
Debtors	1,657
Insurance prepaid	15
Cash at bank	328

He owed £600 to H. Sinclair who had made him a loan at 10 per cent interest per annum, £1,308 to suppliers and £81 in respect of expenses.

On 31st December 19–5 his stock was valued at £1,075 and his debtors amounted to £1,734. He owed £1,319 to trade creditors, and £39 for expenses. £15 insurance had been prepaid. His bank account was overdrawn by £27.

During the year he had taken goods for his own use which had cost £325 and had drawn £30 per week for his personal use out of the bank. In addition to these matters he had installed new shop fittings which had cost £352. A win of £200 on the football pools had helped in this purchase. £57 is to be provided for depreciation of shop fittings, and £15 interest on loan remained unpaid.

Prepare a statement showing his net profit for the year 19–5 and draw up a Balance Sheet as on 31st December 19–5.

10. P. Hargreaves, a retailer, adds 25 per cent to the cost of goods which he has purchased for resale to arrive at his selling price.

At 30th June 19–4 his financial position was as follows:

Assets:	Premises and equipment	£5,000
	Stock	3,825
	Debtors	7,175
	Cash at bank	2,200
Liabilities:	Creditors	3,000
	Loan from G. Wright	2,000

During the year ended 30th June 19–5 he dealt with the under-mentioned matters:

(a) paid £11,675 to his suppliers for goods;
(b) repaid £500 to G. Wright off the loan;
(c) purchased a motor van for £700;
(d) drew £80 per month from the bank for his own use;
(e) having won £300 in a sweepstake he paid it into his Business Bank Account;
(f) paid £600 income tax.

On 30th June 19–5 his stock was valued, at cost, £4,000; debtors owed him £7,000; he owed his suppliers £3,500; and his balance of cash at the bank amounted to £1,950.

You are required to ascertain:

(a) the gross profit made during the year;
(b) the net profit or loss for the year ended 30th June 19–5.

(I.C.A.)

11. The assets and liabilities of G, a trader, at 31st December 19–4 were as follows:

Freehold land and building	£6,500
Furniture and fittings	1,400
Motor van	600

Stock-in-trade	7,820
Trade debtors	5,370
Bank overdraft	208
Trade creditors	4,912
Accrued expenses	68
Loan from B	1,600

In March 19–5 G sold a private investment for £961 and paid the proceeds into his Business Bank Account. On 30th June 19–5 he paid £840 to B, representing £40 interest and £800 in part repayment of the loan.

On 31st December 19–5 G's current assets were:

Stock-in-trade	£8,115
Trade debtors	5,842
Balance at bank	327

His trade creditors on the same date amounted to £4,081. No fixed assets were bought or sold in 19–5. G's drawings during 19–5 were £3,200.

The expenses charged in the profit and loss account for 19–5 amounted to £10,300, made up as follows:

General expenses (all paid by 31st December 19–5)	£10,020
Depreciation of furniture and fittings	70
Depreciation of motor van	150
Interest on loan (of which £20 was outstanding at 31st December 19–5)	60

G's gross profit was 20% of the selling price of all goods.
You are required:

(a) to calculate the net profit for the year 19–5;

(b) to reconstruct, from the ascertained net profit and the information given above, the trading and profit and loss account for the year 19–5.

(I.C.S.A.)

CHAPTER XIII

Working Capital and Capital Employed

MEASURING THE WORKING CAPITAL OF A BUSINESS

1. The meaning of working capital. Looking back to our earlier studies we recall that we learned that every business required capital (in the form of money) to enable it to be set up and to be put in a position to commence to trade. This capital is used to acquire a number of necessities. For example, every business requires premises, a certain amount of equipment, such as fittings and furniture, and, most important of all, a sufficient stock of goods to enable it to offer an attractive choice to its customers. Finally, it will need to have sufficient cash left over for the purpose of meeting its immediate running expenses.

The term "working capital" is used normally to indicate the amount of surplus funds a business has available at any time to enable it to meet demands requiring immediate settlement. Each week, for example, most businesses will need money for the payment of wages. Once in each month the firm will have to pay those creditors who have supplied it with goods on credit. Sufficient money, therefore, must be forthcoming for the settlement of liabilities such as these.

2. Current assets. The expression "current assets" is used to refer to those assets which are continually on the move. They are sometimes called the circulating capital of a business because they are constantly in motion. Current assets fall under the following heading.

(a) Stock-in-trade.
(b) Debtors.
(c) Payments in advance (a form of debtors).
(d) Cash at the bank.
(e) Cash in hand.

It requires very little thought to appreciate that the above assets are, by their very nature, subject to continual movement.

3. Current liabilities. The term "current liabilities" is given to those

217

creditors which a business must satisfy by a payment in cash in the very near future. They are:

(a) trade creditors (for goods supplied);
(b) accrued expenses (for services rendered);
(c) income tax (payable within the current year);
(d) dividends declared (payable almost immediately);
(e) bank overdraft.

4. Calculating working capital. In order to ascertain the amount of working capital possessed by a firm we subtract the total of the current liabilities from the total of the current assets. The difference between these two totals is the working capital.

EXAMPLE: The Balance Sheet of J. Snodgrass as at 31st December 19–1 was as below.

Capital		£24,000	*Fixed assets*		
			Freehold premises	£8,000	
Current liabilities			Fixtures and fittings	1,280	
Trade					———
creditors	£3,800				9,280
Accrued					
expenses	450		*Current assets*		
	———	4,250	Stock	5,600	
			Debtors	8,420	
			Prepayments	75	
			Cash at bank	4,875	
					———
					18,970
		———			———
		£28,250			£28,250

Calculation of the working capital at 31st December 19–1.

Current assets	£18,970
Less: Current liabilities	4,250
	———
Working capital	£14,720

ALTERATIONS IN THE WORKING CAPITAL

5. Increasing the working capital. The working capital of a business may be increased in the following ways:

(a) by the introduction of more cash capital by the owners;

(*b*) by somebody outside the business lending money to it, e.g., in the case of a limited company by an issue of debentures;

(*c*) by the business making a profit on its trading;

(*d*) by the business selling some of its fixed assets, thereby increasing its cash resources.

6. Decreasing the working capital. A decrease in the working capital will come about as a result of:

(*a*) the owner of a business withdrawing cash for his own use;

(*b*) a company declaring a dividend which has the effect of increasing current liabilities, i.e., by moving some of the net profit from the area of fixed liabilities into the area of current liabilities;

(*c*) a company making a loss on trading;

(*d*) the purchase of a fixed asset for cash, i.e., by replacing cash, which is a current asset, with a fixed asset such as machinery.

STATEMENTS OF FUNDS

7. Problems in examinations. Problems relating to working capital appear regularly in the professional examinations. They are generally referred to as "sources and application of funds" problems. The question usually requires the student to produce a reconciliation:

(*a*) showing by how much the working capital has increased or decreased during a given period (usually of one year);

(*b*) preparing a statement setting out the sources from which fresh working capital entered the business during the period, and in what manner this was applied, i.e., on what items it was spent.

EXAMPLE: The Balance Sheet of J. Snodgrass at 31st December 19–1 was as follows.

Fixed liabilities			*Fixed assets*		
Capital Account	£24,000		Freehold premises		£8,000
			Fixtures and fittings		1,280
					9,280
Current liabilities			*Current assets*		
Trade creditors	£3,800		Stock	£5,600	
Accrued expenses	450		Debtors	8,420	
		4,250	Prepayments	75	
			Cash at bank	4,875	
					18,970
		£28,250			£28,250

During the first week of January 19–2 J. Snodgrass obtained a loan of £10,000 in cash and purchased machinery at a cost of £18,500. The business sold part of its premises which had cost £1,750 for the sum of £4,250. During this week it was closed for trading and so the other assets and liabilities remained as they appeared in the Balance Sheet at 31st December 19–1.

The above transactions would be recorded as follows.

Bank Account

19–2			19–2		
Jan. 1	Balance b/d	£4,875	Jan. 7	Machinery A/c	£18,500
Jan. 7	Loan A/c	10,000	Jan. 7	Balance c/d	625
	Freehold				
	Premises A/c	4,250			
		£19,125			£19,125
Jan. 7	Balance b/d	£625			

Capital Account

			19–2		
			Jan. 1	Bank A/c	£24,000

Loan Account

			19–2		
			Jan. 7	Bank A/c	£10,000

Freehold Premises Account

19–2			19–2		
Jan. 1	Balance b/d	£8,000	Jan. 7	Bank A/c	£4,250
Jan. 7	Transfer to			Balance c/d	6,250
	Capital				
	Reserve				
	(profit on				
	sale)	2,500			
		£10,500			£10,500
	Balance b/d	£6,250			

Capital Reserve

	19–2
	Jan. 7 Freehold
	Premises A/c £2,500

Machinery Account

19–2	
Jan. 7 Bank	
Account £18,500	

The Balance Sheet as at 7th January 19–2 would then show the following position:

Fixed liabilities			*Fixed assets*		
Capital			Freehold premises		£6,250
Account	£24,000		Machinery		18,500
Capital Reserve	2,500		Fixtures and fittings		1,280
	——				——
	26,500				26,030
Loan Account		10,000			
Current liabilities			*Current assets*		
Trade			Stock	£5,600	
creditors £3,800			Debtors	8,420	
Accrued			Prepayments	75	
expenses 450			Cash at bank	625	
	——	4,250		——	14,720
		——			——
		£40,750			£40,750
		═══			═══

NOTE: The profit on the sale of the premises has been shown in a special account called "Capital Reserve" since it is not a profit made in the *ordinary* course of trading. It is, of course, a sum due to the owner.

The working capital calculations are:

	31st December 19–1 £	7th January 19–2 £
Current assets	18,970	14,720
Less: Current liabilities	4,250	4,250
WORKING CAPITAL	£14,720	£10,470

By subtracting £10,470 from £14,720 we calculate that the working capital has decreased by £4,250 in the period.

STATEMENT OF SOURCES AND APPLICATION OF FUNDS

Working capital at 31st December 19–1		£14,720
To this must be *added* special receipts of cash:		
From loan	£10,000	
From sale of property	4,250	
		14,250
		28,970
From this total must be *deducted* special payment in cash:		
Purchase of machinery		18,500
Working capital at 7th January 19–2		£10,470

8. The most usual source of working capital. Although working capital may be introduced into a business by means of loans, fresh capital or even the sale of fixed assets, the most usual way for the working capital to be increased is by the business making a *profit on its trading*.

The truth of this statement can be verified very easily by means of a simple example.

EXAMPLE: A business was started with capital in cash amounting to £1,000. Fixtures costing £100 were purchased before trading started. The Balance Sheet would have appeared as follows

BALANCE SHEET 1ST JANUARY

Capital	£1,000	Fixtures	100
		Bank	900
	£1,000		£1,000

The transactions for the first year of trading were as follows:

Cash purchases	£12,000
Cash sales	£15,000
Expenses (all paid for in cash)	£1,400

All takings were banked and all payments were made by cheque. There was no stock on hand at the end of the year.

Cash Book (Bank Account)

Capital A/c	£1,000	Fixtures A/c	£100
Sales A/c	15,000	Purchases A/c	12,000
		Expenses A/c	1,400
		Balance	2,500
	£16,000		£16,000

Trading and Profit and Loss Account

Purchases	£12,000	Sales	£15,000
Gross profit	3,000		
	£15,000		£15,000
Expenses	£1,400	Gross profit	£3,000
Net profit	1,600		
	£3,000		£3,000

BALANCE SHEET 31st DECEMBER

Capital A/c	£1,000	Fixtures	£100
Add: net profit	1,600	Bank	2,500
	£2,600		£2,600

After the purchase of the fixtures for £100 there was left the sum of £900 as *working capital* at the start.

All of the profit was realised, i.e., all transactions were on a cash basis, and so the net profit of £1,600 can be seen to have been received by the business in cash. To the balance of £900 cash at bank on 1st January there has been added during the year the sum of £1,600, the profit realised in cash, which gives a closing balance of £2,500 cash at the bank on 31st December. Thus the working capital amounts to £2,500, since there are no current liabilities and the only current asset is the cash at the bank. Thus the difference between the opening and closing working capital (£900–£2,500) is £1,600, which of course corresponds to the exact amount of net profit made during the year.

If the business had conducted its operations on a credit basis instead of for cash the same result would apply, since instead of collecting cash from the customers for goods sold a number of debtors would appear on the books. Debtors are, of course, current assets in the same way as is cash. Suppose, then, purely for the sake of illustrating the point, that all the sales had been on credit and that no cash had been received, the net profit would have been exactly the same, i.e., £1,600. If we assume that all the transactions, both buying and selling, were on credit the Balance Sheet would appear as below.

BALANCE SHEET 31ST DECEMBER

Capital A/c	£1,000		*Fixed assets*		
Add: net profit	1,600		Fixtures		£100
	2,600		*Current assets*		
Current liabilities			Debtors	£15,000	
Creditors for			Bank	900	
goods	£12,000				15,900
Accrued					
expenses	1,400				
		13,400			
		£16,000			£16,000

Subtracting current liabilities of £13,400 from current assets of £15,900 we are left with £2,500 as the working capital, as before.

9. Measuring the increase or decrease of working capital. In order to measure the increase or decrease in the amount of working capital over a period of time it is necessary to have *two* Balance Sheets, i.e., one which sets out the position at the start of the period and the other which shows the state of affairs at the end. We calculate the amount of working capital as shown by each of the two Balance Sheets and compare one amount with the other. It thus at once becomes evident whether the working capital has increased or decreased by the end of the period.

CAPITAL EMPLOYED

10. Capital invested in a business. When a person decides to bring a business into existence he has to supply money to finance the venture. This, as we know, is called the capital of the business, and it is used, or employed, almost entirely, for the purpose of acquiring by purchase certain types of assets, e.g., shop fittings, motor vans, stock, etc. It is therefore true to say that at this stage, before any trading has taken place, the capital employed by the business is measured by the amount of capital invested by the proprietor. This invested capital is normally in the form of money, but sometimes a private possession of the owner, e.g., a motor car, may be treated as part of his invested capital.

EXAMPLE: J. Snodgrass, a baker by trade, decided to commence business on his own account. He had £3,000 in savings, all of which he paid into a Business Bank Account. He used this money in the following manner:

Three months' rent of premises paid in advance	£150
Ovens and equipment	2,200
Stocks of raw materials	160
Delivery van	400

The position, immediately before he commenced to trade, was as follows.

BALANCE SHEET

Capital	£3,000	Ovens and equipment	£2,200
		Motor van	400
		Stocks	160
		Rent prepaid	150
		Cash at bank	90
	£3,000		£3,000

We can see from this Balance Sheet precisely how the capital has been employed in order to equip the business for the purpose of starting to trade.

11. Changes in the capital employed. Once trading has started the capital employed will change. The reason for this is that when trading takes place profits and losses have the immediate effect of altering the amount of the owner's capital, for it must be remembered that profit accrues on a *day to day* basis. For the purposes of this section we will assume that no losses are incurred, but it must be remembered that if they do the effect on the capital employed will be that it is reduced.

Any trading profit which has been made and which is retained in the business, i.e., not withdrawn by the owner for his private use, is, in effect, an *additional* contribution of capital. It follows, therefore, that the capital employed is increased by the amount of the profit retained in the business. This addition is, of course, shown by an increase in the amount of the assets.

Capital employed may be increased in other ways. The proprietor may, for example, decide to expand the business and invest a further sum from his private resources. Alternatively, he may borrow money from various sources, e.g., a loan from a finance house or a bank. To be properly regarded as capital employed any such loan should be for a term of several years since short-term loans are regarded as being of a temporary nature, and therefore *not* to be considered as really being *invested* in the business.

EXAMPLE: After trading successfully for three years, Snodgrass felt that his business could be enlarged provided he could obtain a loan of £4,000. A friend of his, D. Miller, was prepared to lend him this sum for an indefinite period.

Let us suppose that the Balance Sheet of Snodgrass's business showed the following position at this time:

Proprietor's capital		Fixed assets	
Capital and retained		Ovens and equipment	
profits	£4,210	less depreciation	£1,540
		Motor van less	
		depreciation	160
Current liabilities		Current assets	
Creditors	630	Stocks	1,270
		Debtors	490
		Bank	1,380
	£4,840		£4,840

He used the loan of £4,000 to purchase the lease of the shop next door which was for sale for £2,000, and he paid £600 for shop fittings. He had additional ovens installed at a cost of £2,380.

For the purposes of this example we will suppose that these matters had been arranged before the above Balance Sheet had been drawn up and that settlement was made immediately afterwards. The Balance Sheet incorporating these matters would appear thus:

Proprietor's capital		Fixed assets	
Capital and retained		Lease of premises	£2,000
profits	£4,210	Ovens and	
Long-term liabilities		equipment	3,920
Loan from		Shop fittings	600
D. Miller	4,000	Motor van	160
Current liabilities		Current assets	
Creditors	630	Stocks	1,270
		Debtors	490
		Bank	400
	£8,840		£8,840

The capital employed would now amount to:

Total assets	£8,840
Less: Current liabilities	630
Capital employed	**£8,210**

12. An alternative method of calculation. In the two preceding
sections we have shown the most usual method of computing the
capital employed. This method equates the net worth of the business with its employed capital and from the point of view of the
proprietor it tells him what he needs to know. There is, of course,
a weakness in this since it takes no account of any long-term loan
capital which may be involved. It is clear from the above
example that the net worth does not constitute the entire capital
employed, because, in this case, the owner has borrowed £4,000
with a view to using it in the expansion of his business.

This leads us to the main alternative method which is to treat
the total of both fixed and current assets as being the capital
employed. There is sound reasoning behind this view because it
takes into consideration the fact that where goods are supplied to
the firm on credit the suppliers are, in fact, supporting the purchaser financially during the period of credit. If they refused to
transact business on a credit basis and insisted on immediate cash
payment the purchaser would have had to supply additional
capital in cash in order to maintain his business on the present scale.
In the last example, therefore, we would consider that the capital
employed amounted to £8,840 using this alternative method of
calculation.

**13. Excluding certain items from the capital employed compu-
tation.** If, for some reason, any of a firm's assets are not used in
the business it is thought proper that they be excluded when calculating the capital employed. The most obvious example is that
of the asset "Investments". At some time earlier in the history of
the business it might have been found that it held, as one of its
assets, cash considerably in excess of its requirements, and a decision was taken to invest this surplus in some form of outside
investment, e.g., in Government or Local Authority stocks. Such
investments would normally be expected to produce income each
year in the form of interest. Although the interest would form
part of the firm's income, the capital locked up in the investment

could not properly be said to form part of its employed capital. The reason for this is simply that this part of the firm's capital is not being used in the process of earning income in the field where the firm's business interests lie.

Another item which should be excluded from the computation is any expense which was incurred when the business was founded, such as the formation expenses of a limited company. Such expenditure, of course, was necessarily incurred in order to comply with the requirements of the law but it would not be regarded, generally speaking, as being capital employed in the earning of profits.

14. The return on capital employed. The importance to the owner of knowing the amount of capital employed is that it enables him to measure the degree of success or otherwise of his trading operations. The larger the profit made in relation to the capital employed the greater is the success achieved. The converse is obviously true in that smaller profits made with the same employed capital reduce the measure of success.

The ratio of the net profit to the capital employed is used widely when calculating the profitability (i.e., the capability to earn profits) of a business. This is, after all, common sense. When we invest money in some venture, be it a business or stocks and shares, for instance, we look to the reward that such an investment will bring us each year. If the yield is unsatisfactory we may well be tempted to make a change in the hope of a greater return in the future.

EXAMPLE: Grimshaw's capital employed amounts to £15,000. His net profit amounted to £2,000 and he was looking for a return of 10 per cent on his investment:

$$\frac{£2,000}{£15,000} \times 100 = 13.3\%$$

Had his profit amounted to £1,200 the position would have been.

$$\frac{£1,200}{£15,000} \times 100 = 8.0\%$$

We can thus assess the position rapidly. However, it is necessary to say at this point that in practice there may well be various other additional considerations to be taken into account.

PROGRESS TEST 13

Theory

1. Define "working capital".   **(1)**

2. How would you ascertain the working capital of a business?   **(2, 3, 4)**

3. What are the principal ways in which working capital may be (*a*) increased; (*b*) decreased?   **(5, 6)**

4. What is the most usual source from which a business obtains additional working capital?   **(8)**

Practice

5. The Balance Sheet of C. Kingsley's business on 31st March shows the following position:

BALANCE SHEET AS AT 31ST MARCH

Capital	£7,290	Premises	£3,700
Trade creditors	1,460	Fixtures and fittings	600
Accrued expenses	190	Stock	2,500
		Trade debtors	1,850
		Cash at bank	290
	£8,940		£8,940

You are required to state the following.

(*a*) The amount of working capital in the business on 31st March.

(*b*) The effect which each of the following transactions would have on the working capital of the business:

(*i*) cheque received for £3,000 representing a long-term loan from P. Ross;

(*ii*) additional fittings purchased, at a cost of £400, from Chromium Plate Ltd on three months' credit;

(*iii*) stock costing £225 and included at that value in the amount of £2,500 shown above now sold for £200;

(*iv*) C. Kingsley withdrew £100 from the Business Bank Account for private use;

(*v*) C. Kingsley brought her private sewing machine into the business at a valuation of £30.

6. George Butcher's financial year ends on 31st December annually. The Balance Sheets as on 31st December 19–4 and 31st December 19–5, were prepared by Butcher's accountant and are set out below:

	19–4	19–5		19–4	19–5
Capital at 1st Jan.	£8,000	£8,200	Fixed assets at cost	£5,800	£8,900
Further cash introduced	—	1,250	Less: Total depreciation provided to date		
Profit for the year	2,600	3,400		600	1,380
	10,600	12,850		5,200	7,520
Less:					
Drawings	2,400	3,300	Stock	2,600	2,265
	8,200	9,550	Debtors	1,400	1,815
			Bank	800	—
Bank overdraft	—	970			
Creditors	1,800	1,080			
	£10,000	£11,600		£10,000	£11,600

When Butcher compared the two Balance Sheets he expressed some doubts as to the correctness of the profits for 19–5 (amounting to £3,400). He pointed out that he had started the year with £800 in the bank whereas at the end of the year 19–5 he owed the bank £970, i.e., a net decrease of £1,770; and this in spite of the fact that he had actually paid in additional cash of £1,250. He maintained that if he had really made a profit of £3,400 his bank balance must have shown a considerable increase.

You are required:

(a) to prepare a statement showing Butcher how the net worth of the business has increased during the year, setting out in detail the factors which have brought this about;

(b) to compute the amount of Butcher's working capital at 31st December 19–4 and at 31st December 19–5 and to prepare a statement reconciling these two amounts by showing the sources of any increase in the working capital and in what manner any decreases have taken place.

7. Herring and Bone are contemplating the purchase of a business. They have consulted you on the matter and have asked you to advise them as to the average amount of working capital that would require to be invested during the first year's operations.

You are given the following estimates to which you propose to add a further 10 per cent to allow for unforeseen contingencies:

		Figures for year
(*a*)	Average amount locked up in stocks:	
	Finished goods and work in progress	£2,000
	Stocks of materials	3,200
(*b*)	Average period of credit allowed to debtors:	
	Home sales—6 weeks credit	124,800
	Export sales—1½ weeks credit	31,200
(*c*)	Lag in payment of wages and expenses:	
	Wages—1½ weeks	104,000
	Materials—1½ months	19,200
	Rent, rates and insurance—6 months	4,000
	Salaries of office staff—½ week	4,160
	Manager's salary—½ month	3,000
	General expenses—1½ months	24,000
(*d*)	Payments in advance:	
	Overseas salesmen's commission (paid quarterly in advance)	3,200
(*e*)	Undrawn profits retained in the business:	
	On the average	4,400

Set out your calculation of the average amount of working capital the business will require.

CHAPTER XIV

Interpretation and the Use of Ratios

INTERPRETATION

1. The meaning of "interpretation". The *Concise Oxford Dictionary* defines the word "interpret" as "explaining the meaning of abstruse words, writings, etc." Applying this definition to balance sheets and revenue accounts we find that this requires the *analysis* of statements, documents and other relevant material to enable us to build up a picture of a firm's strong points as well as its weak ones. All of this information will relate to events which have happened in the past; that is to say, it is of *historical* significance.

The object of interpreting accounts is to try to look into the future and predict what is going to happen. Future operations may be planned differently from those of the past, but if there is to be a radical departure in methods used any change would require careful thought. It could be that in such circumstances past results might have a very considerable influence on future financial decisions. That this is so can be readily seen in our own personal lives. We take certain decisions from time to time which we know will almost certainly affect our future. Such decisions will, consciously or unconsciously, be made partly by what has happened to us in the past and partly by what we hope will happen to us in the future.

2. The need for comparison. We frequently find in our everyday life that we make comparisons before deciding upon a particular course of action. If, for example, we have to buy some goods we first of all look at the price and then compare it mentally with the price of similar goods in another shop. If the comparison is favourable we probably decide to buy. If, on the other hand, it is unfavourable we will almost certainly go elsewhere. In business life comparisons will also be made not only in the purchasing pattern of goods and materials, but in longer-term aspects.

By the use of accounting ratios we are able to relate certain figures to other ones and to draw conclusions which will, we hope, be of help in making decisions affecting the future of the business. For example, we may look at the ratio (or percentage) of gross profit to sales; this may lead us to the conclusion, for instance, that we are selling too cheaply and cause us to raise our prices forth-with. To be of benefit to a firm there must be a *significant relationship* between the figures used. It would be of little use to the management in comparing the cost of the telephone with, say, the cost of machinery purchased. There needs to be some direct con-nection between the figures which will be of real significance. Ratios can be used to show the strength or otherwise of a firm's financial position. Vitally important matters such as the trend of profits over a period and the growth of the business can be measured.

There are three main standards of comparison which are nor-mally used. These standards compare the most recent figures against:

(a) those of previous periods (usually yearly);

(b) those of other organisations; and,

(c) those which have been budgeted at an earlier date based on the anticipated sales of the next period of trading; a form of educated guesswork.

RATIOS

3. Ratios: general. If one is asked to interpret a balance sheet and accounts it is normally because the person making the request feels that he cannot understand the *significance* of the figures contained therein. He wants clarification and simplification. Because trends are of immense importance in the interpretation of accounts it is highly desirable that balance sheets and revenue accounts for several earlier years are available for study. The most recent figures by themselves will not reveal the amount of information which can be ascertained from an examination of the three or four previous years' trading results set alongside the latest available accounts.

If one refers to various textbooks one is struck by the frightening number of ratios which sometimes appear therein. It is suggested that the majority of these will only be of use in particular cases and it is of little use, therefore, quoting most of them, especially in an examination. For the average student asked to deal with an exam-ination question the chief problem is: "Where do I start?" The three areas which are of general importance are:

(a) profitability;

(b) liquidity; and

(c) stability.

Before looking at these points in detail we need first to consider the interests of certain parties.

INVESTORS AND LENDERS

4. Interested parties. We will understand the matter of accounting ratios more readily if we first consider who is to be classified as an "interested" party. They may conveniently be placed in two groups:

- (*a*) investors; and,
- (*b*) lenders.

5. Investors. In the first group we will place *investors*. They can be classified in the following sub-groups:

- (*a*) possible shareholders in limited companies;
- (*b*) possible partners in private firms;
- (*c*) possible small investors.

These three categories of possible investors are, in the majority of cases, people *outside* the business who therefore have not got access to *inside* information. The most likely exception is the "possible" partner. The use of the word "possible" is intended to imply that the people concerned are not, as yet, committed to investing their money in a particular business. Their interest stems from the fact that they have a certain amount of money available for investment and they will be looking for something that will give them:

- (*a*) security of the money invested; and,
- (*b*) an annual income from their investment.

We give security of the investment pride of place here simply because if that is lacking in the long term the prospect of an annual income becomes uncertain. Such a prospect obviously renders the investment undesirable.

6. Lenders. Under the heading of "lenders" we have two broad classes:

- (*a*) suppliers of goods and services *on credit*; and
- (*b*) direct lenders of money such as banks and finance houses.

Suppliers who sell on credit, whether it be goods or services, do, in fact, *lend* money to their customers even though it be only for a short time. We must, therefore, class them as "interested parties".

PROFITABILITY

7. The ability of a business to make profits. This is usually expressed in the single word "profitability" and is, without question, the most important attribute which a business can possess.

With few exceptions, e.g., charities, people enter business with only one aim, that of making money. In business terms this is called "profit". If profits are not made a business will ultimately close down. There is certainly no possible hope of finding favour with investors where such conditions prevail.

It is hoped that the following tables will help to crystallise the position in the student's mind. Dealing with the two groups we have:

GROUP I: INVESTORS

Interested Party	Main Interest	Area of Interest
Existing share-holders and possible new shareholders	(a) Dividend (b) Market price of shares	(a) Maintenance of present profit margins (b) Possibilities of growth and capital gains
Possible partners	Sufficient profit to make the investment worthwhile	(a) Maintenance and improvement of present profit margins (b) Possibilities of growth

GROUP II: LENDERS

Trade and expense	Ability to pay within the normal terms of credit	(a) Record of firm according to debt-collecting agencies' reports (b) Recent years' earnings record; Composition of *net* worth in recent years per balance sheets filed with registrar of companies
Banks and finance houses	Security of loan	(a) Ability to pay interest on due dates (b) Adequacy of cash flow

8. The significant ratios. In order to decide which ratios can be classed as being "significant" we must assume that recent balance sheets and profit and loss accounts are available for scrutiny.

Interested parties shown in the above tables who would certainly demand their production would be banks, possible partners and potential purchasers of shares in *private* companies.

The significant ratios would be:

Net operating profit : Capital employed
Gross profit : Sales
Net profit : Sales
Net profit : Investor's personal investment

Before dealing with the ratios in detail it will be appropriate to show a Balance Sheet and Profit and Loss Account under Example 1.

EXAMPLE 1: The following Balance Sheet and Revenue Account will be a suitable basis for illustrating calculations of the accounting ratios described later in this chapter.

(a)

BALANCE SHEET AT 31ST DECEMBER 19–1

	£000s	£000s
Fixed assets at cost less depreciation		3,400
Current assets		
Stocks	2,600	
Debtors	500	
Bank	600	
		3,700
TOTAL ASSETS		£7,100
Less: Current liabilities (including provision for taxation)		1,600
CAPITAL EMPLOYED		£5,500
Represented by:		
Ordinary shares		2,000
Preference shares		400
General reserve		1,800
Profit and Loss A/c		500
Loans		800
		£5,500

NOTE: The working capital is calculated as follows:

Current assets	3,700
Less: Current liabilities	1,600
WORKING CAPITAL	£2,100

(b) *Profit and Loss Account for year ended 31st December 19–1*

	£000s
Sales	5,200
Less: Cost of sales	3,760
Gross Profit (27.69%)	1,440
Less: Administration expenses	640
Net profit on trading (after charging depreciation)	800
Less: Loan interest	75
PRE-TAX PROFIT	725
Provision for taxation	375
	350
Preference dividend	32
PROFIT AVAILABLE FOR ORDINARY SHAREHOLDERS	£318

NOTE: The opening figure of stock at 1st January 19–1 was £900,000 at cost price.

9. Profitability: the return on capital employed. The profitability of a business is usually the direct result of the manner in which the firm has been operated. It may be said, therefore, that the most important of the *significant* ratios is the return on capital employed. This is obtained by measuring: NET OPERATING PROFIT: CAPITAL EMPLOYED

As was pointed out in XIII, **13**, if any of a firm's assets are not used in the business it is deemed proper to exclude them in the calculation of capital employed, e.g., investments. It follows that income received from such investments should, logically, be excluded from the net operating profit.

It is customary, when calculating the net operating profit for the purposes of ratios, to exclude any interest paid to the suppliers of finance, e.g., loan interest. Dividends paid are also excluded from the calculation. Payments of this type are *rewards* for investing money in the business and are *not* part of the *operating costs*. So, when we speak of operational cost we are speaking only of those expenses which form part of the productive and distributive processes and the sales revenue which arises from them. It is the normal practice to use the figure of profit *before* any deduction of tax. After all, *tax is the share of profit* which is taken by the Government.

$$\text{RETURN ON CAPITAL EMPLOYED} = \frac{\text{Profit before interest and taxation}}{\text{Capital employed}}$$

Applying the figures in Example 1 we have:

$$\frac{£800,000}{£5,500,000} \times 100 = 14.54\%$$

So the return for every £100 invested in this particular year amounts to £14.54.

10. Profitability: the percentage return on sales. Accountants usually call this the "Gross Profit percentage". What they mean by this term is, the amount of gross profit made on every £100 worth of sales. They express it as a percentage of the sales.

The sales made by a firm are its most important feature, for without sales there can be no profit. Sales make profit. We already know that the capital invested in a business (from whatever source it comes) is the capital employed. It is employed for the sole purpose of generating profit. The capital is employed, i.e., has been spent, on the acquisition of various fixed assets and on stock. There is thus a very clear connection between profit and capital employed.

The percentage of *net* profit on sales is calculated in the same manner but after deduction of administration and selling expenses.

(*a*) To calculate the percentage of gross profit we employ the following formula:

$$\text{GROSS PROFIT PERCENTAGE} = \frac{\text{Gross profit} \times 100}{\text{Sales}}$$

Applying the figures in Example 1:

$$\frac{£1,440,000 \times 100}{£5,200,000} = 27.69\%$$

(*b*) The percentage of net profit on every £100 worth of sales is calculated similarly:

$$\text{NET PROFIT PERCENTAGE} = \frac{\text{Net profit} \times 100}{\text{Sales}}$$

Applying the figures in Example 1 (*before* charging loan interest but *after* charging depreciation) we have:

$$\frac{£800,000 \times 100}{£5,200,000} = 15.38\%$$

11. Profitability: the percentage return on invested capital. In this test of profitability we compare the net profit (after taxation) with the total investment of the owner. In the case of a sole trader this is very simple. We take the net profit after the estimated (or, actual, if available) amount of taxation which the profit will attract, multiply by 100 and divide by the amount of capital the proprietor has invested in the business. To ascertain the figure for a limited company we take the final figure of profit, i.e., after tax and also after provision for any dividend which is due to the *preference* shareholders.

If we take the appropriate figures from Example 1 it can be seen that the profit available for the ordinary shareholders amounts to £318,000, while the ordinary share capital is £2,000,000. Thus:

$$\frac{£318,000 \times 100}{£2,000,000} = 15.9\%$$

This is not an over-all measure of profitability but is concerned with the return which ordinary shareholders could possibly expect. In fact, in this case nothing has been set aside from the profits to reserve (or "ploughed back") and so the return which the shareholders could expect, in reality, would probably be some £150,000 less, i.e., around £170,000 or 8.5 per cent.

LIQUIDITY

12. Solvency and liquidity. Solvency and liquidity are not necessarily interchangeable terms. A business may be solvent but yet have liquidity problems. To be solvent a business must be in a position to be able to pay its creditors without undue difficulty even though for the moment it may lack the cash or debtors to do so. Provided that it can obtain overdraft facilities from its bank no problem is likely to arise. Not that the bank is a fairy godmother. Banks are run by people whose job is to manage money—other people's money! A banker is not going to put money which does not belong to him to any avoidable risk; on the other hand if he is satisfied that the firm which wishes to arrange an overdraft to meet its immediate liabilities has sufficient underlying strength, e.g., owning its land and buildings or possessing realisable investments, his bank will normally be perfectly willing for an overdraft facility to be granted.

On the other hand, the underlying position of the business may be rather weak. Let us suppose, for example, that it does not own any fixed assets of substance; it perhaps rents its premises, its plant is out of date and its motor vehicles are old. There is nothing here to tempt a bank to allow much in the way of an overdraft because there is no real security for it to fall back on to recover its money. The business might be carrying on but would certainly be regarded as being close to insolvency because it has insufficient financial strength and cannot offer any assets as security.

The dictionary defines "solvency" as "having sufficient money to meet one's liabilities". A state of "liquidity" is defined as "owning assets which are easily convertible into cash".

For a firm to be liquid it should have enough cash and "near-cash" (debtors) to enable it to meet the immediate demands of:

(a) creditors for goods supplied;

(b) creditors for services rendered such as telephone, electricity supply, etc.; and

(c) wages and salaries of employees.

The use of the word "immediate" does not mean "instantaneous". In the context of a business we would have perhaps a period of four to six weeks in which to satisfy the demands of creditors for goods and services. On the other hand there would be a shorter period available for the payment of employees. Wages are normally payable each week and salaries usually at the

end of each month. If the workforce is large the weekly requirement of cash will be large and so it is clear that judging the
liquidity of a business is a matter for the individual firm.

13. Short-term liquidity. The ability of a business to pay its short-
term creditors can be measured in the two following ways:

(*a*) by means of the "current" or "working capital" ratio; and
(*b*) by the so-called "acid test" ratio (sometimes called the
"quick assets" ratio).

14. The "current" or "working capital" ratio. This ratio is the
most commonly used of all balance sheet ratios and its purpose is
to measure the adequacy of current assets cover for current
liabilities. It is generally regarded as desirable that the current
liabilities should be covered at least twice by the current assets,
i.e., for every £1 of current liabilities there should be £2 of current
assets. This, it must be understood, is an approximate figure and
is not laid down as a hard and fast line. The circumstances of the
business concerned will have an important bearing in deciding
what is, in fact, a satisfactory ratio. It may well be that even
though a firm's current assets are no more than, say 1.5:1 its
underlying strength will make the obtaining of overdraft facilities
easy. In such circumstances no problem arises.

The ratio is calculated very simply as shown below:

$$\frac{\text{Current assets}}{\text{Current liabilities}}$$

If we refer to the Balance Sheet in Example 1 we obtain the
following figures:

$$\frac{\text{Current assets}}{\text{Current liabilities}} = \frac{£3,700,000}{£1,600,000} = 2.31:1$$

which appears to be a satisfactory ratio.

15. The "acid test" or "quick assets" ratio. To calculate this ratio
we will *exclude* the closing stock from our workings. We take
only those current assets and "short-term" investments which can
be turned into cash in a very short time.

QUICK ASSETS

(*a*) Cash in hand;   (*c*) Short-term investments;
(*b*) Cash at bank;   (*d*) Debtors.

Normally, we would not consider that "prepayments" should rank as "quick" for the reasons (a) they cannot usually be turned into cash, and (b) they are almost always only a tiny proportion of the total of quick assets.

Stocks are invariably left out of the quick assets calculation because they are not considered to be *readily* realisable. All stocks have to go through two processes which could take several months before being turned into cash. The more difficult of the two processes is the selling of the goods which may take quite a long time. The other process is collecting the debt from the customer.

The ratio is calculated thus:

$$\frac{\text{Current assets } \textit{less } \text{stocks}}{\text{Current liabilities}}$$

Based on the figures in Example 1 we obtain the following result:

$$\frac{\text{£}3,700,000 \textit{ less } \text{£}2,600,000}{\text{£}1,600,000} = \frac{\text{£}1,100,000}{\text{£}1,600,000} = 0.688:1.000$$

In theory, 0.688:1.000 is not an entirely satisfactory ratio. A ratio of 1:1 would be regarded as satisfactory since it would mean that all the immediate liabilities could be settled without the firm being forced to sell stock off cheaply, or even having to sell some of its fixed assets to raise funds. We must use a measure of commonsense, however. In real life a "quick asset" ratio of about 0.7:1.0 would be regarded as adequate in nearly all circumstances.

FINANCIAL STABILITY

16. The use of assets. The degree of profitability which a business achieves is bound to be reflected by the way in which it employs its capital, and, therefore, its assets. If machines are left idle they are being underutilised and the capital which is locked up in them is being partially wasted. In the same way, if *too much* money is locked up in stocks or debtors then the capital represented by these assets is being used inefficiently.

17. Stock turnover. When we speak of the "turnover of stock" we mean the *sale* of those goods specifically bought for the purpose of being sold. Thus a trader might spend £2,000 on his opening stock of goods when he first starts up in business. When these goods have all been sold we say that he has "turned his stock over". By selling (or turning over) his stock he makes a certain amount of profit. It follows that the *more often* he turns his stock over the *greater* will be his profit.

EXAMPLE: A, B and C all open similar businesses on the same day, each one investing £2,000 in the purchase of goods for resale. The gross profit made for each business was at the rate of 33⅓ per cent of the selling price. Mr. A turns his stock over once in this first year of trading. Mr. B turns his stock over twice during the same period, while Mr. C turns his over four times.

The amounts of gross profit will therefore be:

Number of times stock turned over during the year	Sales for the year	Gross Profit
Mr. A 1	£3,000	£1,000 (33⅓% × £3,000)
Mr. B 2	£6,000	£2,000 (33⅓% × £6,000)
Mr. C 4	£12,000	£4,000 (33⅓% × £12,000)

From this example it is plain to see that the *speed* of turnover, i.e., the number of times the stock is sold out, replaced and then sold again, has a tremendous bearing on the amount of profit made in a trading period.

18. The rate of stock turnover. The *rate* at which stock is sold is an indication of whether the quantity of stocks held are justified in relation to the total sales. If stock is sold quickly (at, of course, a normally acceptable rate of gross profit) the liquidity position should be healthy. Stocks which lie for months (sometimes years) on the shelves or in the storeroom represent "dead" money. That is to say, money which could otherwise be used to buy more up-to-date and more readily saleable lines and so produce profit in place of stagnation.

To measure the rate at which stock is turned over, i.e., bought, sold and replacements purchased, basically, we simply divide the sales by the stock. There is a snag here, however, because different *bases of valuation* are used. While sales are made at "cost price plus *mark-up*", stocks are valued *at cost*. To overcome this difficulty we use the device of *reducing* the sales to cost price, i.e., opening stock plus purchases less closing stock which gives us the *cost of goods sold*. We then divide this result by the stock. Thus we show the formula:

$$\frac{\text{Cost of sales}}{\text{Stock at cost}}$$

which gives us the rate of stock turnover.

Finally, the stock figure which must be used in the calculation is the *average* figure of stock held during the period. For examination purposes we find that usually only the opening and closing stock figures are given and so we take the *average* of these. This will be, of course, only an approximate figure. A much closer figure would be the average of the stocks held at the end of each month of the period in question, but unless this is given there is nothing to be done about it. Only the management of the business would have access to such figures in real life situations.

From Example 1(*b*) let us take the "cost of sales" which is shown as being £3,760,000, while Example 1(*a*) gives the closing stock the value of £2,600,000. The note at the foot of Example 1(*b*) states that the value of the opening stock, at cost, was £900,000. Thus the opening and closing stocks totalled £3,500,000 which gives the *average* stock held as £1,750,000. Applying the formula we obtain the rate of stock turnover.

$$\frac{\text{Cost of sales}}{\text{Average stock at cost}} = \frac{£3,760,000}{£1,750,000} = 2.15 \text{ times}$$

Should it be impossible to calculate the "cost of sales" an alternative is available. We add the profit "mark-up" to the average stock thus raising it to the selling price and use the formula of:

$$\frac{\text{Sales (at selling price)}}{\text{Average stock (at } selling \text{ price)}}$$

thus comparing like figures with like.

One of the principal benefits of ascertaining the rate of stock turnover is that by comparing the result with the previous year or years the trend, if there is any variation, becomes apparent and, if necessary, steps can be taken to rectify deviations. If the rate is *declining* this means that the volume of stock in terms of money has *increased* in relation to sales. This is a bad sign because it means that the investment of capital (money) in stock is not producing the amount of profit that it was hitherto, and therefore, the result must be judged as being an *inefficient* use of capital.

Consider the following tables assuming that there has been *no inflation* of the currency:

TABLE I

	Year 1	Year 2	Year 3
Cost of sales / Average stock	£40,000 / £3,600	£44,000 / £3,600	£50,000 / £3,600
Rate of stock turn	11.11 times	12.22 times	13.89 times

In Year 1 the average stock carried was a little too high when compared with the two following years, since the stock figure has remained *constant* against the *increase* in sales. This suggests an alert and efficient management.

TABLE II

	Year 1	Year 2	Year 3
Cost of sales / Average stock	£40,000 / £4,000	£44,000 / £5,000	£50,000 / £7,000
Rate of stock turn	10.00 times	8.80 times	7.14 times

Note that in both Tables the sales have remained identical. In Table II the stock increases.

In Year 3 the amount of money locked up in stock has nearly doubled when compared with Year 1. The *rate* of stock turnover has dropped alarmingly suggesting that something could be seriously wrong somewhere. At the same time it is important that other matters should be considered before jumping to the conclusion that inefficiency is at the root of the trouble. For instance consider the following points.

(a) It may have been decided that larger or more varied stocks may be carried in order to satisfy the demands of customers.

(b) How does the rate of stock turnover compare with similar firms? Is the rate of decline general or is our firm the exception?

(c) Do the figures used for calculating the average stock represent fairly the stock figures carried throughout the year? Perhaps the Christmas trade requires an enormous volume of stock, whereas when the year ends on, let us say, 30th June, only a small amount of stock is carried. If this is the case and the *average* of opening and closing stock taken, the rate of turnover could be wildly astray.

19. The usage of fixed assets. This is an important feature when measuring a firm's performance. The *higher* the rate of use of fixed assets the more effectively they are being used. In a manufacturing firms fixed assets are used to generate sales, i.e. the product manufactured has a certain rate of sales which brings profits to the business.

Looking at Example 1 we see that under (*a*) the fixed assets are valued at £3,400,000, and under (*b*) the sales amounted to £5,200,000. The formula in this case is:

$$\frac{\text{Sales}}{\text{Fixed assets}}$$

Translated into the figures of Example 1 we have:

$$\frac{£5,200,000}{£3,400,000} = \text{a usage of 1.53 times.}$$

Suppose that the sales had amounted to £6,200,000 instead of £5,200,000 we would find that the usage was 1.82 times. This is a considerable improvement in the utilisation of the fixed assets when compared with the figures of Example 1.

20. Debtor control. This feature is yet another instance of how a firm may test the efficiency with which it employs its capital. By the use of this ratio we measure the average time allowed to debtors for the settlement of their accounts. It must be noted that here we are specifically dealing with *trade* debtors, i.e. customers, and we are assuming that all the sales are made on credit.

The *average* of daily credit sales is obtained by dividing the total sales for the year by 365. We then divide the average so found into the total debtors at the year end. The result shows the number of days' sales represented by the debtors, i.e. how many days credit they are taking before paying for their goods.

From Example 1(*b*) we see that the sales for the year amounted to £5,200,000. Applying the above method we obtain:

$$\frac{£5,200,000}{365} = £14,247 \text{ sales per day.}$$

From Example 1(*a*) we find that the debtors at the year end amounted to 500,000.

$$\frac{£500,000}{14,247} = 35,$$

meaning that 35 days credit can be said to be given to each customer.

To test the efficiency of the debtor control we need to ascertain the *expected* period of credit given to customers (often referred to as "the terms of trade"). If thirty days' credit is normal in the example above then there is inefficiency; if forty days' was the normal time allowed to customers then the debtors control will be regarded as being efficient.

THE CAPITAL RATIOS

21. The ratio of capital employed to total indebtedness. The assets of a private business are normally owned by the proprietor. When, however, we come to examine the finances of limited companies we find that the money supplied to buy the assets is often contributed, in part anyway, by outsiders with spare cash to invest, and not by the *owners* of the business, the shareholders. In addition to these outsiders we have to add creditors for goods and services, since they too help to finance any business. If a firm had to pay immediate cash for everything then it would need to obtain extra capital to that which it had already. Thus the significance of the amount of loan capital supplied by creditors becomes apparent.

To assess the significance of this we need to measure the total volume of the assets against the total owed to outsiders, i.e. people who are *not* shareholders (assuming that we are dealing with a limited company).

Referring to Example 1(a) we see that:

Fixed assets	£3,400,000
Current assets	3,700,000
TOTAL ASSETS	£7,100,000
Current liabilities	£1,600,000
Loans	800,000
OWING TO OUTSIDERS	£2,400,000

So,

$$\frac{\text{Outside creditors}}{\text{Total assets}} = \frac{2,400,000}{7,100,000} = 0.34 : 1.00$$

In this example we have used the total assets as being the measure of the capital employed. There are other methods by which the capital employed is calculated.

22. The ratio of capital employed to fixed assets. The object of this ratio is to show the extent to which the fixed assets are covered by the proprietors' funds. It should be noted that this ratio is usually used in the appraisal of the capital structure of a limited company. The money invested in a limited company comes mainly from people who purchase its shares. They are called shareholders and, as such, are the proprietors of the business. All other investors are *lenders* or *loan creditors*. In most cases they are called debenture-holders. These debenture-holders are regarded as being *outsiders*, i.e., not owners of any part of the company but merely casual people who have *lent* the company some money. It is the shareholders who *own* the company.

Where the fixed assets are not fully owned by the shareholders there is always the risk that the outsiders will demand repayment of their loan and thus force the company into liquidation.

Taking the appropriate figures from Example 1(a) we find:

	£000s	£000s
Shareholders' funds:		
Ordinary shares	£2,000	
Preference shares	400	
General reserve	1,800	
Profit and Loss Account	500	
		£4,700
Fixed assets		£3,400

So,

$$\frac{\text{Shareholders' funds}}{\text{Fixed assets}} = \frac{4,700}{3,400} = 1.38 : 1.00$$

From these calculations we see that the shareholders have invested £1.38 in the fixed assets as against the outsiders' investment of £1.00. This position can be regarded as being satisfactory.

23. The management and business ratios. We have set out above the more usual ratios in which the management of a firm may be particularly interested. All the information needed to calculate them should be readily available from the firm's records. On the other hand much of the information required for the calculation of these ratios is not available to the investing public although it would have to be made available to, say, a bank manager if a loan were being considered. Similarly, if a private firm was seeking a new partner such information would be bound to be made available to him to enable him to reach a decision. It is the general public, interested in purchasing shares in limited companies, who do *not* have access to this inside information and have to rely upon such calculations as the price/earnings ratio, dividend cover, etc., which may be obtainable from investment analysis. Banks and stockbrokers can help here. All the same, it cannot be denied that a lot of their calculations must be guesswork, even though it may be "inspired" guesswork. Some of these matters are dealt with in the author's *Company Accounts* (2nd edition, 1978) which is available in the Macdonald & Evans Handbook series.

Students may rest assured that examination questions requiring calculations will give all the relevant figures to enable the correct answer to be obtained. On the other hand, many questions are so framed that a knowledge of each type of ratio is needed in case details are asked for.

Finally, it should be apparent that the application of some or all of the ratios dealt with in this chapter can open up a new dimension to the accountancy student, and it is hoped that his appetite may have been suitably whetted.

GENERAL EXAMPLE:

Oriental Enterprises Ltd., has a subsidiary company, Confucian Ltd., of which it owns 55 per cent of the ordinary shares. Confucian Ltd. has enjoyed a marked degree of autonomy in the past, but recently its managing director retired suddenly because of ill health. As a preliminary to further investigation the chairman of Oriental Enterprises Ltd., has asked you to report to him on the current situation of Confucian Ltd., as revealed by the information set out below.

CONFUCIAN LTD.
BALANCE SHEET AS AT 31ST MARCH

	19–0	19–1
Ordinary share capital	£150,000	£150,000
General Reserve	35,000	40,000
Profit and Loss A/c	4,880	5,240
Debentures (secured on land and buildings)	50,000	25,000
Trade creditors	32,790	58,520
Current taxation	8,000	10,000
Dividend payable	15,000	15,000
Bank overdraft	—	50,000
	£295,670	£353,760
Land and buildings (revalued 19–0)	£75,000	£75,000
Plant (cost less depreciation to date)	65,000	113,000
Vehicles	10,000	12,000
Stock	50,940	73,235
Debtors	49,730	60,525
Quoted investments	44,000	20,000
Cash	1,000	—
	£295,670	£353,760

Sales revenue for the year to 31st March 19–1 was £240,000. Depreciation for the same period on plant was £9,750, and vans £4,000.

(A.C.A.)

To: The Chairman,
    Oriental Enterprises Ltd.
From: Chief Accountant   10th June 19–1

*Report on the current situation of
Confucian Ltd.*

(a) Profitability
The return on gross capital employed for the year ended March 31st 19–1 is modest at 8.6 per cent as disclosed by the primary ratio:

Net profit before tax: Gross capital employed
£30,360: £353,760 = 8.6%

NOTE. To find net profit see working on p. 255.

The principal reason for the poor return would appear to be under-utilisation of resources; in addition the net profit margin on sales may also be capable of improvement. This is indicated by the secondary ratios:

Net profit: Sales
£30,360: £240,000 = 12.7%
Sales: Capital employed
£240,000: £353,760 = 68%

(b) *Solvency*
Working capital has diminished drastically in 19–0/–1 compared with the previous year, as revealed by the following ratios:

	Year ended March 31st	
	19–0	*19–1*
Current assets	£145,670	153,760
Less: Current liabilities	55,790	133,520
	£89,880	£20,240
Working capital ratio	2.6:1	1.2:1
Quick assets ratio (see note on p. 255)	1.7:1	0.6:1

The imminent need to meet dividends of £15,000 in the absence of liquid resources is rather disquieting and may necessitate the realisation of investments or recourse to further borrowing. Should the bank press for a substantial reduction in the overdraft and further debentures become payable in the near future disaster could conceivably ensue.

Assuming that all sales are on credit terms and spread evenly, in terms of sterling, over the year, the company effectively extends some three months' credit to its customers: this may be considered excessive and call for more effective credit control and/or a reduction in the period of credit allowed, provided that this is not inimical to the company's business.

(c) *Movement of Funds*
The utilisation of short-term finance to meet the costs of expansion, i.e. the long-term application of funds, may be illus-

trated by the following statement for the year ended 31st March
19–1:

Opening cash		£1,000
Cash flow: Net profit (after tax)	£20,360	
Depreciation	13,750	
	34,110	
Less: Dividend	15,000	
		19,110
		20,110
Application of funds:		
Purchase of plant		
£(48,000 + 9,750)	57,750	
Purchase of vehicles		
£(2,000 + 4,000)	6,000	
Debentures repaid	25,000	
		88,750
Decrease in working capital		(68,640)

	Source	Application
Changes in working capital:		
Creditors	£25,730	
Taxation	2,000	
Bank overdraft	50,000	
Quoted investments	24,000	
Stock		£22,295
Debtors		10,795
	£101,730	£33,090
Net source		68,640

From the above statement it will be apparent that expenditure of
approximately £64,000 on fixed assets and £33,000 on current

assets has been financed in the main by an increase in creditors and the bank overdraft, while the redemption of debentures has been met by the sale of investments. It seems clear that the company has embarked upon a programme of expansion, although it is difficult to see how the day-to-day costs of this are to be met in the light of the precarious solvency position. In view of this, consideration might be given to raising further capital, if any remains unissued.

There appears to be some disparity between the increases in the items associated with expansion, as follows:

	At 31st March 19–0	Increase during year ended 31st March 19–1	
Plant (at written down values)	£65,000	£48,000	74%
Stock	50,940	22,295	44%
Debtors	49,730	10,795	22%

The reasons for the disparity may be many and varied, while the increased percentage in the plant acquired (probably at inflated prices) at written down values will not necessarily be accompanied by a corresponding percentage increase in the value of stocks and debtors. If an analysis of stocks between raw materials and finished stocks, and the exact date when additional machinery was purchased were available, further conclusions could be drawn. Assuming that the additional plant was purchased early in 19–0/–1 the respective growth rates suggest either that expansion is not yet complete, or point to a long production cycle, so that the expansion may not yet have been fully realised, as suggested by the low turnover of capital employed. However, the presence of excessive quantities of finished stocks at 31st March 19–1 would tend to upset these conclusions by indicating dilatory salesmanship or an abortive venture.

(d) *Ownership*

The increased amount due to outsiders can be seen by comparing total indebtedness with shareholders' funds, as follows:

Year ended 31st March 19–0
£105,790:£189,880 = 0.6:1

Year ended 31st March 19–1
£158,520:£195,240 = 0.8:1

At 31st March 19–1 shareholders' funds (£195,240) were less than the fixed assets (£200,000) while more than one-third of the gross capital employed was provided by short-term creditors, i.e., current liabilities amounting to £133,520.

(e) *Dividend Cover*
The dividend was the same for both years at 10 per cent; the cover being as follows for the year ended 31st March 19–1:

Profits *available* for dividend : Dividend
£20,360 : £15,000 = 1.4 : 1

The cover was, therefore, fairly low, leaving approximately one-quarter of the profits available for retention.

_____ (Signed)
Chief Accountant

NOTE 1:
Working to find net profit
Net profit before tax for year ended 31st March 19–1:

Increase in general reserve	£5,000
Increase in Profit and Loss Account	360
Current taxation	10,000
Dividend payable	15,000
	£30,360

NOTE 2: The quick assets ratio is calculated on the following basis:

Debtors + Quoted Investments + Cash : Current liabilities.

PROGRESS TEST 14

Theory

1. What do you understand by the word "interpretation" as applied to accountancy? **(1)**
2. What are the main standards of comparison used when examining the results of a period of training? **(2)**

3. There are three main areas of importance to be looked at when interpreting a balance sheet and revenue account (Profit and Loss Account). What are these three areas? (3)

4. People are sometimes interested in investing money in a business. Classify the people who are likely to be interested and state to what aspects of a business they might pay particular attention. (4, 5, 6, 7)

5. In the course of examining the accounts of a firm with a view to investing money therein what important ratios would you look at in relation to the earning capacity of the business? (8, 9, 10, 11)

6. Explain the difference between solvency and liquidity. (12)

7. What is meant by the "current" or "working capital" ratio? How would you calculate it? (14)

8. What are "quick" assets? Explain what you understand by the term "acid test". (15)

9. We meet the expression "stock turn" or "stock turnover" in considering the financial stability and efficiency of a business. Why is speed of turnover regarded as being of great importance? (16, 17)

10. Stock turnover can be a useful indicator of the efficiency of a business. How is this so? (18)

11. How do we calculate the rate of stock turnover? (18)

12. What can the rate of use of fixed assets tell us? (19)

Practice

13. The sales and gross profit of a business for the last three years were:

	19–5	*19–6*	*19–7*
Sales	£35,171	£37,609	£38,938
Gross Profit	£14,380	£10,558	£13,452

Calculate the percentage of gross profit to sales in each year.

If you find that the annual percentages vary, state what, in your opinion, might be the cause or causes of these variations.

14. Calculate the ratio of gross profit to sales for the years ending on 31st December 19–8, and 19–9, from the figures set out below:

	19–8	19–9		19–8	19–
Stock at start of period	£6,170	£4,920	Sales	£59,940	£65,930
materials purchased	16,810	22,150			
	22,980	27,070			
Less: Closing stock at end of period	4,920	4,060			
	18,060	23,010			
Manufacturing Wages	14,750	16,960			
Factory expenses	8,990	9,880			
	41,800	49,850			
Gross profit	18,140	16,080			
	£59,940	£65,930		£59,940	£65,930

What do you consider to be the reasons for the fall in the gross profit percentage?

Your answer should be supported by the percentage rise or fall in the various items of expenditure and income.

You are to assume that the volume of production was the same in each year.

15. You are required to:

(a) explain what is meant by the following terms, giving also the context in which each one is commonly used:

    (i) Lead time,
    (ii) Period of credit,
    (iii) Cash forecast,
    (iv) Cash budget,
    (v) Funds statement,
    (vi) Cash flow,
    (vii) Liquidity,
    (viii) Insolvency;

(*b*) define the two accounting ratios most commonly used for management control purposes explaining any terms used in each definition and also the reasons why each one is valuable.

(I.C.A.)

16. Describe the principal ratios which you consider significant when interpreting accounts and explain the inferences which may be drawn from their use.

(I.C.A.)

Examination Technique

Preparation

The only road to certain success in accountancy examinations is for the student to have acquired a *thoroughly sound knowledge* of double-entry book-keeping. Unless his knowledge is soundly based, he will forever find himself in a twilight world where some things are understood dimly and where a great deal is completely incomprehensible. Many students regrettably fall into this category and, as a result, fail miserably in their efforts to master the subject.

It must be pointed out that to have a thoroughly sound knowledge of the principles of book-keeping the student must first of all know *why* things are done. It can be claimed with some justification that book-keeping is a logical discipline and this is manifest to anyone who really understands book-keeping. When one accepts that book-keeping *is* logical, it follows that reasoning can be applied to its problems. This is the key to making good progress. There is, indeed, a basic reason for everything that is done in book-keeping, and since the principles of book-keeping are applied one hundred per cent to accountancy problems it follows that without a thorough knowledge of the fundamentals, examination success will be very hard to attain.

There is a second ingredient which is required for success in accountancy examinations. This is *practice* in the working of problems. Furthermore, this practice must be a continuous exercise. In the months of preparation before the examination, a very great deal of the student's time must be devoted to the working of problems. Accountancy is not a subject which can be mastered just by reading. It is an intensely practical subject and practical subjects can only be mastered by *constant* practice. Ideally, at least two hours a day for five days a week should be spent on working practical problems in accountancy during the months of preparation for your examination. For this you should acquire as many past examination papers *with worked solutions* as you can. It does not matter which examining body's papers you obtain; they will all afford you the opportunity for plentiful and varied practice. (Quite a number of organisations specialise in supplying past examination papers and they usually advertise in the professional journals.)

In addition, you should obtain *several* books on accountancy. Do not rely on just one book. One finds that some books deal with specific aspects of accountancy better than others. Again, the approach of one author may appeal to one student but not to another. Hence a little variety in your textbooks may prove to be of great value.

At the examination

In these hints on examination technique, two assumptions have been made. These are:

(*a*) that the student has covered the syllabus; and

(*b*) that he has a reasonable grasp of the principles of the subject.

To these a third could well be added, i.e., that no student can reasonably hope to achieve 100 per cent of the available marks, neither is it necessary for him to do so to pass the examination. This is not only a comforting thought but it is also common sense and should be borne in mind when in the examination hall. It is better to answer some of the questions *really well* and gain sufficient marks in that way than to answer all inadequately and probably fail.

Most of the professional bodies require the candidate to answer five questions in accountancy examinations. It is only very occasionally that the answers to six questions are called for. Some bodies give a choice, e.g., seven questions are set with five to be answered.

Choice. Where a choice of questions is offered, the student should be very careful to answer only one of the alternatives.

It is by no means uncommon to find students disregarding this point. Whether they do so in error or because they find that they can answer both, it must be pointed out emphatically that they will be credited only with the marks attaching to *one* of their answers. Which one will depend upon the view taken by the examiner. He may adopt the view that the first one dealt with by the candidate is the one which is to count. On the other hand, he may be more charitable and take the trouble to mark both answers, crediting the candidate with the higher scoring answer. Both questions would, of course, carry the same possible maximum mark.

Allocation of marks. In accountancy examinations, marks are allocated to certain parts of the answers. It is most important for the student to realise this. A simple illustration will make the point easier to appreciate.

Suppose a question set out the Trial Balance of a firm and beneath it a number of adjustments which had to be incorporated in the final accounts and balance sheet. The total marks for the question might be 25.

Three marks might be awarded for dealing correctly with the provision for doubtful debts, one mark for deducting a pre-payment from the Profit and Loss Account charge for insurance and a fifth mark for entering the balance under current assets in the Balance Sheet. Two marks might be given to the correct treatment of goods on sale or return in the Trading Account and yet another mark for the inclusion of the item in the closing stock in the Balance Sheet. This pattern will be continued throughout the remainder of the question. Finally, an award of, say, three marks might be given for presentation.

Many students seem to think that because they have managed to balance both sides of the balance sheet they will score full marks. This is far from reality. Conversely, many feel that because they have not balanced they will score no marks. This again is far from true.

Time wasted. If the student has prepared himself reasonably well for the examination, he will expect to find some questions, at least, of a type that he recognises and which he can make a fair attempt at answering. Often, however, having worked through a question, he finds that he must have gone wrong at some point since his final answer is clearly incorrect.

There is a great danger here that he will spend an inordinate amount of time trying to locate his mistake. At this stage he should do no more than quickly run over his answer, making a pencil cross against any points of doubt—unless, of course, he can see the cause of his error at once. In this latter case the necessary adjusting entries should be made. It is more likely, however, that his error will not be immediately apparent and, in that case, his best plan is to leave matters as they stand and *not to waste any time at all* at this stage.

Many students have failed examinations because they wasted a vast amount of time in a fruitless effort to discover an error. In so many cases its discovery would have made only a very small difference to the number of marks earned.

If the mistake is not immediately apparent, *move to the next question at once.*

Allocating time to questions. If you have a watch, place it on the desk in front of you.

The normal maximum marks for an accountancy paper is 100. The normal time allowance is three hours and this allows nearly two minutes per mark. Nearly every professional examination shows the number of marks allocated to each question, so you can make a rough calculation of the number of minutes that you can afford to devote to each question.

It is at this point that your attention is drawn to the opening remarks of this section, i.e., that none but the most gifted student can hope to score full marks. If you score sixty you will be sure of passing. Are you capable of scoring sixty? Do the questions appear to give you that hope? Can you answer four of the five well, or only three? These questions can only be answered by the candidate with the examination paper in front of him. If the reply to the first question is favourable, then take care to allocate the appropriate amount of time per question before settling down to work. But remember that if, for example, you answer four questions out of five, your sixty marks must be earned from a total of, perhaps, eighty possible marks only. It would be wise, therefore, to leave half an hour at the end for going on to another question to earn a few bonus marks and for "polishing up" your answers.

By adopting this technique, quite a lot of the "pressure" will be eased. The result will almost certainly be that a far better paper will be handed in than would otherwise be the case.

Suggested Answers to Examination Questions

Chapter I

5

TRIAL BALANCE

Capital		£4,436
Stock—typewriters	£3,650	
—adding machines	775	
Equipment	688	
Bank overdraft		568
Cash	138	
Rent	29	
Wages	23	
Stationery	5	
Electricity	8	
Creditors (£93 + £320)		413
Debtors (£45 + £176)	221	
Repairs	10	
Sales		230
Purchases	100	
	£5,647	£5,647

6(a) BALANCE SHEET 31ST DECEMBER 19–4

Capital at			Fixed assets		
1st January	£5,500		Goodwill		£500
Add: net			Premises		5,000
profit	1,703		Motor van		
	———		(£350 − £70)		280
	7,203		Fixtures		
Less:			(£300 − £30)		270
drawings	1,1000				———
	———	£6,203			6,050
Current liabilities			Current assets		
Trade creditors	600		Stock	£400	
Wages accrued	12		Debtors £1,200		
Bank overdraft	900		*Less:*		
	———	1,512	Provision 60		
				——— 1,140	
			Rates prepaid	50	
			Cash	75	
				———	1,665
		———			———
		£7,715			£7,715
		═══			═══

7

TRIAL BALANCE

Capital		£5,000
Bank	£371	
Cash	30	
Goodwill	1,291	
Shop fittings	795	
Stock	600	
Motor car	450	
Creditor for motor car		300
Trade creditors		770
Sales		1,266
Debtors	420	
Purchases	1,040	
Lease	2,100	
Wages	80	
National insurance	24	
Postage	8	
Sundries	7	
Drawings	100	
Rent	20	
	£7,336	£7,336

NOTE: On the basis of a purchase price of £4,000 for the assets of the business the goodwill amounts to £941. However, you have undertaken to pay off the creditors (£350) as well. You will, therefore, be out of pocket by a total of £4,350 in respect of the overall purchase of the business. The usual way in which the acceptance of liabilities is dealt with is to debit Goodwill Account with the amount of the liability *in addition to* the value attributed to goodwill in the purchase price. So goodwill becomes £1,291 (£941 + £350). An alternative to this treatment is to debit the Capital Account and credit Creditors Account.

Trading and Profit and Loss Account

Stock	£600	Sales	£1,266
Purchases	1,040		
	1,640		
Less: Closing stock	674		
	966		
Gross profit	300		
	£1,266		£1,266
Wages and N.I.	104	Gross profit	300
Rent	20		
Postage	8		
Sundry expenses	7		
	139		
Net profit	161		
	£300		£300

BALANCE SHEET

Capital	£5,000	Fixed assets			
Add: Net		Goodwill			£1,291
profit	161	Lease			2,100
		Shop fittings			795
	5,161	Motor car			450
Less: Drawings	100				
	£5,061				4,636
		Current assets			
Current liabilities		Stock		674	
Trade creditors	770	Debtors		420	
Creditor for		Bank		371	
car	300	Cash		30	
	1,070				1,495
	£6,131				£6,131

9

Report to Mr. F. Taylor

In order to be able to draw any useful conclusions from the results of your trading for 19–4 and 19–5 it is necessary to convert the *actual* figures of gross profit and net profit into *percentages* based on the turnover (sales) of each of the two years.

	Year 19–4	Year 19–5
Gross profit percentage	33.0%	30.0%
Net profit percentage	12.0%	12.5%

The following points emerge.

(1) Although the turnover of 19–5 exceeded that of 19–4 by £16,000 the percentage of gross profit fell from 33% to 30%.

(2) The net profit (which, in the final analysis, is the really vital figure for any business, i.e., it is the profit which becomes available for the proprietor's personal use and/or for further investment in the business) of 19–5 exceeded that of 19–4 by 0.5 per cent.

(3) The expenses of 19–4 amounted to £19,320 whereas in 19–5 they actually fell to £18,900. These figures are obtained by deducting the net profit from the gross profit.

For each £100 of sales you have made a gross profit of £33 in the first year. This fell to £30 per £100 in the second year. Your net profit in 19–4 was £12.00 per £100 but in 19–5 this increased to £12.50 per £100. In actual terms of money you made a gain of £2,460 as compared to 19–4.

The conclusions to be drawn are:

(*a*) you *reduced* your prices in 19–5 and so increased your sales from £92,000 to £108,000, an increase of £16,000;

(*b*) the increased sales raised your gross profit by £2,040, i.e., £32,400 against £30,360, which coupled with a decrease in your operating expenses of £420, gave you an increased total of net profit of £2,460.

10

Stock on premises, 5th April		£25,370
Stock held by customer on sale or return,		
5th April	£400	
Less: 25%	100	
	——	300
Sales 1st to 4th April	£2,840	
Less: Despatched 7th April	720	
	2,120	
Less: 25%	530	
	——	1,590
Goods purchased on 31st March but not received until 7th April		123
		27,383
Deduct:		
Goods sold on 31st March but not despatched until 7th April	£184	
Less: 25%	46	
	—— 138	
Returns inwards 1st to 4th April	168	
Less: 25%	42	
	—— 126	
Purchases, 1st to 4th April	1,835	
	——	2,099
Stock for annual accounts		£25,284

Chapter II

8 The annual profit or loss of a particular company can be found by taking the difference between net worth of the business, found from the balance sheet, at one date from net worth a year later. By following accepted accounting conventions, accountants could report different profits for the same company, depending on the method of valuation of assets.

Areas where differences can occur include:

(*a*) *Work in progress.* Valuation of work in progress, particularly for a long-term contract, could be on a conservative basis, so that cost to the date of the balance sheet only is taken, which would allow for the possibility of things going wrong. Alternatively, valuation could be on cost plus a proportion of the profit that should arise when the contract has been completed. Even here, differences could arise depending on what proportion of profit is taken.

(b) *Depreciation*. (See VIII, **11**) With several accepted methods of depreciation, differences in profit could arise simply depending on the method used, e.g., equipment having an expected life of ten years could be depreciated on the straight-line basis with 10 per cent of cost written off each year; alternatively, 20 per cent could be taken each year on the reducing balance method. Again, differences could arise on the length of the "expected life" of an asset, and even if the same expected term of life is agreed one accountant could suggest that a shorter time span be used in case it is decided to adopt new methods involving new equipment before the allotted time is up. Further differences arise as to whether historical cost or replacement cost is used as a basis for calculation, while a further problem could arise through interpretation and treatment of obsolescent equipment.

(c) *Stocks*. Valuation of stock can cause profit to vary widely depending on the method of valuation used, e.g., LIFO, FIFO, or the interpretation of the terms "at cost" and "net realisable value", e.g., what overheads are included? Although a company's products are selling profitably sales may be falling and perhaps one accountant would value on a direct cost basis, whereas another might value by making allowance for an expected fall in selling price. Again, are the effects of inflation taken into account?

(d) *Bad debts*. Although companies may make provison for bad debts, the decision as to what rate to charge may be purely arbitrary, one accountant adopting a more prudent approach than another.

(e) *Research and development*. Different treatment of research and development may arise with one accountant advocating charging the full amount against profits in the year the costs arise, while another would write the amount off over a period of years. Another method may be simply to capitalise the expenditure and charge nothing against profits.

(f) *Advertising*. The cost of a large-scale advertising campaign can pose a problem on which accountants' treatment may vary. Should the full amount be charged against profits in the year of expenditure or should it be spread over a number of years on the basis that the benefits will continue for some time? If the latter method is adopted, for how many years should the expense be carried over?

(g) *Buildings.* What value to place on freehold property can cause differences in net worth, i.e., to value on historical cost or present market value? If the latter, who can determine present value? Different accountants may obtain varying valuations for the same property from different valuation experts.

9 The expression "conservatism in accounting" means, to put the matter simply, "prudence". (See S.S.A.P.2.)

The dictum "anticipate no profit; provide for all possible losses" should always be aimed at as being the epitome of conservatism. The following rules should always be applied:

(a) Understate: (i) assets, and (ii) income.

(b) Overstate: (i) liabilities, and (ii) expenditure.

(c) Always value stock at cost (and at market value if lower than cost).

(d) Always take occurred expenses into account.

(e) Always take prepayments into account.

(f) Always value fixed assets at cost (less depreciation).

(g) Only take credit for a sale when the goods have been delivered and not when ordered.

10 A common mistake made by the layman is to assume that the trading profit can be found by comparing the income of the period against the expenditure, no account being taken of accrued expenses or of payments in advance. This is called the "accruals concept" (S.S.A.P.2). The "realisation concept" which S.S.A.P.2 calls the "prudence concept" is closely allied to the "accruals concept" in that the decision to take profit at the time of the delivery of the goods/services to the customer is the point at which profit should be taken, and not the time at which the customer pays his account.

To obtain the appropriate figures to complete the matching process it is necessary to *accrue* all items of expenditure *unpaid* and, at the same time, to *deduct* any expenses which have been *paid in advance*, so that the figures for expenditure relate to the trading period only.

Provisions for depreciation and, likewise, provisions for doubtful debts, are also relevant to this concept of "matching" costs against revenue. (S.S.A.P.2.)

In the same way, any income received *in advance* must also be excluded when matching costs against revenue. Income of this type could arise where premises are sublet since landlords are most unlikely to permit tenants of business premises to pay in arrears. Another possible example of cash received in advance would be where it is customary for clubs to accept membership fees to cover future periods.

Chapter III

6 *See* **1** and **2** for an explanation of the phrase "Bank Reconciliation Statement".

(*a*) The fact that two cheques for £100 and £50 respectively have not been cleared by the bank will have no affect on the balance in the Cash Book. Before the balance was struck these items had been entered on the credit side as payments and, as a consequence, the balance will automatically have been reduced accordingly. The fact that the payee (the person in whose favour the cheque has been drawn) has, in neither case, presented his cheque for payment, has no bearing on the matter.

(*b*) As the bank has debited the Trader's Account in its ledger a few days earlier than usual for this particular Standing Order (which has the effect of reducing the amount owed to him by the bank), the trader should take appropriate action and credit the Bank Account in his Cash Book thus reducing the balance which appears therein.

7   *Cash Book*

Balance	£2,000	Standing Orders	£100
		Bank interest and	
		charges	132
		Balance c/d	1,768
	£2,000		£2,000
Balance b/d	£1,768		

Memorandum Bank Statement Account—J. Rogers

Unpresented cheques	£1,060	Balance b/d	?
		Credit transfers not credited by bank	£545
Balance c/d	£1,768	Correction of cheque wrongly charged by bank	25
	£2,828		£2,828
		Balance b/d	£1,768

When every item has been entered in *both* sets of books, i.e., in the Cash Book of J. Rogers and in the ledger of the bank, then the closing balances must be equal to each other.

In this particular case we can see that the missing opening balance which has now to be inserted in the ledger of the bank is on the credit side, i.e., as the first item. The balance standing to the credit of J. Rogers's account in the bank's ledger at 31st December 19–4 must therefore have amounted to £2,258.

8

B. Bee's Account in the Bank's Ledger
(or *"Bank Statement Account"*)

Unpresented cheques	£616	Balance, 31st May	£230
Balance c/d	19	Cheques not credited	405
	£635		£635

Cash Book

Balance, 31st May	£29	Standing Order (not previously entered in Cash Book	£25
Dividend paid directly into bank (not previously entered in Cash Book	15	Balance (as now adjusted and agreeing with the balance on B. Bee's account in the bank's ledger) c/d	19

Bank Reconciliation Statement

Balance per Bank Statement	£230
Add: Cheques not yet credited by bank	405
	635
Less: Unpresented cheques	616
Balance per Cash Book	£19

9   *C. Courage's Account in the Bank's Ledger*
                        (or *"Bank Statement Account"*)

Balance overdrawn, 31st December	£460	Cheques not yet credited	£622
Cheques drawn but not yet presented for payment	308	Balance c/d overdrawn	146
	£768		£768

Cash Book

Balance overdrawn as ascertained per bank's ledger	£146	Balance, 31st December	£118
		Payments not previously entered in Cash Book·	
		Subscription	10
		Bank Charges	18
	£146		£146

Bank Reconciliation Statement

Balance per Bank Statement	£460
Add: Unpresented cheques	308
	768
Less: Cheques not yet credited	622
Balance per Cash Book	£146

10

(a) *Cash Book*

Balance at 31st March	£832	Standing Orders paid on 28th February:		
Amount paid into bank by a customer	68	Trade subscription	£6	
		Hire-purchase instalment	27	
			—	33
		Balance c/d		867
	———			———
	£900			£900
	══			══
Balance b/d	£867			

(b) *F.V.'s Account in the Bank's Ledger*

		Balance (per Bank Statement)	?
Cheques drawn but not yet presented	£259	Cheques paid in but not credited by the bank	£174
Balance per Cash Book after adjustment— see above	867		
	———		———
	£1,126		£1,126
	══		══
		Balance b/d	£867

The balance required to be entered is £952. This is the answer required under (b) in the question.

(c)

Net profit as shown by the Profit and Loss Account		£4,128
Less: Discount allowed	£2	
Trade subscription	6	
	—	
		8
		£4,120

11

(a) The balance on the debit side of the Cash Book on 1st June was £774.

(b) Unpresented cheques at 30th June:

Porter	£19
Forrester	108
Woods	29
	£156

(c) Bank Reconciliation at 30th June:	
Balance per Bank Statement	£815
Add: Cheques not credited by the bank	139
	954
Less: Unpresented cheques	156
Balance per Cash Book	£798

Chapter IV

6   JOURNAL

Sundry assets:	*Dr*		
Shop equipment A/c		£625	
Delivery van A/c		380	
Stock A/c		942	
Debtors A/c		207	
Rent A/c (prepaid)		90	
To Sundry liabilities:			
Creditors A/c			£144
Electricity A/c			19
Telephone A/c			16
Capital Account			2,065
		£2,244	£2,244

7   JOURNAL

Sept. 1 Sundry assets:	*Dr*		
Land and Buildings A/c		£7,240	
Shop Fittings A/c		1,329	
Shop Equipment A/c		576	
Delivery Van A/c		440	
Stock A/c		3,687	
Debtors A/c		966	
Bank A/c		1,201	
Cash A/c		43	
To Sundry liabilities:			
Creditors A/c			£1,168
Telephone A/c			31
Light and Heat A/c			27
Advertising A/c			64
Capital Account			14,192
		£15,482	£15,482

BOSWORTH: JOURNAL

			Dr	Cr
Nov. 1	Building Equipment A/c To Purchases A/c Adjustment of item of capital expense wrongly treated as revenue expenditure	*Dr*	£118	£118
Nov. 9	Purchases A/c To Grant & Co. A/c Invoice previously omitted from books	*Dr*	79	79
	Drawings A/c To Wages A/c Correction of an item of private expenditure wrongly charged as a business expense		165	165
Nov. 18	Bank Charges A/c To Insurance A/c Adjustment of item charged to wrong account	*Dr*	14	14
Nov. 23	Purchases A/c To Harley & Sons A/c Adjustment of (*a*) under-cast of £100 in the Purchase Day Book and (*b*) omission of similar amount which should have been posted to the account of Harley & Sons	*Dr*	100	100
Nov. 26	Cash A/c To A. Vance A/c Drawings A/c To Cash A/c Entries previously omitted from the books	*Dr* *Dr*	45 45	 45 45

9

			Dr	Cr
June 4	Purchase A/c	Dr	£1,560	
	To Hornbeams Ltd.			£1,560
	Invoice previously omitted from the books			
June 10	Hotel Cash Receipts A/c	Dr	127	
	To Bar Cash Receipts A/c			127
	Correction of entry, i.e., hotel receipts wrongly credited as bar receipts			
June 15	Drawings A/c	Dr	30	
	To Bar Sales Receipts A/c			30
	Entry previously omitted from books			
June 21	Stocktaker's A/c	Dr	12	
	To Bar Sales Receipts A/c			12
	Entry previously omitted from books			

10

(a)	Creditor's A/c	Dr	£16	
	To Sales A/c			£16
(b)	Sales A/c	Dr	£15	
	To J. Wilkins A/c			£15
(c)	Drawings A/c	Dr	£75	
	To Wages A/c			£75
(d)	Purchases A/c	Dr	£88	
	To Creditors A/c			£88

The following adjustments will have an effect on the Balance Sheet:

(a)	Creditors—reduced by £16	
(d)	—increased by £88	−£16
		+£88
	Net increase in creditors	£72
(b)	Debtors—reduced by £15	−£15
(c)	Capital A/c—credit balance reduced by drawings of £75	−£75

The net profit will be reduced by (d) and (b), a total of £103. It will be increased by (a) and (c), a total of £91. Net decrease in profit = £12.

BALANCE SHEET (as corrected)

Capital (£3,132			Assets—Premises	£2,450
− £75 − £12)	£3,045		Fixtures	520
Creditors			Stock	487
(£617 + £72)	689		Debtors (£189 − £15)	174
Loan	430		Bank	510
			Cash	23
	£4,164			£4,164

DAVID CLONCURREY: JOURNAL

		Dr	*Cr*

June 4	Motor Vehicles A/c *Dr*
	    To Superior Motor
	        Garages A/c
	Cost of new car to replace old
	Cresta
		£1,741.16	£1,741.16

June 4	Motor Expenses A/c *Dr*
	    Road Fund Tax 25.00
	    Insurance 62.00
	    Delivery petrol 1.37
	
	    To Motor Vehicle A/c
	Transfer of revenue expense
	items included in invoice
		88.37	88.37

June 11	Superior Motor
	    Garages A/c *Dr*
	        To Motor Vehicle A/c
	Value allowed on old car
	taken in part settlement
		500.00	500.00

June 11	Superior Motor
	        Garages A/c *Dr*
	    To Bank A/c
	Payment of balance of pur-
	chase price of new Cresta
		1,241.16	1,241.16

June 11	Profit and Loss Account *Dr* To Motor Vehicle A/c Transfer of loss on sale of old Cresta	42.00	42.00

12(a)

JOURNAL OF LOMAX MOTORS

19–4				
October 31	*Sundries:*	Dr		
	Rates		£60	
	Legal expenses		317	
	Freehold			
	property		10,000	
			£10,377	
	To sundries:			
	Rent (Lomax)			£140
	Rent (McLintock)			42
	Water rate			1
	Bank			10,194
				£10,377

(b) The value to be attributed to the freehold property in the Balance Sheet of Lomax Motors will be £10,000.

Chapter V

6   JOURNAL

Suspense A/c	Dr	£100	
To General Expenses A/c			£100
Office Furniture A/c	Dr	£600	
To Office Expenses A/c			£600
Discount A/c	Dr	£40	
To Suspense A/c			£40
Suspense A/c	Dr	£148	
To Returns Outwards A/c			£148
Suspense A/c	Dr	£90	
To Sales A/c			£90

7   *Suspense Account Part I*

Discount A/c	£100	General Expenses A/c	£100
		Discount A/c	60
Difference c/d to		Sales Day Book	90
Part II	298	Returns Outward	148
	£398		£398

NOTE: Each item set out in Part I above has been regarded individually and each entry is the one which would have to be made assuming that *each* one of the above matters had, in itself, been *the only error* in the Trial Balance. Thus, the credit entry of £100 in regard to the overcast on the General Expenses Account would have had to be made to balance the Trial Balance if we assumed that it was the only mistake which had been made. The remainder are then dealt with on the same basis.

Suspense Account Part II

General Expenses A/c	£100	Difference b/d from	
Returns Outwards A/c	148	Part I	£298
Sales A/c	90	Discount A/c*	40
	£338		£338

* The discounts have been shown here net, thus conforming with the solution given in the previous problem.

8   *Suspense Account*

(a) John Gunn A/c	£42.86	(b) Office Equipment	
(d) Kendall and Co.		A/c	£101.50
A/c	5.70	(c) Balance on	
(e) Purchases A/c	28.06	Weedon and Co.	
		A/c omitted from	
	76.62	the Trial Balance	65.26
Original difference in			
Trial Balance	90.14		
	£166.76		£166.76

9(a) Effects, if any, on the Trial Balance.

(*a*) No effect on the Trial Balance.

(*b*) A debit of £0.63 has been omitted and a credit of £63.00 inserted, resulting in an overcredit in the Trial Balance of £63.63.

(*c*) A debit of £5 has not been entered in the personal account in the Sales Ledger, resulting in an overcredit in the Trial Balance of £5. (Calculation: $4/12 \times 5/100 \times £300 = £5$)

(*d*) An overdebit of £1.80 in the Trial Balance.

(*e*) An overdebit of £11.97 in the Trial Balance. *N.B.* It is assumed that the personal account of the debtor has been correctly debited with £13.30 to close it off.

(*f*) No effect on the Trial Balance because the closing stock does not appear therein. The profit will, of course, be reduced by £40.

(*g*) An overcredit of £45.15 in the Trial Balance.

(*h*) The Trial Balance would have an overdebit of £3.75.

(b) Taking item (*c*) above as a simple example for explanatory purposes: there we have an item of £5 credited to the Interest Receivable Account but there is no corresponding debit entry in the Personal Account, i.e., we have an overcredit in the Trial Balance. In order to make the Trial Balance agree we would debit the Suspense Account with £5. It is most important that this entry is recognised for what it is—a *single* entry!

Suspense Account

Error in Trial Balance	£5

The books would now balance—temporarily. When the error was finally discovered a *double* entry would have to be made in order to correct matters, i.e., credit the Suspense Account and debit the customer's account in the Sales Ledger.

The Suspense Account would finally appear as follows:

Suspense Account

Purchase Day		Bought Ledger	
Book (*d*)	£1.80	Account	£63.63
Bad Debts Account	11.97	Sales Ledger Account	5.00
Bank Deposit		Sales Account re.	
Interest Account	3.75	trade discount	45.15
Original difference	96.26		
	£113.78		£113.78

Chapter VI

10   *Books of Johnson Account with Williams*

Jan. 4 19–2 Cash (one half of proceeds of bill)	£492.50	Jan 1 19–2 Bills receivable (Three months bill from Williams)	£1,000.00
Jan. 1 19–2 Bill payable (Three months bill to Williams)	400.00	Jan. 4 19–2 Cash (One half of proceeds of bill)	197.00
Feb. 4 19–2 Charges (Adjustment of discounting charges) £15 Suffered by Johnson £6 Suffered by Williams — £9 Half chargeable to Williams	4.50	April 4 19–2 Bill receivable (Three months bill from Williams for £1,000 plus interest at 5% for three months)	1,012.50
April 1 19–2 Bill dishonoured (Williams' bill met by Johnson)	1,000.00	Oct. 31 19–2 Cash (First and final dividend 50p in £ from Williams' trustee in bankruptcy)	356.25
April 4 19–2 Interest chargeable (to Williams on new bill)	12.50	Oct. 31 19–2 Bad Debt (Balance on Williams Account, now irrecoverable)	356.25
July 1 19–2 Bill dishonoured (due to Williams' bankruptcy)	1,012.50		
	£2,922.00		£2,922.00
Dec. 5 19–3 Bad Debts A/c (Amount agreed to be paid by Williams after his discharge)	356.25	Feb. 10 19–3 Cash (From Williams)	356.25
	356.25		£356.25

WORKINGS

Bills Receivable Account

Williams (Three month bill)	£1,000.00	Cash £985.00 Discounting charges £15.00	£1,000.00
Cash (Williams dishonoured)	1,000.00	Williams (Bill dishonoured)	1,000.00
Williams (Three month bill)	1,012.50	Williams (Bill dishonoured)	1,012.50
	£3,012.50		£3,012,50

Bills Payable Account

Cash	£400.00	Williams (Three month bill)	£400.00
	£400.00		£400.00

Interest Receivable Account

Profit and Loss A/c	£12.50	Williams (Interest on bill $5\% \times £1,000 \times \frac{3}{12}$)	£12.50
	£12.50		£12.50

Discounting Charges Account

Bill receivable ($6\% \times £1,000 \times \frac{3}{12}$)	£15.00	Williams (Adjustment of charges)	£4.50
		Profit and Loss A/c	10.50
	£15.00		£15.00

11 Entries in Black's books:

LEDGER

Brown's Account

July 1 Balance b/d	£650	July 1 Bills Receivable A/c	£400
Oct. 10 Bills Receivable A/c	175	July 5 Bills Receivable A/c	175
		Oct. 15 Bank A/c	250
	£825		£825

White's Account

July 8 Bills Receivable A/c	£175	July 1 Balance b/d	£740
July 9 Bills Payable A/c	574	July 9 Interest on Bills A/c	9
	£749		£749
Oct. 10 Bank A/c	£175	Oct. 10 Bills Receivable A/c (re. Grey)	£175

Bills Receivable Account

July 1 Brown's A/c	£400	July 8 White's A/c (re. Grey)	£175
July 5 Brown's A/c (re. Grey)	175	Oct. 4 Bank A/c	400
Oct. 10 White's A/c (re. Grey)	175	Oct. 10 Brown's A/c	175
	£750		£750

Bills Payable Account

Oct. 12 Bank A/c	£574	July 9 White's A/c	£574

Interest on Bills Account

July 9 White's A/c	£9	

Bank Account

Oct. 4 Bills Receivable A/c	£400	Oct. 10 White's A/c	£175
Oct. 15 Brown's A/c	250	Oct. 12 Bills Payable A/c	574

12   *Brown Account*

June 16 Bills Receivable (No. 2)	£150	June 1 Purchases A/c	£860
June 20 Bills payable	720	June 20 Interest A/c	10
	£870		£870
Sept. 17 Bank A/c	150	Sept. 17 Jones A/c—re. Bill Receivable dishonoured	150

Jones Account

June 1 Sales A/c	£570	June 1 (Bills Receivable (No. 1)	£400
		June 14 Bills Receivable (No. 2)	150
Sept. 17 Brown A/c (Bill Receivable dishonoured)	150	Sept. 20 Bank A/c	85
		Sept. 20 Balance c/d	85
	£720		£720
Sept. 21 Balance b/d	£85		

Bills Receivable Account

June 1 Jones A/c		June 16 Brown A/c	
(No. 1)	£400	(No. 2)	£150
June 14 Jones A/c		Sept. 3 Bank A/c	
(No. 2)	150	(No. 1)	400
	£550		£550

Bills Payable Account

Sept. 23 Bank A/c	£720	June 20 Brown A/c	£720

Interest Account

June 20 Brown A/c	£10	

Bank Account

Sept. 3 Bills Receivable	£400	Sept. 17 Brown A/c	£150
Sept. 20 Jones A/c	85	Sept. 23 Bills Payable	720

13   BARNES: JOURNAL

Purchases A/c	*Dr*	£100	
To Simpson's A/c			£100
Purchase of goods on credit			
Simpson's A/c	*Dr*	100	
To Bills Payable A/c			95
Discount Received A/c			5
Acceptance of Bill for £95 drawn in favour of Byers, in full settlement of debt for £100			
Bills Payable A/c	*Dr*	95	
To Bank A/c			95
Byers's Bill being paid on presentation			
Bank A/c	*Dr*	100	
To Bills Payable A/c			100
Substitution of Byers's Bill by Northcountry Bank			

14   *W. Reckitt Account*

Mch. 2	Cash	£120	Mch. 1 Goods	£250
	Bills Payable	100	Apl. 4 Bills Payable	
Mch. 26	Bills Receivable	30	(bill withdrawn)	100
Apl. 4	Cash	60		
	Bills Payable	40		
		£350		£350

F. Kelly Account

Mch. 14 Cash	£40	Mch. 14 Goods	£70
Apl. 30 Balance c/d	30		
	£70		£70

S. Pearce Account

Mch. 8 Goods	£120	Mch. 9 Bills	
Apl. 13 Cash—Bills Rec.		Receivable	£120
dishonoured	120	Apl. 20 Returns	40
		Apl. 30 Balance c/d	80
	£240		£240

H. Bradford Account

Mch. 23 Goods	£50	Mch. 23 Cash	£20
Apl. 30 Balance c/d	15	Bills Receivable	30
		Apl. 18 Returns	15
	£65		£65

Bills Receivable Account

Mch. 9 S. Pearce	£120	Mch. 9 Cash	£120
Mch. 23 H. Bradford	30	Mch. 26 W. Reckitt	30
	£150		£150

Bills Payable Account

Apl. 4 W. Reckitt	£100	Mch. 2 W. Reckitt	£100
Apl. 30 Balance c/d	40	Apl. 4 W. Reckitt	40
	£140		£140

Discounting Charges Account

Mch. 9 Cash	£2

Chapter VII

8

(*a*)   *Bought Ledger Control*

Cash paid	£16,000	Balance at 1st Jan.	
Discounts received	210	19–4	£7,000
Returns outward	20	Purchases	19,000
	16,230		
Balance at 31st Dec.			
19–4	9,770		
	£26,000		£26,000

(b)   *Sales Ledger Control*

Balance at 1st Jan.		Cash received	£35,000
19–4	£6,000	Discounts allowed	400
Sales	40,000	Bills receivable	1,500
		Returns inward	300
		Bad debts written off	500
			37,700
		Balance at 31st Dec.	
		19–4	8,300
	£46,000		£46,000

9   *Bought Ledger Total Account*

19–5		19–4	
June 30 Cash paid to		July 1 Balances	
suppliers	£229,035	b/d	£20,652
Discounts received	4,763		
Transfer to Sales		19–5	
Ledger	3,827	June 30 Purchases	240,931
Purchase returns	247		
	237,872		
Balances c/d	23,711		
	£261,583		£261,583

The figure stated to be the total of the Bought Ledger balances, i.e., £23,701, is £10 less than the balancing figure required for the Total Account. We can, therefore, assume that an error has occurred in extracting the list of balances from the ledger.

Sales Ledger Total Account

19–4			19–5	
July 1 Balances b/d	£29,028		June 30 Cash received	
19–5			from customers	£339,179
June 30 Sales	£350,753		Discount allowed	5,932
			Sales returns	473
			Bad debts written off	278
			Transfer from	
			Bought Ledger	3,827
				£349,689
			Balances c/d	30,092
	£379,781			£379,781

10 *Sales Ledger Control Account*

Balances			Balances, 1st January	£34
1st January	£10,840		Cash	111,935
Sales	121,400		Bills Receivable	6,250
Bills Receivable			Bad debts	227
dishonoured	375		Discount allowed	2,780
Interest charged to			Returns inwards	1,165
customer	10		Transfer to Bought	
			Ledger	492
Balances,				
31st December	40		Balances,	
			31st December	9,782
	£132,665			£132,665

Bought Ledger Control Account

Balances, 1st January	£15	Balances,	
Cash	91,575	1st January	£8,760
Discounts received	1,930	Purchases	96,320
Returns outwards	218	Balances,	
Transfers from Sales		31st December	63
Ledger	492		
Balances,			
31st December	10,913		
	£105,143		£105,143

Bills Receivable Account

Balance	£520	Bank A/c	£6,770
Sales Ledger			
Control A/c	6,250		
	£6,770		£6,770

Bank Account

Bills Receivable		Sales Ledger	
discounted	£6,770	Control A/c	£375

11   THORNLEY

Sales Ledger Control Account

Balances, 1st		Balances,	
January 19–4	£15,279	1st January 19–4	£133
Sales	142,789	Cash	136,182
Cash refund	64	Returns	1,016
Balances, 31st		Bad Debts	1,002
December 19–4	184	Balances,	
		31st December 19–4	19,983
	£158,316		£158,316

Purchases Ledger Control Account

Balances		Balances,	
1st January 19–4	£216	1st January 19–4	£12,491
Cash	93,438	Purchases	96,241
Returns	838	Balances,	
Balances, 31st		31st December 19–4	149
December 19–4	14,389		
	£108,881		£108,881

12   CUNNINGHAM

	−	+
(a) *Reconciliation of balances*		
Balances as extracted from the Purchase Ledger		£35,560
(d) Balances omitted from the list	40	540
(e) Undercast on Holmes' account		20
(i) Credit balances listed as debit balances (£70)		140
(j) Balance on creditors list to be reduced		
by payments to Snodgrass Brothers	240	
	£280	£36,260
	−	280
Amended total of balances		£35,980

Purchase Ledger Control Account

(g) Discounts for		(a) Purchase returns	
March	£30	(overcast)	£200
(h) Purchase returns	80	(f) Bad debt written off	4
(c) Contra	900	(b) Advertising transfer	360
			564
Balance (as corrected per			
amended list)	35,980	∴ the opening balance	
		must have been	
		(balancing figure)	36,426
	£36,990		£36,990

Chapter VIII

10 *Manufacturing, Trading and Profit and Loss Account*

Raw materials		Cost of manufacture	
Stock at 1st Jan.		transferred to	
19–4	£11,464	Trading Account £218,047	
Purchases	115,826		
	———		
	127,290		
Less: Stock at			
31st Dec. 19–4	12,162		
	———		
Raw materials			
consumed	115,128		
Manufacturing			
wages	72,242		
	———		
PRIME COST	186,370		
Factory expenses			
General			
expenses £19,324			
Rent and			
rates 6,000			
Depreciation			
of plant 8,000			
———	33,324		
	———		
	219,694		
Deduct:			
Work in progress—			
at 31st Dec.			
19–4 £19,941			
Less: at 1st			
Jan 19–4 18,294			
———	1,647		
	———		
FACTORY COST AT			
PRODUCTION	£218,047		£218,047

Manufacturing, Trading and Profit and Loss Account
(continued)

Stock of manufactured goods at 1st Jan. 19–4	£14,881	Sales	£284,369
Manufactured goods transferred from Manufacturing Account	218,047		
	232,928		
Less: Stock of manufactured goods at 31st Dec. 19–4	14,238		
	218,690		
Gross profit	65,679		
	£284,369		£284,369

Rent and rates of office	3,000	Gross profit	65,679
General administration expenses	21,642		
Salesmen's salaries	6,162		
Motor expenses	3,984		
Other selling expenses	7,046		
Depreciation of motor vans	1,800		
	43,634		
Net profit	22,045		
	£65,679		£65,679

11   *Oldhamlet Manufacturing Company:*
        Manufacturing, Trading and Profit and Loss Account
            for the year ended 31st December 19–5

Raw materials:			Factory cost of
Stock at 1st Jan.			production trans-
19–5	£3,315		ferred to Trading
Purchases	38,942		Account £117,646
	42,257	
Less: Stock at 31st		
Dec. 19–5	2,973	
Raw materials		
consumed	39,284	
Manufacturing wages 52,681		
Prime cost	91,965	
Production overheads:		
Factory		
expenses £15,656		
Depreciation		
of plant 6,500		
Factory		
power 3,670		
	25,826	
	117,791	
Deduct:		
Work in progress		
at 31st		
Dec.		
19–5 £1,894		
Less: at		
1st Jan.		
19–5 1,749		
	145	
Factory cost of		
production £117,646		£117,646

[*Continued*

Oldhamlet Manufacturing Company (continued)

Stock of finished goods, 1st Jan. 19–5	5,064	Sales	£145,600
Factory cost of production	117,646		
	122,710		
Less: Stock of finished goods at 31st Dec. 19–5	7,138		
Cost of sales	115,572		
Gross profit	30,028		
	£145,600		£145,600
Office and administration expenses	£7,450	Gross profit	£30,028
Salesmen's salaries and commission	4,630		
Advertising	1,035		
Delivery van: Running expenses £1,425 Depreciation 1,250	2,675		
	15,790		
Net profit	14,238		
	£30,028		£30,028

12   *Manufacturing and Trading Account*
          for the year 31st December 19–4

Raw materials:			Factory cost of		
Stock at 1st Jan.			production trans-		
19–4	£5,415		ferred to Trading		
Purchases	16,190		Account		£52,260
Less: Stock at 31st					
Dec. 19–4	5,910				
Raw materials					
consumed	15,695				
Productive wages	19,260				
Prime cost	34,955				
Factory overheads:					
Non-produc-					
tive wages	£5,830				
Power and					
light	1,675				
Rent, rates &					
insurance	1,560				
Repairs to					
machines	600				
Depreciation					
of machines	2,750				
Works					
manager's					
salary	5,200				
	17,615				
	52,570				
Add: Work in progress					
at 1st Jan. 19–4	4,920				
	57,490				
Less: Work in progress					
at 31st Dec. 19–4	5,230				
Factory cost of					
production	£52,260				£52,260

Manufacturing and Trading Account (continued)

Stock of finished goods, 1st Jan. 19–4	7,245	Sales	69,080
Cost of finished goods transferred from Manufacturing A/c	52,260		
	59,505		
Less: Stock at 31st Dec. 19–4	7,970		
Cost of sales	51,535		
Gross profit (25.4%)	17,545		
	£69,080		£69,080

Chapter IX

9   *Subscriptions Account*

19–4		19–4	
Jan. 1 Balance b/d (in arrears)	87	Jan. 1 Balance b/d (in advance)	71
Dec. 31 Income & Expenditure A/c	1,143	Dec. 31 Cash A/c	1,214
Dec. 31 Balance c/d (in advance)	108	Dec. 31 Balance c/d (in arrears)	53
	£1,338		£1,338

10 *Subscriptions Account for year to 30th September 19–5*

19–4			19–4	
Oct. 1 Balance b/d	£21		Oct. 1 Balance b/d	£9
19–5			19–5	
Sept. 30 Income and			Sept. 30 Cash A/c	384
Expenditure A/c	375		Sept. 30 Balance c/d	15
Sept. 30 Balance c/d	12			
	———			———
	£408			£408
	▬▬			▬▬
19–5			19–5	
Oct. Balance b/d	£15		Oct. 1 Balance b/d	£12

11 *Subscriptions Account for year to 31st December 19–5*

19–5			19–5	
Jan. 1 Balance b/d	£69		Jan. 1 Balance b/d	£43
Dec. 31 Income and			Dec. 31 Cash A/c	837
Expenditure A/c	858		Dec. 31 Balance c/d	76
Dec. 31 Balance c/d	29			
	———			———
	£956			£956
	▬▬			▬▬
19–6			19–6	
Jan. 1 Balance b/d	£76		Jan. 1 Balance b/d	£29

12

DRIFTERS CLUB

Opening Statement

Bank	£360	
Premises	5,000	
Stock	618	
Creditors		£450
Wages accrued		25
Furniture	3,620	
Capital fund		9,043
Subscriptions received		
in advance		80
	£9,598	£9,598

(*a*) *Bar Trading Account*

Stock	£618	
Purchases	6,040	
Sales		£8,000
Closing stock		548
Gross profit	1,890	
	£8,548	£8,548

(*b*) *Income and Expenditure Account
for year ending 31st December 19–4*

Wages	£2,125	Gross profit on bar	£1,890
Printing, etc.	140	Subscriptions	2,740
General expenses	1,830		
Surplus	535		
	£4,630		£4,630

(c)   BALANCE SHEET 31ST DECEMBER 19–4

Capital fund				Premises		£5,000
Balance at				Furniture	£3,620	
1st Jan.				Additions	650	
19–4	£9,043				———	4,270
Add:				Stock		548
Surplus	535			Bank		380
	———	£9,578				
Creditors						
Goods	490					
Wages	30					
Subscriptions						
received in						
advance	100					
	——	620				
		———				———
		£10,198				£10,198

13   THE WELCOME CLUB

Bar Trading and Profit and Loss Account for 19–5

(*a*)				
Opening Stock		£4,100		Sales £53,800
Purchases	40,380			
+	2,284			
	———			
	42,664			
−	2,040			
	———	40,624		
		———		
		44,724		
Less: Closing stock		5,968		
		———		
		38,756		
Gross profit		15,044		
		———		———
		£53,800		£53,800

Wages		8,420	Gross profit	15,044
Rent and Rates		2,400	Subscriptions	6,200
General			Interest	2,080
expenses	2,680			
−	80			
	2,600			
+	124			
		2,724		
Depreciation		1,520		
		15,064		
Surplus		8,260		
		£23,324		£23,324

BALANCE SHEET AS AT 31ST DECEMBER 19–5

Accumulated Fund			Investments		£37,600
Jan. 1 19–5		£48,420	Furniture and		
Add: Current surplus		8,260	Equipment		
				15,200	
		56,680	−	1,520	
					13,680
Creditors					
Bar	2,284		Bar Stocks	5,968	
Expenses	124		Bank	1,840	
		2,408			7,808
		£59,088			£59,088

(b) (i)	£	£
Cost of Building		88,000
Funds available		
Bank balance	1,840	
Loan	10,000	
Proceeds sale of investments	40,160	52,000
Maximum overdraft		£36,000

(*ii*)
Annual cash flow:

Surplus		8,260
Depreciation		1,520
		9,780
Less: Interest not now receivable	2,080	
Loan from member	1,000	3,080
		6,700
Add: Rent not payable	1,500	
Rent receivable	800	2,300

Annual amount available for payment of bank interest and for reduction of overdraft.   **£9,000**

---

14   *Capital Fund 1st January 19–7*

Equipment		920
Savings Bank		500
Bank		54
Cash		4
		1,478
Less:		
Rent owing	74	
Subs received in advance	90	164
		£1,314

*Income and Expenditure Account for the year ended
31st December 19–7*

Rent	296	Entrance fees		22
Wages	416	Subscriptions		604
Production expenses	20	Interest (Savings Bank)		12
Sundry expenses	176	Profit on refreshments		150
Bank interest	4	Excess of expenditure		
Depreciation on		over income		264
equipment	140			
	£1,052			£1,052

BALANCE SHEET AS AT 31ST DECEMBER 19–7

Capital fund		*Fixed assets*		
Balance Jan. 1		Equipment	£920	
19–7 £1,314		*Less:* Sales	30	
			890	
Less: Excess of		Additions	80	
expenditure over			970	
income 264		*Less:* Depn.	140	
	1,050			830
Current liabilities		*Current assets*		
Bank overdraft	40	Savings Bank 412		
Subscriptions in advance	84	Cash 6		
Rent outstanding	74			418
	£1,248			£1,248

Chapter X

8   *Debtors Account*

Balance at 1st Jan. 19–5	£840	Cash A/c	£5,609
Sales A/c	**5,686**	Balance c/d (31st Dec. 19–5)	917
	£6,526		£6,526
Balance b/d	£917		

Sales Account

		Debtors A/c	**£5,686**

9   *Debtors Account*

Balance at 1st Feb. 19–5	£674	**Cash A/c**	£4,995
Sales A/c	4,949	Balance c/d (31st Jan. 19–6)	628
	£5,623		£5,623
Balance b/d	£628		

Cash Account

Debtors A/c	**£4,995**	

10   *Debtors Account*

Balance at 1st Mar. 19–5	£2,105	Cash A/c	£22,993
Sales A/c	23,741	**Balance c/d** (29th Feb. 19–6)	**2,853**
	£25,846		£25,846
Balance b/d	**£2,853**		

11 *Debtors Account*

Balance at 1st Apr. 19–5	**£2,544**	Cash A/c	£15,801
Sales A/c	16,486	Balance c/d (31st Mar. 19–6)	3,229
	£19,030		£19,030
Balance b/d	£3,229		

12 *General Expenses Account*

Cash A/c	£922	Balance b/d (1st May 19–5)	£147
Balance c/d (30th Apr. 19–6)	135	**Profit & Loss A/c**	**910**
	£1,057		£1,057
		Balance b/d	£135

Profit and Loss Account

General expenses	**£910**	

13 *Electricity Supply Company Account*

Cash A/c	£105	Balance (1st June 19–5)	£24
Balance (31st May 19–6)	27	**Light and Heat A/c**	**108**
	£132		£132
		Balance b/d	£27

Light and Heat Account

Electricity Supply Co. A/c	**£108**

14 *Richard Barton and Co. Opening Statement*

Capital A/c		£5,200
Stock	£1,250	
Fixtures etc.	675	
Goodwill	3,075	
Bank	200	
	£5,200	£5,200

Suppliers Account

Bank	£31,978	Purchases A/c	£32,349
Balance c/d	371		
	£32,349		£32,349
		Balance b/d	371

Cash Account

Sales	£45,453	Purchases	£2,310
		Wages	1,517
		Expenses	274
		Drawings	1,764
		Bank A/c	39,480
		Balance c/d	108
	£45,453		£45,453
Balance c/d	108		

Purchases Account

Suppliers	£32,349	
Cash A/c	2,310	
	£34,659	

Electricity Account

Bank	£167		
Balance c/d	£58		
	£225		
		Balance b/d	£58

Customers Account

Sales A/c	£95		
	£95		

Sales Account

		Cash A/c	£45,453
		Customers A/c	95
			£45,548

Rates Account

Bank	£300		
Balance c/d	100		
	£400		
		Balance b/d	£100

Rent Account

Bank	£1,500	Balance c/d	£300
	£1,500		
Balance b/d	£300		

Drawing Account

Bank	£1,790	
Cash	1,764	
	£3,554	

Trial Balance 31st December 19–4

Capital		5,200
Stock (1st Jan. 19–4)	1,250	
Fixtures	675	
Goodwill	3,075	
Cash	108	
Wages	1,517	
Expenses	274	
Hire of equipment	125	
Bank	3,820	
Debtors	95	
Sales		45,548
Creditors		371
Purchases	34,659	
Electricity	225	
,, creditor		58
Rates	400	
,, creditor		100
Rent	1,200	
,, paid in advance	300	
Drawings	3,554	
	£51,277	£51,277

*Trading and Profit and Loss Account
for the year ended 31st December 19–4*

Stock at 1st Jan. 19–4	£1,250	Sales	£45,548
Purchases	34,659		
	35,909		
Less: Stock at 31st Dec. 19–4	1,860		
	34,049		
Gross profit (27.44%)	11,499		
	£45,548		£45,548
Rent	1,200	Gross profit	11,499
Rates	400		
Electricity	225		
Wages	1,517		
Expenses	274		
Hire of equipment	125		
Net profit	7,758		
	£11,499		£11,499

BALANCE SHEET AS ON 31ST DECEMBER 19–4

Capital A/c			*Fixed assets*		
Cash paid in £5,200			Goodwill at cost	£3,075	
Add: Net			Fixtures, etc.		
profit	7,758		at cost	675	
	12,958				3,750
Less:					
Drawings 3,554					
		9,404			
Current liabilities			*Current assets*		
Creditors for			Stock	1,860	
supplies	371		Debtors	95	
Accrued expenses:			Prepayment		
Electricity	58		Rent	300	
Rates	100		Bank	3,820	
			Cash	108	
	—	529		—	6,183
		£9,933			£9,933

15   BOBBIN: CASH BOOK

	Cash	Bank		Cash	Bank
Capital A/c		£6,000	Vendor		£3,750
Cash A/c		12,050	Purchases	£158	10,000
			Rent		300
Sales A/c			Rates		190
(being the			Electricity		45
balancing			Fittings		
figure			(new)		100
required to			Bank A/c	12,050	
complete			Wages	597	
the Cash			Sundry		
Account)	£13,645		expenses	104	
			Drawings	624	
			Balance c/d	112	3,655
	£13,645	£18,050		£13,645	£18,050

Trading and Profit and Loss Account for year to 31st March 19–5

Stock (1st Apr. 19–4) £1,250		Sales	£13,645
Purchases (£10,000 + £158 + £268)	10,426		
	11,676		
Less: Stock (31st Mar. 19–5)	1,456		
	10,220		
Gross profit	3,425		
	£13,645		£13,645

Wages	£597	Gross profit	£3,425
Rent (£300 + £100)	400		
Electricity (£49 + £17)	66		
Rates	196		
Sundries	104		
Depreciation	60		
Net profit	2,002		
	£3,425		£3,425

BALANCE SHEET AS ON 31ST MARCH 19–5

Capital Account			Fixed assets		
Cash introduced		£6,000	Goodwill		£2,000
Add: Net profit		2,002	Fittings at cost £600		
		————	*Less:* De-		
		8,002	preciation	60	
Less: Drawings		624		———	540
		————			————
		7,378			2,540
Current liabilities			Current assets		
Creditors:			Stock	£1,456	
Suppliers	£268		Bank	3,655	
Electricity	17		Cash	112	
Rent (3 months)	100			———	5,223
	———	385			
		————			————
		£7,763			£7,763
		═════			═════

16　　　　　　　　　*R. Honeybone: Trading Account*

Stock at 1st Jan. 19–4	£2,086	Sales	£10,560
Purchases to 31st May			
19–4	8,608		
	———		
	10,694		
Gross profit (20% on			
sales)	2,112		
	———		
	£12,806		

The value, at cost, of the stock which was saved amounted to £604.

As can be seen from the Trading Account which has been deliberately left in an incomplete state there is a shortage on the credit side amounting to £2,246. Deducting the stock salvaged (£604) from the deficiency (£2,246) we obtain £1,642 as the remainder. This amount, £1,642, is the value of the stock destroyed and a claim will be made accordingly on the insurance company.

17   *Philip Stevens*

Drawings		£2,506
Add: Increase in assets during 19–4	£176	
Decrease in liabilities during 19–4	99	
	———	275
Net profit for 1974		£2,781

Chapter XI

5

(*a*)   *Bank Account*

Balance at 1st Jan. 19–5	£685	Trade creditors	£17,660
Trade debtors	24,130	Wages	2,472
Sale of furniture	22	General expenses	843
		Drawings	2,198
		Balance c/d	1,664
	£24,837		£24,837
Balance b/d	£1,664		

(*b*)   *Trading and Profit and Loss Account*

Stock at 1st Jan. 19–5	£1,248	Sales	£24,750
Purchases	18,500	Stock at 31st Dec. 19–5	1,367
Gross profit	6,369		
	£26,117		£26,117
Wages	2,472	Gross profit	6,369
Discounts allowed	530	Discounts received	775
General expenses	914		
Loss on sale of furniture	108		
Net profit	3,120		
	£7,144		£7,144

BALANCE SHEET

Capital, 1st Jan.			Furniture and fittings	£795
19–5	£2,705		Stock	1,367
Add: Net			Debtors	1,580
profit	3,120		Bank	1,664
	5,825			
Less:				
Drawings	2,198			
		£3,627		
Creditors		1,725		
Accrued expenses		54		
		£5,406		£5,406

Debtors Account

Bal. at 1st Jan.		Discounts	530
19–5	1,490	Bank	24,130
Sales	24,750	Balance	1,580
	£26,240		£26,240

Creditors Account

Discounts	775	Bal. at 1st Jan.	
Bank	17,660	19–5	1,660
Balance	1,725	Pur-	
		chases	18,500
	£20,160		£20,160

6   *Cash Account*

Balance, 1st Jan.		Wages	£724
19–5	£15	General Expenses	627
Sales	19,429	Paid into Bank	14,614
		Drawings	3,460
		Balance c/d	19
	£19,444		£19,444

Bank Account

Balance, 1st Jan. 19–5	£1,291	Creditors	£11,487
Cash paid in from		Rent	750
takings	14,614	Light, etc.	198
		Balance c/d	3,470
	£15,905		£15,905

Creditors Account

Bank	£11,487	Balance, 1st Jan. 19–5	£1,777
Discount	293	**Purchases A/c**	**11,901**
Balance c/d	1,898		
	£13,678		£13,678

Purchases Account

Creditors A/c	**£11,901**

Trading and Profit and Loss Account

Stock at 1st Jan. 19–5	£1,302	Sales	£19,429
Purchases	11,901		
	13,203		
Less: Stock at 31st Dec. 19–5	1,421		
	11,782		
Gross profit	7,647		
	£19,429		£19,429
Wages	£724	Gross profit	£7,647
Rent	750	Discounts received	293
Light, heat and insurance	198		
General expenses	627		
	2,299		
Net profit	5,641		
	£7,940		£7,940

BALANCE SHEET

Capital at 1st Jan. 19–5	£1,358		Shop fittings	£527
Add: Net profit	5,641		Stock	1,421
	6,999		Cash at bank	3,470
Less: Drawings	3,460		Cash in hand	19
		£3,539		
Creditors		1,898		
		£5,437		£5,437

NOTES:

(a) The opening capital position is calculated as follows:

Shop fittings	£527	
Stock	1,302	
Cash	15	
Bank	1,291	
Creditors		£1,777
Capital		1,358
	£3,135	£3,135

(b) The complete double entry has not been recorded in this solution for considerations of space. Students are recommended, however, not to neglect this when preparing their answers to this type of problem. Never fail to complete the **Trial Balance.**

7

(a)   *Bank Account*

Capital A/c	£3,000	Shop Fittings A/c	£640
Debtors A/c	12,675	Rent A/c	240
		Rates A/c	309
		Light and Heat A/c	108
		Telephone A/c	43
		General expenses A/c	572
		Insurance A/c	144
		Drawings A/c	2,680
		Creditors A/c	8,979
		Balance c/d	1,960
	£15,675		£15,675
Balance b/d	£1,960		

(b)   *Trading and Profit and Loss Account*
            to 31st December 19–5

Purchases	£11,206	Sales	£14,208
Less: Stock at 31st			
Dec. 19–5	2,722		
	8,484		
Gross profit (40.29%)	5,724		
	£14,208		£14,208
Rent	240	Gross profit	5,724
Rates	228		
Light and heat	108		
Telephone	43		
Insurance	96		
General expenses	644		
Depreciation	32		
	1,391		
Net profit	4,333		
	£5,724		£5,724

BALANCE SHEET AT 31ST DECEMBER 19–5

Capital (1st			Shop fittings at		
May 19–5)	£3,000		cost	£640	
Add: Net			*Less:*		
profit	4,333		Depreciation	32	
	7,333				£608
			Stock	2,722	
Less:			Debtors	1,533	
Drawings	2,680		Prepayments	129	
		£4,653	Cash at bank	1,960	
Creditors					6,344
Suppliers	2,227				
Expenses	72				
		2,299			
		£6,952			£6,952

Chapter XII

7 ALBERT MUNN: STATEMENT OF ASSETS AND LIABILITIES

	1st Jan. 19–4		31st Dec. 19–4	
Stock	£2,000		£4,750	
Bank	400		1,875	
Debtors	3,200		3,625	
Creditors		£1,800		£6,150
Capital		3,800		4,100
	£5,600	£5,600	£10,250	£10,250

Capital Account

Drawings	£5,000	Balance (1st Jan. 19–5	£3,800
Balance (31st Dec. 19–5)	4,100	Cash introduced	250
		Net profit	5,050
	£9,100		£9,100

8 L. SPEED: OPENING BALANCE SHEET AT 1ST JANUARY 19–5

Creditors	£2,229	Fixed assets	£4,725
Capital	7,978	Current assets	5,482
	£10,207		£10,207

CLOSING BALANCE SHEET AT 31ST DECEMBER 19–5

Creditors	£2,579	Fixed assets £4,725		
Bank overdraft	318	*Less:*		
Capital	9,225	Depreciation 475		
			£4,250	
		Motor vehicle £1,260		
		Less:		
		Depreciation 252		
			1,008	
		Current assets	6,864	
	£12,122		£12,122	

Capital Account

Drawings	£2,160	Balance at 1st Jan.	
Balance	9,225	19–5	£7,978
		Cash paid in	500
		Net profit	**2,907**
	£11,385		£11,385

9 BALANCE SHEET AT 31ST DECEMBER 19–4

Loan from Sinclair	£600	Shop fittings	£794
Creditors:		Stock	991
Goods £1,308		Debtors	1,657
Expenses 81		Insurance prepaid	15
	1,389	Bank	328
Capital	1,796		
	£3,785		£3,785

BALANCE SHEET AT 31ST DECEMBER 19–5

Loan from			Shop fittings		
Sinclair	£600		At 31st Dec.		
Add: Interest			19–4	£794	
due	15		Additions	352	
	——	615		——	
Creditors:				1,146	
Goods	£1,319		*Less:*		
Expenses	39		Depreciation	57	
	——	1,358		——	£1,089
Bank overdraft		27	Stock	1,075	
Capital		1,913	Debtors	1,734	
			Insurance		
			prepaid	15	
				——	2,824
		£3,913			£3,913

Capital Account

Drawings:			Balance at 31st Dec.	
Goods	£325		19–4	£1,796
Cash	1,500		Cash paid in—pools win	200
	——	£1,885	Net profit	1,802
Balance at 31st Dec.				
19–5		1,913		
		——		——
		£3,798		£3,798

10   OPENING STATEMENT AT 30TH JUNE 19–4

Premises and equipment	£5,000	
Stock	3,825	
Debtors	7,175	
Bank	2,200	
Creditors		£3,000
Loan		2,000
Capital		13,200
	——	——
	£18,200	£18,200

CLOSING BALANCE SHEET AT 30TH JUNE 19–5

Creditors		£3,500	Premises and	
Loan from			equipment	£5,000
Wright	£2,00		Motor van	700
Less: Repaid	500		Stock	4,000
		1,500	Debtors	7,000
Capital		13,650	Bank	1,950
		———		———
		£18,650		£18,650

Capital Account

Drawings	£960	Balance (30th June	
Income Tax paid	600	19–4)	£13,200
Balance per Balance		Cash won on	
Sheet at 30th June		sweepstake	300
19–5	13,650	Net profit	1,710
	———		———
	£15,210		£15,210

Creditors Account

Bank	11,675	Balance	
Balance		(30th June	
(30th June		19–4)	£3,000
19–5)	3,500	Purchases	
		A/c	12,175
	———		———
	£15,175		£15,175

Cost of Sales Calculation

Opening stock	£3,825
Add:	
Purchases	12,175
	———
	16,000
Less: Closing	
stock	4,000
	———
Cost of sales	£12,000

Sales	£15,000
Less: cost of sales	12,000
	———
Gross profit	£3,000

11

(*a*) To calculate the opening capital we set out the assets at 31st December 19–4 and deduct the total of the liabilities. This gives us:
Total assets, £21,690, less total liabilities, £6,788 = £14,902.

(*b*) The Balance Sheet at 31st December 19–5 is set out below:

BALANCE SHEET

Loan from B	£800		Land and buildings		£6,500
+ interest	20		Furniture	1,400	
		£820	*Less:* Dep'n	70	
					1,330
Creditors		4,081	Motor van	600	
			Less: Dep'n	150	
Capital		17,663			450
			Stock		8,115
			Debtors		5,842
			Bank		327
		£22,564			£22,564

(*c*) *Capital Account*

Drawings	£3,200	Balance at 1st Jan.	
Balance c/d	17,663	19–5	£14,902
		Bank (investments	
		sold)	961
		Profit	5,000
	£20,863		£20,863

(*d*) Having ascertained the net profit as £5,000 we now add the various expenses which amounted to £10,300. This gives us a total of £15,300 which must be the figure of gross profit.

We are told that the gross profit amounted to 20 per cent of the sales. Thus the sales must have been £76,500.

Both the opening and closing stocks are given and so we can deduce that the purchases total is £61,495.

NOTE: In questions of this type it is advisable to build up the Profit and Loss Account and the Trading Account in conventional form, working upwards from the figure of net profit.

Chapter XIII

5

(a) The working capital at 31st March consists of:

Stock		£2,500
Trade debtors		1,850
Cash at bank		290
		4,640
Less: Trade creditors	£1,460	
Accrued expenses	190	
		1,650
Working capital		**£2,990**

(b) The effect on the working capital would be as follows:

(*i*) An *increase* of £3,000, i.e., to £5,990.

(*ii*) A *decrease* of £400, i.e., to £2,590, since the creditors (*current liabilities*) would be increased by £400 and *fixed* assets by a similar sum.

(*iii*) A *decrease* of £25, i.e., to £2,965. Current asset of stock is *reduced* by £225 and current asset of cash *increased* by £200.

(*iv*) A *decrease* of £100, i.e., to £2,890. The capital account is reduced by £100 but this has no effect on the current liabilities whereas *current asset* of cash is *reduced* by £100.

(*v*) This would have no effect on the working capital. The owner's capital would be increased by £30 and the fixed assets (fixtures and fittings) by a like amount.

6	(a)	Net worth at 31st December 19–5	£9,550
		Net worth at 31st December 19–4	8,200
		Increase in net worth	**£1,350**

The decrease in the net worth during the year 19–5 is attributable to the following factors:

	Increase in value of	Decrease in value of
Fixed assets	£2,320	
Stock		£335
Debtors	415	
Bank		1,770
Creditors	720	
Increase in net worth		**1,350**
	£3,455	£3,455

(b)

Working capital at 31st December 19–4 (£4,800 less £1,800)
= £3,000

Working capital at 31st December 19–5 (£4,080 less £2,050)
= £2,030

Reconciliation

Working capital at 31st Dec. 19–4		£3,000
Add: Additional cash introduced	£1,250	
Net profit	3,400	
Depreciation for year	780	
		5,430
		8,430
Less: Cost of new fixed assets	£3,100	
Drawings	3,300	
		6,400
Working capital at 31st Dec. 19–5		£2,030

7   *Calculation of average amount of working capital required*

	Figure for year	Period	Average amount
Average amount locked up in stocks:			
Finished goods and work in progress	£2,000	12 months	£2,000
Materials	3,200	12 months	3,200
Average period of credit:			
Home sales	124,800	6 weeks	11,400
Export sales	31,200	1½ weeks	900
Payments in advance (overseas salesmen's commission)	3,200	3 months	800
			18,300
Deduct: Lag in payments			
Wages	104,000	1½ weeks	£3,000
Materials	19,200	1½ months	2,400
Rent, rates and insurance	4,000	6 months	2,000
Staff salaries	4,160	½ week	40
Manager's salary	3,000	½ month	125
General expenses	24,000	1½ months	3,000
			10,565
			7,735
Less: Average amount of undrawn profits			4,400
			3,335
Add: 10% for contingencies			333
			£3,668

13   The percentage of gross profit on sales for each year is as follows:

19–5	40.88%
19–6	28.07%
19–7	34.55%

One explanation of the differences in the gross profit percentage in each of the three years could be that purchase invoices amounting to some £2,500 had been omitted from the 19–5 Trading Account, and placed, in error, in the 19–6 purchases.

If we deduct £2,500 from the 19–5 gross profit we obtain £11,880 as the new figure, which gives 33.78 per cent. Adding the £2,500 to the 19–6 gross profit we obtain 34.72 as the corrected percentage. Thus, the gross profit percentage for the three years would be as follows:

19–5	33.78%
19–6	34.72%
19–7	34.55%

These percentages are reasonably close to each other and suggest that the wide fluctuations were caused by this error.

Other factors which could have caused the trouble in whole, or in part, are: (*a*) a mistake in the valuation of the closing stock; (*b*) the sales being incorrectly calculated; (*c*) shortages in stock due to fraud or undue waste; (*d*) an increase in the price of purchases without any alteration in selling prices.

14 The main reason for the fall in the gross profit percentage which can be deduced from the figures are as follows.

(*a*) Purchases. There has been a marked rise in the cost of raw materials. In 19–9 the cost had increased by 31.77 per cent on the 19–8 figures.

(*b*) Manufacturing wages were up by 14.98 per cent.

(*c*) Factory expenses had risen by £890, an increase on 19–8 of almost 10 per cent.

(*d*) Sales had risen by about 10 per cent also.

The Table shown below gives the percentage comparison based on sales for each of the two years:

	19–8	*19–9*
	%	%
Cost of materials used	30.13	34.90
Manufacturing wages	24.61	25.72
Factory expenses	15.00	14.98
	69.74	75.60
Gross profit	30.26	24.40
	100.00%	100.00%

The percentage increase of the items of expenditure in 19–9 compared with the 19–8 figures show the following:

	Increase %	Decrease %
Cost of materials used	4.77	
Manufacturing wages	1.11	
Factory expenses		0.02
Gross profit		5.86
	5.88	5.88

15 (a) The following is an explanation of each of the terms referred to:

(i) *Lead time* refers to the interval which will elapse between the ordering of goods and their delivery. To avoid hold-ups in production it is therefore vital that this period be taken into account when ordering materials.

(ii) *Period of credit* is the normal time given to a customer in which to pay for goods supplied to him. This may vary from business to business but the management's policy will indicate a consistency within businesses of the same type.

This is of particular importance in ensuring adequate credit control is exercised over debtors.

(iii) *Cash forecast* is a statement drawn up in columnar form which discloses an analysis of the cash payments and receipts for the future. Such forecasts may be short and medium term forecasts (drawn up on a monthly basis covering future periods of six to twelve months) or long-term forecasts (over three to five years) linked with capital expenditure involving the building of factories, plant, etc.

These are principally concerned when considering the cash needs of the business in the future and enable management to consider the extent to which additional funds must be obtained to finance business expansion.

(iv) *Cash budget* is a statement which links the profit which is expected to result from the activities of the business with the items to be paid, which are not shown in operating statements, e.g., capital expenditure, tax payments and dividends, and increases and decreases in stock, debtors, and liabilities. The result of making such adjustments will produce a vertical statement showing for a stated period the expected changes in the cash position for the period.

(v) *A funds statement* is a statement used to give a clear picture of the source and application of the funds of a business over a period of time. Principally it is employed as a supporting schedule to Balance Sheets where it is desired to give full information as to the deployment of the business funds since the previous Balance Sheet date.

(vi) *Cash flow* is the term used to identify profit plus depreciation. Depreciation is a non-cash *charge* and as such should be added to the profits after taxation but before appropriation of profit when considering the extent to which the business *has provided from trading* a flow of funds to support additional capital investment and other cash outlays.

(vii) *Liquidity* refers to the cash or near cash assets such as debtors and short-term investments and indicates the extent to which a business can meet its current liabilities.

The term is found in the analysis of balance sheets in particular when additional finance is required and when comparing the balance sheets of associated companies with a group (inter firm comparison).

(viii) *Insolvency* refers to the financial state of a person or business when it is found that due to insufficient liquid resources the creditors cannot be paid as they fall due.

This term is associated in particular with a business during the period prior to liquidation or bankruptcy.

(b) Two accounting ratios most commonly used for management control purposes:

(i) Debtors' ratio
Sales : Debtors

For this purpose the sales figure used is the net credit sales, (i.e., sales less returns but not cash discounts, which are a financial expense), compared with the debtors' balances from trading which will exclude any items such as prepayments and investment grants receivable.

The significance of this ratio (used for credit control purposes) lies in the fact that the proportion should be consistent and in line with management's policy. Where the proportion of debtors to sales is increasing the ratio will fall and at once steps can be taken to investigate the reasons for this.

(*ii*) **Current ratio**

Current assets : Current liabilities

The current assets are those assets such as stock and other assets in their stages of conversion into cash, e.g. debtors; the current liabilities are those provisions and liabilities which are due for payment in the next accounting period, usually the following month.

The significance of this ratio is that it indicates the financial strength of the business, because if a business is solvent its current ratio would normally be greater than 1.

16 The principal ratios which can be used when interpreting accounts, and the inferences which may be drawn from their use, are as follows:

(*a*) Ratio of current assets to current liabilities. The significance of the *current ratio* lies in the fact that it serves two purposes, first, as an index of solvency and, secondly, as an index of the strength of working capital.

(*b*) Ratio of current assets to fixed assets. This ratio should be treated with some caution, as different industries will tend to show different standards. A comparison, however, with similar firms in the same industry, may prove informative. This ratio, *computed from several successive balance sheets*, will indicate whether or not a particular enterprise is improving or receding in financial strength.

(*c*) Ratio of net worth to total liabilities. This ratio gives some indication at a particular date of the financial interests of the proprietors of the business as *contrasted with* those of the creditors. The higher the net worth in relation to total liabilities the stronger should be the business, and those directing it are, therefore, unlikely to be unduly influenced by the views or opinions of the creditors.

(*d*) Ratio of net worth to fixed assets. This ratio has come to be regarded as a test of the soundness of the capital structure, since it is associated with the view that the proprietors of an undertaking should provide the fixed assets and contribute some part of the working capital if the enterprise is to be adequately financed in relation to its capital structure.

(*e*) Ratios of cost of goods sold and gross profit to sales. These should be compared with the ratios in previous years and in similar businesses. Changes may be due to variations in the rates of Value

Added Tax or other duties, but, if not otherwise explained may point to errors in stocktaking or to misappropriation of goods or takings.

(*f*) Ratios of the various management, selling and distribution expenses, the cost of finance, etc., to turnover. Comparison of these with the corresponding ratios in previous years may afford valuable information as to directions in which economies ought to be effected.

(*g*) Ratios of cost of average stock to net sales. This shows the number of times the stock is "turned over" during an accounting period, and may afford useful information as to whether capital is being locked up in slow-moving stock, or whether the gross profit might be increased by reducing prices in order to induce a more rapid rate of turnover.

(*h*) Ratio of debtors to net sales. This will indicate the effectiveness of the organisation in respect of the granting of credit and the collection of debts.

(*i*) Ratio of net profit to capital employed. This will indicate the net earning capacity of the business and will enable *invaluable comparisons* to be made with other periods and other businesses.

Index

M & E Handbooks

Law

'A' Level Law/B Jones
Basic Law/L B Curzon
Cases in Banking Law/P A Gheerbrant, D Palfreman
Cases in Company Law/M C Oliver
Cases in Contract Law/W T Major
Commercial and Industrial Law/A R Ruff
Company Law/M C Oliver, E Marshall
Constitutional and Administrative Law/I N Stevens
Consumer Law/M J Leder
Conveyancing Law/P H Kenny, C Bevan
Criminal Law/ L B Curzon
Equity and Trusts/L B Curzon
Family Law/P J Pace
General Principles of English Law/P W D Redmond, J Price,
    I N Stevens
Jurisprudence/L B Curzon
Labour Law/M Wright, C J Carr
Land Law/L B Curzon
Landlord and Tenant/J M Male
Law of Banking/D Palfreman
Law of Contract/W T Major
Law of Evidence/L B Curzon
Law of Torts/J G M Tyas
Meetings: Their Law and Practice/L Hall, P Lawton, E Rigby
Mercantile Law/P W D Redmond, R G Lawson
Private International Law/A W Scott

Business and Management

Advertising/F Jefkins
Basic Economics/G L Thirkettle
Basics of Business/David Lewis
Business Administration/L Hall
Business and Financial Management/B K R Watts
Business Organisation/R R Pitfield
Business Mathematics/L W T Stafford
Business Systems/
    R G Anderson
Data Processing Vol 1: Principles and Practice/R G Anderson
Data Processing Vol 2: Information Systems and Technology/
    R G Anderson
Economics for 'O' Level/L B Curzon

Human Resources Management/H T Graham
Industrial Administration/J C Denyer, J Batty
International Marketing/L S Walsh
Management, Planning and Control/R G Anderson
Managerial Economics/J R Davies, S Hughes
Marketing/G B Giles
Marketing Overseas/A West
Microcomputing/R G Anderson
Modern Commercial Knowledge/L W T Stafford
Modern Marketing/F Jefkins
Office Administration/J C Denyer, A L Mugridge
Operational Research/W M Harper, H C Lim
Production Management/H A Harding
Public Administration/M Barber, R Stacey
Public Relations/F Jefkins
Purchasing/C K Lysons
Retail Management/Roger Cox, Paul Brittain
Sales and Sales Management/P Allen
Statistics/W M Harper
Stores Management/R J Carter

Accounting and Finance

Auditing/L R Howard
Basic Accounting/J O Magee
Basic Book-keeping/J O Magee
Capital Gains Tax/V Di Palma
Company Accounts/J O Magee
Company Secretarial Practice/L Hall, G M Thom
Cost and Management Accounting – Vols 1 & 2/W M Harper
Elements of Banking/D P Whiting
Elements of Insurance/D S Hansell
Finance of Foreign Trade/D P Whiting
Investment: A Practical Approach/D Kerridge
Practice of Banking/E P Doyle, J E Kelly
Principles of Accounts/E F Castle, N P Owens
Taxation/H Toch

Humanities and Science

European History 1789 – 1914/C A Leeds
Land Surveying/R J P Wilson
Physics for 'O' Level/Chapple
Sociology 'O' Level/F Randall
Twentieth Century History 1900–45/C A Leeds
World History: 1900 to the Present Day/C A Leeds